OF FIRE

MERIDIAN

Crossing Aesthetics

Werner Hamacher
& David E. Wellbery
Editors

Translated by
Charlotte Mandell

Stanford
University
Press

———

Stanford
California

THE WORK
OF FIRE

Maurice Blanchot

'The Work of Fire'
was originally published in French
in 1949 under the title
'La Part du feu'
© 1949, Editions Gallimard

Assistance for this translation
was provided by the French
Ministry of Culture.

"Literature and the Right to Death" was
published in Maurice Blanchot, *The Gaze of
Orpheus and Other Literary Essays*, ed. P. Adams
Sitney, trans. Lydia Davis (Barrytown, N.Y.:
Station Hill Press, 1981); reprinted by
permission of Station Hill Press.

Stanford University Press
Stanford, California

Printed in the United States of America

CIP data appear at the end of the book

Original printing 1995
Last figure below indicates year of this printing:
04   03   02   01   00   99   98   97   96   95

Stanford University Press publications
are distributed exclusively by
Stanford University Press within
the United States, Canada, Mexico, and
Central America; they are distributed
exclusively by Cambridge University Press
throughout the rest of the world.

Contents

Translator's Note

Maurice Blanchot is celebrated for the subtlety of his language and his style. We cannot even enter the present text without witnessing a typical measure of his craft. The original title of this collection of essays is *La Part du feu*. The most literal, simply verbal translation would be "the part of fire." But the word "part" has, as in English, the two meanings of "division of some whole" and "role," as in a play. It has further senses of "advantage," "political party," and others. So we might begin by thinking of The Role of Fire, the Work of Fire, the Partisans of Fire, and so on. But then we reflect that *feu* also has a range of meanings broader than the English "fire." It can mean "light," "lights" (as in traffic lights, tail lights), "signal flares," the "warmth" of feelings or of someone's prose style, the frenzy of someone's piano playing. Now we start thinking of the Role of Light, Signals, Flares, the Side of Light; we are caught up in a tangle of speculations about illumination, work, taking sides, destruction (for fire does destroy what it briefly illuminates), signs and signals, various self-consuming artifacts—in short, we are already in the highly charged paradoxical world of Blanchot's profound interrogations of literary texts. Now add to all this the phrase *faire la part du feu*—which means "to cut a firebreak" to stop the spread of fire in the woods and, metaphorically, "to cut one's losses" in business. So in offering the present work with the English title *The Work of Fire*, I am sensible of how inadequate the phrase is to all portended by the original.

Such inadequacy, to be sure, is part and parcel of any translation. Blanchot's celebrated and intricate style, almost paratactic in its taste for long strings of phrases and clauses loosely kept coherent by grammatical concords in French that English lacks, poses a formidable challenge, especially if the translator believes, as I do, that one ought to do one's best to preserve the sentential structures of the author. At times I have felt it clearer or safer to break a very long sentence into two smaller ones, or silently repeat a noun when a pronoun's antecedent has grown implausibly remote, all in the interest of making readable sentences that are offered to the reader, by the author, as deeds of attention. The reader of Blanchot is meant to ponder, not hasten to conclusions.

Save in the previously translated last essay, I have followed Blanchot's own minimalist style of citation. When Blanchot cites texts from other languages, I have straightforwardly translated his French version, so that the reader can see what he saw. (Thus the passage from Hölderlin's "Germania" used as one of the epigraphs to this book and cited in the essays "Mystery in Literature" and "The 'Sacred' Speech of Hölderlin" is rendered in three different versions.) For citations from works originally in English, I have, when possible, provided that original.

And I would ponder here, with much gratitude, those friends who have helped me in matters of French and of English: Pierre Joris, Nicole Peyrafitte, Claudine Heron, Michèle Conteh, and my husband, Robert Kelly, who still persists in believing books can be translated.

—CHARLOTTE MANDELL

It behooves mortals
To speak with restraint of the gods.
If, between day and night,
One time a truth should appear to you,
In a triple metamorphosis transcribe it;
Though always unexpressed, as it is,
O innocent, so it must remain.

—Hölderlin

The name of the bow is life, but its work is death.

Who will hide from the fire that does not set?

—Heraclitus

§ Reading Kafka

Perhaps Kafka wanted to destroy his works, since they seemed to him condemned to increase universal misunderstanding. When we see the disorder in which this work reaches us—what is made known to us, what is hidden, the fragmentary light thrown on this or that piece, the scattering of the texts themselves, unfinished to begin with and split up even more, and reduced to dust, as if they were relics whose power were indivisible—when we see his silent work invaded by the chatter of commentaries, these unpublishable books made the subjects of endless publications, this timeless creation changed into a footnote to history, we begin to ask ourselves if Kafka himself had foreseen such a disaster in such a triumph. Perhaps his wish was to disappear, discreetly, like an enigma that wants to escape being seen. But this modesty gave him over to the public, this secret made him famous. Now the mystery is spread everywhere, it is in broad daylight, a main attraction. What is to be done?

Kafka wanted only to be a writer, the *Diaries* show us, but the *Diaries* succeed in making us see in Kafka something more than a writer; they foreground someone who has lived rather than someone who has written: from then on, he is the one we look for in his work. This work forms the scattered remains of an existence it helps us to understand, priceless evidence of an exceptional destiny that, without it, would have remained invisible. What is strange

I

about books like *The Trial* and *The Castle* is that they send us back
endlessly to a truth outside of literature, while we begin to betray
that truth as soon as it draws us away from literature, with which,
however, it cannot be confused.

This tendency is inevitable. All the commentators ask us to look
for stories in these stories: events signify only themselves, the
surveyor is indeed a surveyor. Do not substitute "dialectical constructions for the unfolding of events that should be taken as a real
story." But a few pages later one can "find in Kafka's work a theory
of responsibility, views on causality, finally a comprehensive interpretation of human destiny, all three sufficiently coherent and
independent enough of their novelistic form to bear being transposed into purely intellectual terms" (Claude-Edmonde Magny,
The Sandals of Empedocles). This contradiction might seem strange.
And it is true that these texts have often been translated with a
peremptory decisiveness, in obvious disdain for their artistic character. But it is also true that Kafka himself set the example by
commenting occasionally on his tales and trying to clarify their
meaning. The difference is that aside from a few details whose
evolution, but not meaning, he explains to us, he does not transpose the story onto a level that might make it more understandable
to us: his commentarial language embeds itself in fiction and is
indistinguishable from it.

The *Diaries* are full of remarks that seem linked to a theoretical
knowledge that is easily recognized. But these thoughts remain
foreign to the generalization from which they take shape: they are
there as if in exile, they fall back into an equivocal style that does
not allow them to be understood either as the expression of a single
event or as the explanation of a universal truth. Kafka's way of
thinking does not conform to a uniformly valid rule, but neither
does it simply refer to a particular event in his life. His thoughts
swim fleeting between these two streams. As soon as they become
the transcription of a series of events that actually happened (as is
the case in a diary), they move imperceptibly off in search of the
meaning of these events, they want to keep pursuing. Then the
narrative begins to merge with its explanation, but it is not an

explanation, it does not arrive at the point of what it is supposed to be explaining; and, more important, it does not succeed in soaring over it. It is as if it were drawn, by its own gravity, toward the particularity whose closed character it must break: the meaning that it sets in motion wanders around the facts, it is an explanation only if it frees itself from them, but it is an explanation only if it is inseparable from them. The endless wanderings of thought, its new beginnings taking off from an image that breaks that reflection, the meticulous rigor of reasoning applied to a nonexistent object, constitute a style of thinking that plays at generalization but is thought only when caught up in the density of a world reduced to the unique instance.

Mme. Magny notes that Kafka never wrote a platitude, not because of an extreme refinement of intelligence but through a sort of congenital indifference to received ideas. His way of thinking is in fact rarely banal, but that is because it is not completely thinking. It is singular, that is to say, it rightly belongs to a single person; in vain does it use abstract terms, such as positive, negative, good, bad; it resembles a strictly individual story whose occurrences might be obscure events that, having never happened, will never happen again. Kafka, in his attempt at autobiography, described himself as an ensemble of particularities, sometimes secret, sometimes explicit, endlessly throwing himself at the law, and not succeeding at having himself either recognized or suppressed. Kierkegaard went more deeply into this conflict, but Kierkegaard had taken the side of the secret, while Kafka could not take either side. If he hid what was strange about him, he hated both himself and his fate, and considered himself evil or damned; if he tried to make his secret public, the secret was not recognized by the community, which gave it back to him, imposing secrecy on him again.

Allegory, symbol, the mythic fiction whose extraordinary developments his works present to us, are made unavoidable in Kafka by the nature of his thought. It oscillates between the two poles of solitude and the law, of silence and everyday speech. It can attain neither one nor the other, and this oscillation is also an attempt to escape from oscillation. His thinking cannot rest easy in the general, but although it complains sometimes of its madness and its confinement, it is also not absolute solitude, for it speaks about this solitude; it is not non-meaning, for it has this non-meaning for its meaning; it is not outside the law, because its law is this banishment that is at the same time its reconciliation. One could say of the absurdity by which one tries to size up this thinking what he himself says of the wood louse: "Only try to make yourself understood by the wood louse—if you succeed in asking it the goal of its work, you will at the same instant have exterminated the nation of wood lice." As soon as thought meets the absurd, this meeting signifies the end of the absurd.

Thus all Kafka's texts are condemned to speak about something unique while seeming only to express its general meaning. The narrative is thought turned into a series of unjustifiable and incomprehensible events, and the meaning that haunts the narrative is the same thought chasing after itself across the incomprehensible like the common sense that overturns it. Whoever stays with the story penetrates into something opaque that he does not understand, while whoever holds to the meaning cannot get back to the darkness of which it is the telltale light. The two readers can never meet; we are one, then the other, we understand always more or always less than is necessary. True reading remains impossible.

Whoever reads Kafka is thus forcibly transformed into a liar, but not a complete liar. That is the anxiety peculiar to his art, an anxiety undoubtedly more profound than the anguish over our fate, which often seems to be its theme. We undergo the immediate experience of an imposture we think we are able to avoid, against which we struggle (by reconciling contradictory interpretations)—and this effort is deceptive, yet we consent to it, and this laziness is betrayal. Subtlety, shrewdness, candor, loyalty, negligence are all equally the means to a mistake (a deception) that is in the truth of the words, in their exemplary power, in their clarity, their interest, their assurance, their power to lead us on, let us fall, pick us up again, in the unfailing faith in their meaning that does not permit one either to leave it or to follow it.

How can Kafka portray this world that escapes us, not because it is elusive but perhaps because it has too much to hold onto? The commentators are not fundamentally in disagreement. They use almost the same words: the absurd, contingency, the will to make a place for oneself in the world, the impossibility of keeping oneself there, the desire for God, the absence of God, despair, anguish. And yet of whom are they speaking? For some, it is a religious thinker who believes in the absolute, who even hopes for it, who struggles endlessly to attain it. For others, it is a humanist who lives in a world without remedy and, in order not to increase the disorder in it, stays as much as possible in repose. According to Max Brod, Kafka found many paths to God. According to Mme. Magny, Kafka finds his main consolation in atheism. For another, there is indeed a world of the beyond, but it is inaccessible, perhaps evil, perhaps absurd. For another, there is neither a beyond nor a movement toward the beyond; we exist in immanence, what matters is the awareness, always present, of our finiteness and the unresolved mystery to which that reduces us. Jean Starobinski: "A man stricken with a strange sorrow, so Franz Kafka appears to us. . . . Here is a man who watches himself being devoured." And Pierre Klossowski: "Kafka's *Diaries* are . . . the diaries of a sick man who yearns for a cure. He wants health . . . so he believes in health." And again: "We can in no case speak of him as if he did not have a final vision." And Starobinski: "there is no last word, there can be no last word."

These texts reflect the uneasiness of a reading that seeks to conserve the enigma and its solution, the misunderstanding and the expression of this misunderstanding, the possibility of reading within the impossibility of interpreting this reading. Even ambiguity does not satisfy us, for ambiguity is a subterfuge that seizes a shifting, changing truth, whereas the truth that is waiting for these writings is perhaps unique and simple. It is not certain that we could understand Kafka better if we answered each assertion with an assertion that disrupts it, if one infinitely nuanced themes with others oriented differently. Contradiction does not reign in this world that excludes faith but not the pursuit of faith, hope but not the hope for hope, truth here below and beyond but not a summons to an absolutely final truth. It is indeed true that to explain such a work by referring to the historic and religious situation of the one who wrote it, by making him into a sort of superior Max Brod, is an unsatisfying sleight of hand, but it is also true that if his myths and his fictions are without ties to the past, their meaning sends us back to elements that this past makes clear, to problems that would undoubtedly not be present in the same way if they were not already theological, religious, impregnated with the torn-apart spirit of an unhappy conscience. That is why we can be equally constrained by all the interpretations offered us but cannot say that they are all equal to each other, that they are all equally true or equally false, immaterial to their object, or true only in their disagreement.

Kafka's main stories are fragments, and the totality of the work is a fragment. This lack could explain the uncertainty that makes the form and content of their reading unstable, without changing the direction of it. But this lack is not accidental. It is incorporated in the very meaning that it mutilates; it coincides with the representation of an absence that is neither tolerated nor rejected. The pages we read are utterly full; they indicate a work from which nothing is lacking; moreover, the entire work seems given in these minute developments that are abruptly interrupted, as if there were nothing more to say. Nothing is lacking in them, not even the lack that is their purpose: this is not a lacuna, it is the sign of an impossibility that is present everywhere and is never admitted: impossibility of living with people, impossibility of living alone, impossibility of making do with these impossibilities.

What makes our effort to read so full of anguish is not the coexistence of different interpretations; it is, for each theory, the mysterious possibility of seeming sometimes to have a negative meaning, sometimes a positive one. Kafka's world is a world of hope and a world condemned, a universe forever closed and an infinite universe, one of injustice and one of sin. What he himself says of religious knowledge—"Knowledge is at once a step leading to eternal life and an obstacle raised in front of this life"—must be said of his work: everything in it is obstacle, but everything in it can also become a step. Few texts are more somber, yet even those whose outcome is without hope remain ready to be reversed to express an ultimate possibility, an unknown triumph, the shining forth of an unrealizable claim. By fathoming the negative, he gives it the chance to become positive, but only a chance, a chance whose opposite keeps showing through and that is never completely fulfilled.

Kafka's entire work is in search of an affirmation that it wants to gain by negation, an affirmation that conceals itself as soon as it emerges, seems to be a lie and thus is excluded from being an affirmation, making affirmation once again possible. It is for this reason that it seems so strange to say of such a world that it is unaware of transcendence. Transcendence is exactly this affirmation that can assert itself only by negation. It exists as a result of being denied; it is present because it is not there. The dead God has found a kind of impressive revenge in this work. For his death does not deprive him of his power, his infinite authority, or his infallibility: dead, he is even more terrible, more invulnerable, in a combat in which there is no longer any possibility of defeating him. It is a dead transcendence we are battling with, it is a dead emperor the functionary represents in "The Great Wall of China," and in "The Penal Colony," it is the dead former Commandant whom the torture machine makes forever present. As Starobinski notes, isn't the supreme judge in *The Trial* dead, he who can do nothing but condemn to death because death is his power, death—not life—is his truth?

The ambiguity of the negation is linked to the ambiguity of death. God is dead, which may signify this harder truth: death is not possible. In the course of a brief narrative titled "The Hunter Gracchus," Kafka relates the adventure of a Black Forest hunter who, having succumbed to a fall in a ravine, has not succeeded in reaching the beyond—and now he is alive and dead. He had joyously accepted life and joyously accepted the end of his life— once killed, he awaited his death in joy: he lay stretched out, and he lay in wait. "Then," he said, "the disaster happened." This disaster is the impossibility of death, it is the mockery thrown on all humankind's great subterfuges, night, nothingness, silence. There is no end, there is no possibility of being done with the day, with the meaning of things, with hope: such is the truth that Western man has made a symbol of felicity, and has tried to make bearable by focusing on its positive side, that of immortality, of an afterlife that would compensate for life. But this afterlife is our actual life. "After a man's death," Kafka said, "a particularly refreshing silence intervenes for a little time on earth for the dead, an earthly fever has reached its end, they [the dead] no longer see dying going on, a mistake seems to have been removed, even for the living it is a chance to catch one's breath and open the window of the death chamber—until this easing appears illusory and the pain and lamentations begin."

Kafka says again: "Lamentations at the deathbed are really because he is not dead in the true sense of the word. We still have to content ourselves with this way of dying, we go on playing the game." And even more clearly: "Our salvation is death, but not this death." We do not die, it is true, but because of that we do not live either; we are dead while we are alive, we are essentially survivors. So death ends our life, but it does not end our possibility of dying; it is real as an end to life and illusory as an end to death. Thus this ambiguity, this double ambiguity that lends strangeness to the slightest actions of these characters: Are they, like Gracchus the hunter, dead people who are vainly trying to finish dying, beings drowning in who knows what waters and kept afloat by the mistake of their former death, with the sneering that goes with it, but also with its gentleness, its infinite courtesy, in the familiar surroundings of ordinary things? Or are they living people who are struggling, without understanding why, with great dead enemies, with something that is finite and not finite, that they cause to spring up again by pushing it away, that they shove away from them as they try to find it? For that is the origin of our anxiety. It does not come only from this emptiness from which, we are told, human reality would emerge only to fall back; it comes from the fear that even this refuge might be taken away from us, that nothingness might not be there, that nothingness might just be more existence. Since we cannot depart from existence, this existence is unfinished, it cannot be lived fully—and our struggle to live is a blind struggle that does not know it is struggling to die and gets mired in a potential that grows ever poorer. Our salvation is in death, but our hope is to live. It follows that we are never saved and also never despairing, and it is in some way our hope that makes us lost, it is hope that is the sign of our despair, so that despair also has a liberating quality and leads us to hope. ("Not to despair even of what you do not despair of. . . . That is exactly what is called living.")

If each word, each image, each story can signify its opposite— and the opposite of that as well—then we must seek the cause of that in the transcendence of death that makes it attractive, unreal, and impossible, and that deprives us of the only truly absolute ending, without depriving us of its mirage. Death dominates us, but it dominates us by its impossibility, and that means not only that we were not born ("My life is the hesitation before birth") but also that we are absent from our death. ("You talk endlessly of dying but you do not die.") If night suddenly is cast in doubt, then there is no longer either day or night, there is only a vague, twilight glow, which is sometimes a memory of day, sometimes a longing for night, end of the sun and sun of the end. Existence is interminable, it is nothing but an indeterminacy; we do not know if we are excluded from it (which is why we search vainly in it for something solid to hold onto) or whether we are forever imprisoned in it (and so we turn desperately toward the outside). This existence is an exile in the fullest sense: we are not there, we are elsewhere, and we will never stop being there.

The theme of "The Metamorphosis" is an illustration of the torment of literature whose subject is its own deficiency, and that carries the reader off in a whirl where hope and despair answer each other endlessly. Gregor's state is the state of the being who cannot depart from existence; for him, to exist is to be condemned to falling continually back into existence. Turned into a vermin, he continues to live at the level of his degeneration, he sinks into animal solitude, he comes close to the absurdity and impossibility

of living. But what happens? He goes on living. He does not even
try to get out of his unhappiness, but into this unhappiness he
brings a last resource, a last hope: he still struggles for his place
under the sofa, for his little excursions on the coolness of the walls,
for life amid the filth and dust. So we also have to go on hoping
along with him, because he hopes, but we also have to despair of
this frightening hope that goes on, aimlessly, inside the void. And
then he dies: an unbearable death, abandoned and alone—and yet
almost a happy death by the feeling of deliverance it represents, by
the new hope of an end that is final for now. But soon this last hope
is also stripped away; it is not true, there is no end, life goes on, and
the young sister's gesture, her movement of awakening to life, the
call to the sensual on which the story ends, is the height of horror;
there is nothing more frightening in the entire story. It is the curse
and it is revival, hope, for the girl wants to live, when to live is just
to escape the inevitable.

Kafka's narratives are among the darkest in literature, the most
rooted in absolute disaster. And they are also the ones that torture
hope the most tragically, not because hope is condemned but
because it does not succeed in being condemned. However complete the catastrophe is, an infinitesimal margin survives; we do not
know if it preserves hope or if, on the contrary, it dismisses it
forever. It is not enough that God himself submits to his own
verdict and succumbs in the most sordid collapse, in an unheard-of
caving-in of scrap iron and human organs; we still have to wait for
his resurrection and the return of his incomprehensible justice that
condemns us forever to terror and consolation. It is not enough
that the son, obeying the unjustifiable and irrefutable verdict of his
father, throws himself into the river with an expression of calm love
for him; this death must be associated with the continuation of
existence through the strange final sentence: "At this moment the
traffic on the bridge was literally mad," a sentence whose symbolic
import, whose precise physiological meaning Kafka has affirmed.
And finally, most tragic of all, Joseph K. in *The Trial* dies, after a
parody of justice, in the deserted suburb where two men execute
him without a word; but it is not enough that he dies "like a dog,"

he still has to have his share of survival, that of the shame which the limitlessness of a crime he has not committed assigns to him, condemning him to live as well as to die.

"Death is in front of us a little like the painting *Alexander's Battle* on the wall of a classroom. What we have to do, from this life forward, is to dim or even erase the painting by our acts." The work of Kafka is this painting that is death, and it is also the act of dimming it and erasing it. But, like death, it is not able to be dimmed; on the contrary, it shines admirably from the vain effort it made to extinguish itself. That is why we understand it only by betraying it, and our reading revolves anxiously around a misunderstanding.

§ Kafka and Literature

"All I am is literature, and I am not able or willing to be anything else." In his *Diaries*, in his letters, in all phases of his life, Kafka dealt with himself as a writer of literature, and he prided himself on claiming a title that most people scorn today. For many of his commentators, to admire Kafka is first to place him outside of his status as a writer. He knew how to give a religious meaning to literary work, Jean Starobinski says. We should place his life and work in the category of sanctity and not of literature, says Max Brod. He not only had to create a body of work, Pierre Klossowski says, but also to deliver a message. But this is what Kafka says: "My situation is unbearable because it contradicts my only desire and my only calling: literature." "Everything that is not literature bores me." "Everything that does not have to do with literature, I hate." "My chance to use my talents and every potential in some manner lies entirely in the domain of literature."

One sometimes has the impression that Kafka offers us a chance of catching a glimpse of what literature is. But one must not begin by judging unworthy of him a category that, far from disparaging, he valued as the only sort that could save him, if he could attain it. It is strange that a man who took nothing for granted regarded words with a certain confidence; he did not feel threatened by what has become for us the worst threat (for us and also, let us not forget it, for many writers of his time. Kafka chose Goethe and Flaubert as his masters, but he lived during the era of the expressionist avant-garde). He doubted only his capacity to write, not the possibility of writing or the value of art.

Kafka sought above all to be a writer. He was driven to despair each time he thought he was prevented from becoming one. He wanted to kill himself when, having been placed in charge of his father's factory, he thought that he would not be able to write for two weeks. The longest section in his *Diaries* concerns the daily struggle he had to keep up against business, against other people, and against himself just to be able to write a few words in his *Diaries*. This obsession is impressive, but we know that it is not all that unusual. In Kafka's case, it seems more natural if one recognizes how he chose to fulfill his spiritual and religious destiny in literature. Having devoted his entire existence to his art, he saw all of it in danger when this activity had to give way to another: then, in the true sense of the word, he stopped living.

How can existence be completely devoted to a concern for arranging a certain number of words in some order? That is what is not so clear. Let us admit that for Kafka writing was not a matter of aesthetics; he did not have the creation of a valid literary work in mind, but his salvation, the accomplishment of the message that is in his life. The commentators would like to keep separate completely artistic preoccupations, which they consider secondary, from interior preoccupations, the only things worth being explored for themselves. "Aesthetic deliberation," we are told, "has no place here." So be it. But then look at what literature becomes. Strange activity, this: if it has a mediocre purpose (for example, producing a well-written book), it demands an approach that is attentive to the whole and to details, mindful of the technique and composition, and aware of the power of the words; but if it aims higher (for example, examining the very meaning of life), then its approach is free of all these conditions, it can come about by completely neglecting the very substance of which it is made. Let us note that this idea of literature, understood as an activity capable of being practiced without consideration for the means, is not a simple theoretical dream—it has the well-known name of "automatic writing"; but such a form was foreign to Kafka.

He wrote stories, novels. In his *Diaries*, he describes the scenes at which he was present, the people he met. He passes judgments on his work: "The description of R. did not seem effective to me." Often he describes objects in detail. Why? Is it because, as Max Brod claims, the truth being visible everywhere, he finds it everywhere? Is it not rather the case that he is practicing, that he is trying to learn? We know that he carefully studied Kleist's chilly style, and that Goethe and Flaubert taught him to recognize the value of a perfectly wrought form. "What I am lacking," he wrote to Pollack, "is discipline . . . I want to work with zeal, for three months running. Today I know this more than anything: art has more need of craft [*métier*] than craft has of art. I do not believe, of course, that one can force oneself not to have children, but I do believe, rather, that one can force oneself to educate them." Kafka asked more of literature, and got more from it, than many others have. But he had first of all the honesty of accepting it in all its forms, with all its constraints, as both craft and art equally, as a task and as a privileged activity. From the moment one writes, he thought, one cannot do it without writing well.

It would be too easy, for someone who writes out of concern for life or morality, to find himself freed from all aesthetic considerations. Literature is not an apartment house where everyone can choose a flat, where if someone wants to live on the top floor, he will never have to use the back stairs. The writer cannot just drop out of the game. As soon as he starts writing, he is within literature and he is there completely: he has to be a good artisan, but he also has to be an aesthete, a word seeker, an image seeker. He is compromised. That is his fate. Even the famous instances of total sacrifice in literature change nothing in this situation. To master literature with the sole aim of sacrificing it? But that assumes that what one sacrifices exists. So one must first believe in literature, believe in one's literary calling, make it exist—to be a writer of literature and to be it to the end. Abraham was willing to sacrifice his son, but what if he was not sure he had a son, and what he took for his son was really just a ram? And then, silence is not enough to make a writer more than a writer, and whoever tries to leave art to become a Rimbaud still remains an incompetent in the silence. We cannot even say that Kafka rejected his work because he judged it morally bad, or unfaithful to the message he wanted to deliver, or inferior to the silence. He might have wanted to destroy it simply because he considered it imperfect in literary terms. How does one distinguish between the messenger who says, "Pay no attention to my message," and the artist who declares, "My work is a failure, let it be destroyed"? In one sense, the artist alone has the right to make such a decision. The messenger is not master of his words; even if they are bad, they are beyond his control, for that might be their very meaning, to be bad; all that one is able to grasp is that the will to destroy it may be incorporated in the message itself: the secret desire of speech is to be lost, but this desire is a vain one and speech is never lost.

What is strange is not only that so many writers believe their entire existence is devoted to the act of writing, but that by devoting themselves to it, they still give birth to works that are masterpieces only from the aesthetic point of view, which is precisely the point of view they condemn. Moreover, the very ones who want to give a fundamental meaning to their activity, a search that implies the whole of our condition, succeed only in carrying this activity through by reducing it to the superficial meaning they exclude, the creation of a work well done, and this creation forces them, at least momentarily, to separate themselves from existence, to disengage themselves, to lose interest in it. "Write with blood," said Zarathustra, "and you will learn that blood is mind." But it is the opposite that is true: one writes with the mind and one thinks one is bleeding. Kafka himself: "I will not give way to fatigue, I will dive completely into my story, even if I gash my face." The image is certainly dramatic: the writer emerges from his work, his face crisscrossed with cuts, but it is only an image. Camus's Caligula has the heads cut off of people who do not share his artistic emotions. No Caligula for the writer. His overbearing (and, for some, degrading) situation comes in part from his success: he claims to undergo great risk in his work, but the risk he runs is perhaps no risk at all; far from succumbing, he gets himself out of it with an admirable work that enlarges his existence. Hence the alibi for so many bloody words—there is no blood. Hence, too, all the scornful words about those with pen in hand.

One can imagine Racine writing under constraint of a "truth" to seek. One can also imagine him led by this search to a kind of asceticism, to a disgust with the harmonious, to a refusal of perfection, in short, not to the silence of *Phaedra*, but rather to some *Phaedra* by Nicolas Pradon.* That is the problem. We have seen writers renounce writing out of dislike for it or out of a need to go beyond literature by sacrificing it. We have seen others ready to destroy masterpieces because these masterpieces seemed to them to be a betrayal. But we have never seen anyone give up being a good writer out of devotion to his inner life, continue to write because writing was necessary, but continue to write more and more badly. A Rimbaud never became a Sully-Prudhomme. How strange that is! Even Hölderlin, in his insanity, went on being a good poet. And Kafka could condemn his work, but he never condemned himself to the emptiness of mediocre language, to death from banality and stupidity (only Flaubert sometimes makes us think of this suicide).

Why did a man like Kafka feel lost if he did not become a writer? Was that his calling, the true form of his mandate? But how did he come by this half-certainty that while he might not fulfill his destiny, his own way of missing it was to write? Countless texts show that he attributed an immense importance to literature. When he notes, "The immensity of the world I have in my head. . . . Better to explode a thousand times than hold it back or bury it in me; for that is the reason I am here, I haven't the least doubt about that," he again expresses in his usual way the urgency of a creation that blindly clamors to be let out. It is most often his own existence that he feels is at stake in literature. Writing causes him to exist. "I have found meaning, and my monotonous, empty,

* This inferior dramatist's play, staged two nights after Racine's masterpiece on the same theme, was used by Racine's enemies against him.—TRANS.

misled, bachelor life has its justification. . . . It is the only path that can lead me forward." In another passage: "brave, naked, powerful, surprising as I am usually only when I write." This text tends to reduce literary activity to a means of compensation. Kafka was not very good at living; he lived only when he was writing. All the same, even in this perspective, the main point remains to be explained, for what we want to understand is, why write?—And not an important work, but insignificant words ("The particular kind of inspiration I find myself in . . . is such that I [can do] everything, and not just what is intended for a definite work. When I arbitrarily write a sentence like this: 'He looked out the window,' this sentence is already perfect"); to write "He looked out the window" is already to be more than oneself.

Kafka makes us understand that he is capable of freeing latent forces in himself, or even that at a time when he feels closed in and surrounded, he can discover by this means some close possibilities of which he had not been aware. In solitude, he dissolves. This disintegration makes his solitude very perilous; but, at the same time, something important can spring up from this confusion, provided language grasps it. The drama is that at such a moment it is almost impossible for him to speak. Normally, Kafka found it extremely difficult to express himself, due to the nebulous contents of his consciousness; but now, the difficulty surpassed everything. "My powers are not enough for even a single sentence." "Not one word, when I write, goes with another. . . . My doubts surround each word even before I can make it out, what am I saying, I've made this word up!" At this stage, it is not the quality of the words that matters, but the possibility of speaking: that is what is at stake, that is what one experiences. "Have listened to myself from time to time, perceiving at times inside me something like the mewing of a young cat."

It seems that literature consists of trying to speak at the moment when speaking becomes most difficult, turning toward those moments when confusion excludes all language and consequently necessitates a recourse to a language that is the most precise, the most aware, the furthest removed from vagueness and confusion—

to literary language. In this case, the writer can believe that he is creating "his spiritual possibility for living"; he feels his creation linked, word by word, to his life, he re-creates and regenerates himself. Literature then becomes an "assault on the frontiers," a hunt that, by the opposing forces of solitude and language, leads us to the extreme limit of this world, "to the limits of what is generally human." One could even dream of seeing it develop into a new Cabala, a new secret doctrine from centuries ago that could re-create itself today and begin to exist starting from, and beyond, itself.

That is a work which probably will not reach completion, but it is surprising enough that it could be thought possible. We have said that in the midst of general impossibility, Kafka's trust in literature was still remarkable. He rarely lingers on the inadequacy of art. If he writes, "Art flies around truth, but with the determination not to get burnt by it. Its skill consists of finding a place in the void where the ray of light focuses most powerfully, without knowing beforehand the location of the light source itself," he himself is responding to this other, darker reflection: "Our art is to be blinded by truth: the light on the grimacing face as it pulls back, that alone is true and nothing else." And even that definition is not without hope: it already is something to lose one's sight and, more than that, to see while blind; if our art is not light, it is a form of darkening, a possibility of attaining the flash through the dark.

According to the pious Max Brod, whose commentaries strive to bring the friend he lost closer to himself, art should be a reflection of religious knowledge. One sometimes has the completely different impression that, for Kafka, art went further than knowledge. Knowledge of oneself (in the religious sense) is one of the means of our condemnation: we raise ourselves up thanks only to it, but it also is the only thing that prevents us from raising ourselves; before being acquired, it is the necessary path; afterward, it is the insurmountable obstacle. This ancient idea from the Cabala, in which our downfall seems our salvation and vice versa, perhaps lets us understand why art can succeed where knowledge fails: because it is and is not true enough to become the way, and too unreal to change into an obstacle. Art is an *as if.* Everything happens as if we were in the presence of truth, but this presence is not one, that is why it does not forbid us to go forward. Art claims knowledge when knowledge is a step leading to eternal life, and it claims non-knowledge when knowledge is an obstacle drawn up in front of this life. It changes its meaning and its sign. It destroys itself while it survives. That is its imposture, but that is also its greatest dignity, the same that justifies the saying "Writing is a form of prayer."

Sometimes Kafka, struck, like so many others, by the mysterious nature of this transformation, seems ready to recognize in it the proof of an abnormal power. In the course of literary activity, he tells of having experienced (sometimes) illuminating states, "states during which I lived entirely in each idea, but also realized each one of them," great harrowing states in which he believed himself surpassing his limits and reaching universal limits; but, he adds, "It was not in these states that I wrote my best works." Illumination might thus be linked to the exercise of this special activity of language, without knowing if that presupposes it or provokes it. (The state of dissolution, associated with solitude, of which we spoke earlier, is also ambiguous: there is dissolution from the impossibility of speaking while still within sight of speech; silence and the void seem to exist only to be filled.) In any case, the extraordinary is placed on the level of language, either by causing the magnificence of life to rise up from the deep by the "magic" power of the right word, "which does not create, but invokes," or by turning against the one who is writing, like a dagger in the hands of "spirits." The idea of spirits and magic explains nothing by itself; it is a warning that says: There is something mysterious here, you must be on your guard.

This is the mystery: I am unhappy, so I sit down at my table and write, "I am unhappy." How is this possible? This possibility is strange and scandalous to a degree. My state of unhappiness signifies an exhaustion of my forces; the expression of my unhappiness, an increase in my forces. From the side of sadness, there is the impossibility of everything—living, existing, thinking; from the side of writing, the possibility of everything—harmonious words, accurate exposition, felicitous images. Moreover, by expressing my sadness, I assert a negation and yet, by asserting it, I do not transform it. I communicate by the greatest luck the most complete disgrace, and the disgrace is not made lighter. The more luck I have, that is to say, the more gifted I am in making my unhappiness felt by description, embellishments, and images, the more the bad luck this misfortune reports is respected. It is as if the possibility that my writing represents essentially exists to express its own impossibility—the impossibility of writing that constitutes my sadness. Not only can it not put it in parentheses, or accommodate it without destroying it or being destroyed by it, but it really is possible only because of its impossibility. If language and, in particular, literary language did not constantly hurl itself eagerly at its death, it would not be possible, since it is this movement toward its impossibility that is its nature and its foundation; it is this movement that, by anticipating its nothingness, determines its potential to be this nothingness without actualizing it. In other words, language is real because it can project itself toward non-language, which it is and does not actualize.

In the text on which we have just commented, Kafka writes: "Could never understand that it was possible, for almost anyone who wanted to write, to objectify pain while in pain." The word "objectify" attracts attention, because literature tends precisely to construct an object. It objectifies pain by forming it into an object. It does not express it, it makes it exist on another level, it gives it a materiality which is no longer that of the body but the materiality of words which represent the upheaval of the world that suffering claims to be. Such an object is not necessarily an imitation of the changes that pain makes us live through: it shapes itself to *present* pain, not *represent* it; first of all, this object must exist, that is, it must be an always indeterminate conjunction of determined relationships. There must always be in it, as in everything that exists, a surplus that one cannot account for. "To write a story, I do not have the time to extend myself in all directions, as I should." This regret of Kafka indicates the nature of literary expression: it radiates in all directions, and indicates the nature of movement inherent in all literary creation: one makes it genuine only by looking for it in all directions, pursued by it but outrunning it, pushed everywhere by pulling it everywhere. The "I am unhappy" is unhappiness only when it becomes thicker in this new world of language, where it takes form, sinks down, is lost, is darkened, and survives.

It seems striking to many commentators, in particular to Claude-Edmonde Magny, that Kafka grasped the fecundity of literature (for himself, for his life, and to go on living) from the moment that he felt literature was the passage from *Ich* to *Er*, from I to He. That is the great discovery of the first important story he wrote, "The Judgment," and we know that he commented on this event in two ways: to bear witness to this overwhelming encounter with the possibilities of literature, and to make clear to himself the connections this work permitted him to make clear. It is, Mme. Magny says, borrowing a phrase of T. S. Eliot, that he had succeeded in constructing an "objective correlative" for his originally incommunicable emotions; she adds that it is a question of a kind of annihilation of the self, agreed to by the artist, not for the sake of inner progress but to give birth to an independent and complete work of art. No doubt. And yet it seems that something even more curious is happening. For, from all the evidence, when Kafka wrote "The Judgment" or *The Trial* or "The Metamorphosis," he was writing narratives about beings whose story belongs only to them, but at the same time about Kafka and his own story, which belongs only to him. It seems the further he got from himself, the more present he became. Fiction's narrative shapes a distance, a gap (itself fictive) inside the one writing, without which he could not express himself. This distance must become even deeper as the writer participates more in his narrative. He is implicated, in both senses of the ambiguous term: he questions himself, and he is also in question in the story—though almost effaced.

So it is not enough for me to write "*I* am unhappy." As long as I write nothing else, I am too close to myself, too close to my unhappiness, for this unhappiness to become really mine in the form of language: I am not yet truly unhappy. It is only from the moment I arrive at this strange substitution, "*He* is unhappy," that language begins to be formed into a language that is unhappy for me, to sketch out and slowly project the world of unhappiness as it occurs in him. So, perhaps, I will feel myself implicated, and my unhappiness will be felt by this world from which it is absent, in which I and it are both lost, where it cannot be consoled or appeased or amused, where, foreign to itself, it neither stays nor disappears, and lasts without possibility of lasting. Poetry is deliverance; but this deliverance signifies that there is nothing more to deliver, that I have become involved in another in whom, however, I no longer find myself. (This partly explains why Kafka's stories are myths, extraordinary tales, beyond the plausible and the realistic: it is because he expresses himself in them by this immeasurable distance, by the impossibility of recognizing himself in them. It is not possible that this vermin is himself: so it is he in his most intimate and irreducible essence.)

Impersonal and mythic narrative, taken as faithful to the essence of language, necessarily creates certain contradictions. We have noted that language is real only from the perspective of a state of non-language, which it cannot realize: it is striving toward a dangerous horizon where it seeks in vain to disappear. What is this non-language? We do not have to clarify that here. But we should remember that it constitutes a reminder to all forms of expression of their inefficiency. Language is possible because it strives for the impossible. Inherent in it, at all its levels, is a connection of struggle and anxiety from which it cannot be freed. As soon as something is said, something else needs to be said. Then something different must again be said to resist the tendency of all that has just been said to become definitive, to slip into the imperturbable world of things. There is no rest, either at the level of the sentence or at that of the whole work. Nor is there any in regard to the struggle that cannot make any assertion without correcting itself—and none, either, in silence. Language cannot be realized by being mute; saying nothing is a manner of expressing oneself, the illegitimacy of which throws us back into speech. Moreover, it is inside words that the suicide of words must be attempted, a suicide that haunts them but cannot be achieved, that leads them to the temptation of the white page or to the madness of a word lost in insignificance. All these solutions are illusory. The cruelty of language comes from the fact that it endlessly evokes its death without ever being able to die.

The Great Wall of China was not finished by its builders. The story "The Great Wall of China" was not finished by Kafka. The fact that the work is connected with the theme of failure by its own failure must be regarded as the sign of uneasiness that is at the root of all literary designs. Kafka cannot prevent himself from writing, but writing prevents him from writing: he interrupts himself, he begins again. His effort is as endless as his passion is without hope—only the absence of hope sometimes becomes the most tenacious hope, while the impossibility of ever being done with it is only the impossibility of going on. What is most striking is that this struggle (without which there is no language, or literature, or authentic research, but which is not enough to guarantee research, or literature, or language; which does not exist before its object and is as unforeseeable in its forms as the movement it reverses) shows through in Kafka's very style, and that this style is often the almost naked manifestation of it.

We know these developments that, particularly in the *Diaries*, are built up in such a strange way. There is a primary assertion, around which secondary assertions are arranged, that support it as a whole, all the while initiating partial reservations. Each reservation leads to another that completes it and, linked to each other, all of them together make up a negative structure, parallel to the central one, that keeps going on and ending at the same time: having reached the end, the assertion is at once completely developed and completely withdrawn; we do not know if we are grasping the outside or the inside, whether we are in the presence of the building or the hole into which the building has disappeared. It is impossible to find out what face the thought turns toward us, it turns toward and away so much, as if, like a weight hanging by a string, its only object were to reproduce its torsion. Kafka's words, by the fact that they attempt a veritable regression to the infinite, give as much the impression of leaping beyond themselves in a dizzying way as of pressing against the void. One believes in a beyond of words, a beyond of failure, in an impossibility that might be more than an impossibility, and thus restore hope to us. ("The Messiah will come only when he is no longer needed, he will come only a day after his arrival, he will not come on the last day, but at the very last." Or again: "Nothing but a word, nothing but a prayer, nothing but a breath of air, nothing but a proof that you are still alive and waiting. No, no prayer, nothing but a breath, not even a breath, nothing but a presence, not even a presence, nothing but a thought, not even a thought, nothing but the calm of sleep.") But when the words stop, we have hope neither for a realized infinity nor for the assurance of something finished; led toward the limitless, we have renounced limits, and finally we must renounce the unlimited as well.

Often, Kafka's language tries to maintain an interrogative mode, as if, under cover of that which eludes yes and no, he hoped to trap something. But the questions repeat themselves while limiting themselves; more and more, they cast aside what they are trying to find, ruining their possibility. They desperately continue in the single hope of an answer, and they can continue only by making any answer impossible—and, even more, by invalidating the very existence of the one who questions. ("What is this? Who is going away under the trees on the bank? Who is completely abandoned? Who can no longer be saved? On whose grave is the grass growing?" Or "What is troubling you? What moves you to the quick? Who is fumbling at the latch of your door? Who is calling you from the street without coming in through the open door? Ah! precisely, it's the one you are troubling, the one you move to the quick, the one at whose door you are fumbling, the one whom, without wanting to come in through the open door, you are calling from the street!") In truth, the language here seems to exhaust its resources and to have no other goal but to go on at all costs. It seems confused with its emptiest possibility, and that is why it also seems to us to have such a tragic fullness, for this possibility is language, frustrated by everything and realizing itself only by the movement of a conflict that finds nothing more to contest.

Literature is the place of contradictions and disputations. The writer who is most connected to literature is also the one most led to disconnect himself from it. It is everything to him, yet he cannot content himself with it or be satisfied. Kafka, so certain of his literary vocation, felt guilty because of all he sacrificed to practice it. He was supposed to conform to the norm (notably by marriage), and instead he wrote. He was supposed to seek God by participating in the religious community, and instead he made do with this form of prayer that is writing. "For a long time now nothing more has been written. God does not want me to write, but as for me, I have to write. There are perpetually highs and lows, but when all is told, God is stronger, and the unhappiness is greater than you can imagine." What was the justification becomes sin and condemnation. He knows "we cannot write our redemption, we can only live it." In the story "Josephine," he shows how futile it is for the artist to think he is the soul of his community, the chief resource of his people in facing the sorrows that strike them; he will not be exempted from his share of work and communal responsibility, his art will suffer from it, even collapse, but what does it matter? His decline "is only a little episode in the eternal consciousness of our people, and our people will soon overcome this loss." This apologia signifies clearly that, even at its highest, art has no rights against the claims of action. It is powerless, but its awareness of this illegitimacy does not resolve the conflict. Witness the fact that, to tell us about it, Kafka has to write another piece of literature, and will actually die while correcting the proofs of one last book. In this sense, whoever sets out to write is already lost. But he can no longer interrupt his work without believing from then on that it is by interrupting it that he will be lost. He will try all the solutions. All, even silence, even action, will be nothing more than more or less inadequate kinds of art from which he will free himself only at the very command of art: Racine's renunciation of tragedy forms a part of tragedy—likewise, Nietzsche's madness or Kleist's death. In recent years we have witnessed how any writer who feels contempt for literature pays for it by multiplying his employment of literary methods. Presently we will observe that when literature tries to forget its gratuitous character by committing itself seriously to political or social action, this engagement turns out to be yet one more disengagement. And it is the action that becomes literary.

Outwardly and inwardly, literature is complicit with what threatens it, and this threat finally is also an accomplice of literature. Literature can only challenge itself, but this challenge restores it to itself. It sacrifices itself, and this sacrifice, far from making it disappear, enriches it with new powers. How can one destroy, when destruction is the same as that which it destroys or even, like the living magic of which Kafka speaks, when destruction does not destroy, but constructs? This conflict adds to all those we have glimpsed in these pages. To write is to engage oneself; but to write is also to disengage oneself, to commit oneself irresponsibly. To write is to call into question one's existence, the world of values, and, to a certain extent, to condemn the good; but to write is always to try to write well, to seek out the good. And then, to write is to take on the impossibility of writing, it is, like the sky, to be silent, "to be an echo only for the mute"; but to write is to name silence, it is to write while preventing oneself from writing. Art is like the temple of which *The Aphorisms* speaks: never was an edifice built so easily, but on each stone a sacrilegious inscription is found engraved, so deeply engraved that the sacrilege will last so long a time that it will become even more sacred than the temple itself. So is art the place of anxiety and complacency, of dissatisfaction and security. It has a name: self-destruction, infinite disintegration. And another name: happiness, eternity.

§ The Myth of
Mallarmé

Henri Mondor's books, the complete edition of Mallarmé (which will, however, remain incomplete, so long as the correspondence to which Mondor has the key is not gathered together)* he published with Jean Aubry and the collection *Proposals on Poetry* that he has just excerpted from that correspondence—all these studies, so remarkable and so worthy of their subject, have certainly brought Mallarmé closer to us. We know him better, and we also know more precisely what we will never know about him. His fame is now that of a classic author. "Such as into himself at last . . ."† Perhaps, however, he is so present to us only because he has distanced himself from us in many respects. Whatever daring there was in his art no longer surprises us. Whatever made his genius mysterious, self-effacing, and profound has disappeared. Especially

---

* Blanchot's complaint is not uncommon. For example, in Charles Mauron's *Introduction to the Psychoanalysis of Mallarmé*, (pp. 23–24) Mauron, speaking of our knowledge of Mallarmé's life, says: "On this score, as everyone knows, we owe almost everything to Dr. Mondor. He has assembled the documents; he has arranged and published most of them in a series of works: *L'Amitié de Verlaine et Mallarmé, Vie de Mallarmé, Mallarmé plus intime,* and *Propos sur la poésie.* Frankly, I regret—and others will join me in this—that the publication of the documents has not been completed and that the little game of releasing now a letter, now the variant of a line, now a poem of his youth, at intervals of several years or more, should be so long drawn out."—TRANS.

† The opening words of Mallarmé's poem "The Tomb of Edgar Poe."—TRANS.

the trust he placed in aesthetic values exclusively, this faith he placed in art above everything, this religion of the poet's solitude, seem to us the signs of a passion that the movement of history no longer permits us to share. Only the pure violence of this passion holds and continues to surprise us.

Valéry never stopped honoring Mallarmé and commenting on his poetic attitude. He remained faithful to him up to his last days, as Plato was to Socrates. But through his own fame; through his infinitely developed researches; through a way of seeing, admiring, and understanding in keeping with these researches, Valéry, like Plato, both lit up and veiled his master's face. By throwing light on him, he relegated him to the shade; he gave him too much, and borrowed too much from him. The two bodies of work are quite distinct, but their ideas are less so; and the extreme singularity of Mallarmé's ideas has been as if erased by the importance they have been accorded from ideas that are almost identical, but that are stronger and especially more strongly and more obstinately put forth, ideas we find in the pages of Valéry's *Variety* or in so many other prose pieces.

Certainly, we know that Valéry scorned literature and that Mallarmé made it his reason to exist. We know that, in literature, the former was mostly interested in the study of the mind's activity, and the latter in the work alone; moreover, Valéry pursued the perfection of art, not for that perfection but for the mastery it implies, and the awareness of self it develops. Mallarmé, however, neither less lucid nor less aware, always kept his concern for art, and even for the *book*, in which this lucidity and this awareness seemed to him to be fully developed. What is there to add? Both lived this everyday paradox of changing their theories by their works. In vain Mallarmé valued the means only in view of the result: the preparation absorbed him, the greatness of the goal turned him away from it, and his last works, admirable and definitive as they are, seem to be the lost moments of secret days, devoted to a more essential and completely interior activity. Valéry, on the other hand, who wrote only to experience the work of one who writes, produced a prodigious body of work, so varied and accomplished that one cannot imagine it has a double even more profound and enclosed in the single silence of the mind. Thus Mallarmé's ideas found in Valéry's work their most complete, if not their most representative, fulfillment. But another result is that Mallarmé's influence, while increasing with his illustrious disciple's, has become the influence of a theory and a method, and has thus lost whatever effectiveness the mystery and beauty of masterpieces adds to the ideas one claims to draw from them.

In a text from *Variety III*, we read this remark: "With Mallarmé, the identification of 'poetic' meditation with the possession of language, and his minute study of their reciprocal relationships, led to a kind of doctrine about which we know, unfortunately, only the leanings." Mallarmé's theoretical writings are numerous but not well developed; they are assertions rather than proofs. What is striking is the importance of reflections on language. No poet felt more strongly that every poem, no matter how tenuous its pretext, was necessarily engaged in the creation of poetic language, and perhaps of all language. Valéry demonstrated and admired this research, but he did little to make it known to us, and it is not certain that he himself continued it in exactly the same sense. The lack of coherence of texts, an anxiety that was not at all logical, the brilliance of certain phrases that do not explain but do show, these make Mallarmé's meditations not easily reducible to the unity and simplicity of a doctrine.

We would like to recall some of these texts and the most constant assertions they contain. Perhaps we will find some preoccupations in them, along with some prejudices rather close to our own. For example, Mallarmé believed in the existence of two languages, one essential, the other crude and immediate. That is a certainty that Valéry will reassert and that has since become very familiar to us. Why? That is less obvious. Mallarmé compared the common word to a currency of exchange, so much so that "to take or place a coin in another's hand in silence" would most often suffice to make us understand. But does he mean, as Valéry's commentary indicates, that this language is worthless because, by being in the service of understanding, it disappears completely in the idea it communi-

cates or in the action it announces? Quite the contrary: "What is
the use of the miracle," said Mallarmé, "of transposing a fact of
nature into its vibratory near-disappearance according to the play
of speech, if it is not so that a pure idea emanates from it, without
the annoyance of a near or concrete reminder?" We find, in this
response, a remarkable specification: the word has meaning only if
it rids us of the object it names; it must spare us its presence or
"concrete reminder." In authentic language, speech has a function
that is not only representative but also destructive. It causes to
vanish, it renders the object absent, it annihilates it.

Up to this point, we can recognize the origin of such remarks.
Mallarmé was struck by the characteristic of language to be both
meaningful and abstract. Every word, even a proper noun, even
Mallarmé's name, designates not an individual event but the general form of this event: whatever it may be, it remains an abstraction. At least, that is what Plato taught us. But is it not remarkable
that poets and writers (since the classical era) have rarely been
satisfied with the law, have tried, rather, to reverse it? They claim to
connect the word to the thing, to confuse it with whatever unique
qualities it has—a name that is mine, not everyone's, that is what
they want. Mallarmé's position is, therefore, exceptional. The one
who, more than anyone else, condemned discourse, which lacks
common qualities—clarity, order, logic, that is to say, everything
that matters to the universal and abstract character of language—is
also the one who appreciates this character as its principal quality
and the very condition of poetic form. If poetry exists, it is because
language is an instrument of comprehension. Here we are far from
Valéry's remarks.

"I say: a flower! and, outside of the oblivion where my voice
relegates no outline, as something other than known calyxes, musically rises the idea itself, suave, the absent one of all the flowers."
We see that all is not so simple. The word distances the object: "I
say: a flower!" and I have in front of my eyes neither a flower, nor an
image of a flower, nor a memory of a flower, but an absence of
flower. "Silenced object." Is this absence, however, the sign of
something else—of truth, for example, in the classic sense—having

value for everyone and in every age? Let us not hasten to conclude this; despite the use of abstract words, "*known* calyxes, *idea*," it is to be felt that the poet is of an order that demands nothing of learning. He does not replace the real absence of an object with its ideal presence. "Suave" and "musically" are assuredly not intellectual concepts asserted by these paths. On the contrary, we note that here we are once again in contact with reality, but a more evasive reality, one that presents itself and evaporates, that is understood and vanishes, one made of reminiscences, allusions, so that if in one respect it is done away with, in another respect it reappears in its most noticeable form, like a series of fugitive and unstable nuances, in the very place of abstract meaning whose emptiness it claims to fill.

At first glance, language's interest is thus to destroy, through its abstract power, the material reality of things and to destroy, through the power of sensible evocation of words, this abstract value. Such an action must lead us rather far. When language contents itself with naming an object, it gives us the picture of it. The thin coating of everyday speech gives way to the pressure of the thing it designates. Since it is ordinary, it vanishes as soon as it is pronounced; it hands us over to the presence from which it was supposed to defend us. Further, "describing, teaching, relating" are acts that reveal crude language, that function of easy and representative medium of exchange. The commonplace, from whose usage Mallarmé desperately fled, has precisely this defect of not offering a strong enough barrier against facts, things, what we see, what we hear. It does not distance us enough; it does not create real absence. If language's distinctive feature is to nullify the presence it signifies, then transparency, clarity, commonplaces are contrary to it, because they thwart its progress toward a signification free of any concrete reference. Thus we understand why essential language grants so much room to what Valéry calls the physique of language. Sounds, rhythm, number, all that does not count in current speech, now become most important. That is because words need to be visible; they need their own reality that can intervene between what is and what they express. Their duty is to draw the gaze to themselves and turn it away from the thing of which they speak. Yet their presence is our gauge for the absence of all the rest.

Clichés annoyed Mallarmé, not because he found only words in them but because words, rather, have disappeared from them. He was hardly frightened of giving precedence to language over thought: how could he fear it? What he wished was to make the word exist, to give it back its material power, to yield the initiative to it by making words shine with "their reciprocal reflections"—all in order to conserve their very worth of meaning. Thought, that is to say, the possibility of being present to things while infinitely distancing oneself from them, is a function of the only reality of words. Where words rule according to the complex relationships they can entertain, thought is accomplished and meaning achieved.

In truth, none of that exists without contradictions. It is clear that, if Mallarmé gives language the mission of referring by absence to what it signifies, it risks entering an impasse. Of what absence is it a question? If it is necessary not to name, but only to qualify the defined void the object creates by disappearing, we will begin to glide toward the image. Allegory is this first step toward absence: "Water cold from boredom in its iced container." But the emancipation is still illusory: as soon as we understand the circumlocution, the object revives and imposes itself again. The fault of simple metaphor is less in its simplicity, which makes its deciphering easy, than in its stability, its plastic solidity; it is as weighty and present as what it represents. It is as if placed immutably in front of us, with its meaning that nothing comes to change. That is why the world of images that Mallarmé seeks is a flight, a negation rather than an affirmation of images. Not only are the figures compressed, placed at an angle, and diffuse, but they follow each other according to a rather brisk rhythm so that none of them allows to the reality it circumscribes any time to exist, time to become present to us by its intermediation. That is the hard part. If I say, "the absent one of all the flowers," undoubtedly I momentarily erase the flower that I would otherwise have to see, but in order to direct my gaze and my mind toward the presence of another thing, no less cumbersome, no less heavy; this must vanish in its turn, under pressure of a more unstable image that will push it away, and thus in succession from figures to figures, anxious images, acts rather than forms, transitions of meaning rather than expressions.

All Mallarmé's researches tend to find a boundary where, by means of terms nonetheless fixed and directed at facts and things, a perspective of parentheses might be sketched out, each opening out into each other to infinity and endlessly escaping themselves. "Allusion," he said, "suggestion." "Speaking has to do with the reality of things only commercially: in literature, it contents itself with making an allusion to them or with abstracting their quality that some idea will incorporate." Thence the impressionism he is accused of, as if he had wanted to portray nature, when he sought only to make it disappear. "Done away with, that pretension (aesthetically an error, although it governs masterpieces) to include in the subtle paper of the volume something other than, for example, the horror of the forest, or the silent thunder scattered in the foliage; not the intrinsic, dense wood of the trees." Mallarmé is not one of those who, to paint an object, incorporate it in their painting. His goal is different: "I call it Transposition."

One also understands why the essential language that does not exclude prose ("In the so-called prose genre there is sometimes some admirable verse, of every rhythm. . . . Every time there is an effort in style, there is versification") is poetry, and implies verse. Verse, substituting more subtle links for syntactic relationships, turns language to a sense of movement, a rhythmic trajectory, in which only passage and modulation count, not the periods, the notes by which one passes. That is what brings poetry and music closer together. Not "Poetry, Music par excellence"—certainly not, because poetry would make a kind of music out of language—but, like it, as an art of movement, it pulls the meaning and effects it wants to attain from duration alone. It is obvious that if verse "makes a complete, new word out of many terms, a word foreign to the language and as if incantatory," it is at first because, in such an instance, words have stopped being "terms" (at which one stops) and have opened themselves up to the intention that makes its way across them, outside any reality that might correspond to them. So it happens that rhythm, enjambment, the special tension of verse create such an eager connection that the word, called to complete it, becomes superfluous, so present is it in the only expectation it demands: by this absence, it is spread out over the length of the sentence as if it had the potential to come into being without an act that would come to exhaust it. "Words, by themselves, are exalted with many a facet recognized as rarest or most valuable to the mind, that center of vibratory suspense, which perceives them, independent of their ordinary connectedness, projected on the cave wall, just as long as their mobility or principle lasts, which cannot be said of discourse: all of them, before extinction, quick to answer signal fires from afar, or from an odd perspective, or angle of contingency."

In *Igitur*, Elbehnon says: "I pour out speech, to plunge it back into its inanity." When one has discovered an exceptional ability in language for absence and questioning, one has the temptation to consider the very absence of language as surrounded by its essence, and silence as the ultimate possibility of speech. Everyone knows that this silence has haunted the poet. What we have sometimes forgotten is that this silence no more marks the failure of his dreams than it signifies an acquiescence to the ineffable, a betrayal of language, a "what's the use" thrown to poetic resources too inferior to the ideal. Silence is undoubtedly always present as the one demand that really matters. But, far from seeming the opposite of words, it is, rather, implied by words and is almost their prejudice, their secret intention, or, rather, the condition of speech, if speaking is to replace a presence with an absence and to pursue a more and more sufficient absence through more and more fragile presences. Silence has so much dignity only because it is the highest degree of this absence that is the whole virtue of speaking (which is itself our ability to give meaning, to separate ourselves from things in order to signify them).

What is striking in Mallarmé is the feeling that a certain arrangement of words might in no way be distinct from silence. "To evoke, in a purposeful shadow, the silenced object, by allusive words, reducing themselves to equal silence, comprises an attempt close to creating. . . . So that an average stretch of words, beneath the comprehending gaze, arranges itself in definitive lines, and silence therewith." Elsewhere, in a witticism, he holds as identical the deed of saying nothing and that of talking about nothing: "Society, that hollowest term, heritage of the philosophes, has this at least in its favor, that since nothing really exists in facts similar to the injunction that its august concept awakens, to discuss it is equivalent to talking about nothing or talking to amuse oneself." With these words, one can make silence. For the word can also make itself empty and by its presence give the feeling of its own lack. "Virgin scattered absence in this solitude," "exquisite vacation of the self," "hollow whiteness, container of nothing," all that is language, but a language that, expressing emptiness, must finally again express the emptiness of language.

When one begins to take part in silence, it demands always a greater part, to the point of wanting to push away, in the end, even that which makes it possible. Mallarmé always claimed to bring unrefined language closer to speech, essential language closer to the written. This seems a surprising claim. Valéry, on the other hand, associated poetry with song, understanding that a language to which one restores its sonorous value requires an organ, other than the eyes, that explores it and shows its obvious power. Moreover, if one wants only to retain the "mobility" of conversation, the essential means of verse, how can one not summon the voice, which alone is able to carry this movement and to engage words in the succession that lightens and volatilizes them? Yet we understand that language, if its purpose is to distance all material presence from us, returns its rights to "the written, the tacit flight of abstract ideas," "facing the fall of bare sounds." The written, by its typographical composition, can even imitate and represent movement, as the preface to *A Throw of Dice* indicates: "The literary . . . advantage, from this copied distance that mentally separates groups of words or the words between them, seems sometimes to accelerate and sometimes to slow down its movement, studying its stresses, even intimating it according to a simultaneous vision of the Page:

this is taken as a whole just as the Verse, or perfect line, is elsewhere. Fiction will rise to the surface and melt away, quickly, according to the mobility of the written, around fragmentary stops of a main sentence, starting from the introductory title and going on from there." The book is the way, par excellence, of language, because it retains of language only the ability to abstract, isolate, transpose, and because it distances chance, the rest of the contingency of things, from it, and because it pushes away man himself from it, the one who speaks and the one who listens. "Impersonified, a volume, so long as one separates oneself from it as author, does not ask the reader to approach. That is how it is, among its human accessories it takes place all alone: a deed, existing." And, we see, this book of which one must dream, which is the Book, equivalent of the world, orphic explanation of the Earth, is not so much the Great Work, destined to sum up the universe, a microcosm that could hold everything, as the hollow of this totality, its other side, its realized absence, that is to say, the ability to express everything, thus an ability that is itself withdrawn from everything and expressed by nothing, what must be called "le jeu par excellence." (The book "replaces everything through lack of anything," he says, implying again that everything must first be missing.) When the poet declares, "I figure, by an undoubtedly ineradicable writer's prejudice, that nothing will remain if it is not uttered," we could judge this claim rather naive. But to say everything is also to reduce everything to nothing, and thus, at the intersection of existence and nothingness, a kind of enigmatic force is asserted, capable, while it summarizes everything "in a virgin scattered absence," of still persisting to complete its task, then of being resorbed into the emptiness it called into being.

To utter everything is also to utter silence. It is, thus, to prevent speech from ever becoming silent again. Mallarmé never freed himself from this impossibility. In vain he asked the white of a white page, the still intact margin, for a material representation of silence.

"The intellectual framework of a poem," he wrote about Poe, "hides itself and holds forth—takes place—in the space that isolates the stanzas and in the midst of the white of the paper: meaningful silence that is not less beautiful to compose than it is verse." Meaningful silence, but also meaningful abandon, for at the very instant language surrounds us with a universal absence and delivers us from the obsession with the word's presence, it is here that silence, to express itself, calls on something material, makes itself present in a manner that ruins the proud building constructed over the void, and it, absence itself, has no other resource, to introduce itself to the world of signified and abstract values, but to be realized as a thing. "To my taste, I do prefer a white page, a spaced design of commas or periods and their secondary combinations, imitating, bare, melody—to a text, even if it were well-written, even sublime, if it were not punctuated." This "spaced design of commas and periods . . . bare melody," preferred over words with a light irony that one undoubtedly should not misjudge, is perhaps the last trace of a language that erases itself, the very movement of its disappearance, but it again seems even more to be the material emblem of a silence that, to let itself be represented, must become a thing, and that thus remains a scandal, its insurmountable paradox.

We see now around what dangerous point Mallarmé's reflections turn. First, language fits into a contradiction: in a general way, it is what destroys the world to make it be reborn in a state of meaning, of signified values; but, under its creative form, it fixes on the only negative aspect of its task and becomes the pure power of questioning and transfiguration. That is possible insofar as, taking on a tangible quality, it becomes a thing, a body, an incarnate power. The real presence and material affirmation of language give it the ability to suspend and dismiss the world. Density and sonorous thickness are necessary to it to extricate the silence that it encloses, and that is the part of the void without which it could never cause a new meaning to be born. It goes on being like this infinitely, to produce the feeling of an absence—and must become like things in order to break our natural relationships with them. The contradiction is rough, it tortures all poetic language, as it tormented Mallarmé's speculations. That is what motivates the poet, recalling Cratylus's doctrine, to seek a direct correspondence between words and what they signify, to miss the clear color of the word "night" [*nuit*] and the dark timbre of the word "day" [*jour*], as if words, far from turning us away from things, had to be their material reproduction: the sensuality of language here carries it away, and the word dreams of uniting itself with the objects whose weight, color, and heavy, sleeping aspect it also possesses.

Likewise, if blanks, punctuation, typographical array, the architecture of the page are all called to play such a large role, it is because written work, too, needs a material presence. It is a qualified space, a living region, a kind of sky that materially represents all events in the very act of understanding. "Everything becomes suspense, fragmentary arrangement with rotation of mirrors, in concord with total rhythm, which would be the silenced poem, with blanks; only translated, in a way, by each pendentive." Language, confused here with the book, raises all the material elements that compose it to a higher existence, like the consciousness of which it is not only the product but also the symbol, and capable, like it, of a mysterious silence, the obscure foundation on the basis of which everything is declared.

We have cited only classic, very clear texts. In an extract from *Music and Literature*, Mallarmé expressed, in a form tinged with idealism, almost the same considerations:

> *Autre chose* . . . ce semble que l'épars frémissement d'une page ne veuille sinon surseoir ou palpite d'impatience, à la possibilité d'autre chose.
>
> Nous savons, captifs d'une formule absolue que, certes, n'est que ce qui est. Incontinent écarter cependant, sous un prétexte, le leurre, accuserait notre inconséquence, niant le plaisir que nous voulons prendre: car cet *au-delà* en est l'agent, et le moteur dirais-je si je ne répugnais à opérer, en public, le démontage impie de la fiction et conséquemment du mécanisme littéraire, pour étaler la pièce principale ou rien. Mais, je vénère comment, par une supercherie, on projette, à quelque élévation défendue et de foudre! le conscient manque chez nous de ce qui là-haut éclate.
>
> A quoi sert cela—
>
> A un jeu.

En vue qu'une attirance supérieure comme d'un vide, nous avons droit, le tirant de nous par de l'ennui à l'égard des choses si elles s'établissent solides et prépondérantes—éperdument les détache jusqu'à s'en remplir et aussi les douer de resplendissement, à travers l'espace vacant, en des fêtes à volonté et solitaires.

Quant à moi, je ne demande pas moins à l'écriture.

Another thing . . . it seems that the scattered trembling of a page wants nothing if not to defer or throb with impatience at the possibility of something else.

We know, captives of an absolute formula, that certainly is not what it is. However, to dismiss forthwith, under some pretext, the delusion would emphasize our inconsistency, negating the pleasure we want to take: for this *beyond* is its agent and, I would say, its engine, if I were not loath to carry out, in public, the impious dismantling of fiction and consequently of the literary mechanism, to flaunt the chief component or nothing. But I admire how, by trickery, one casts up, to some forbidden and lightning-struck elevation, the knowing lack we have of what shines forth up there.

What purpose does that serve—

A game.

In sight of a higher attraction as of a void, we have the right—eliciting it from ourselves by boredom with regard to things if taken as solid and dominant—desperately to detach them until they are filled again with it, and also to endow them with radiance, across empty space, in solitary celebrations at will.

As for me, I ask no less of writing.

What does writing care about? To free us from what is. And what is, is everything, but it is first the presence of "solid and dominant things," all that for us marks the domain of the objective world. This liberation is accomplished by the strange possibility we have of creating emptiness around us, putting a distance between us and things. This possibility is genuine ("we have the right") because it is linked to the deepest feeling of our existence—anguish, say some, boredom, says Mallarmé. We have seen that it corresponds exactly to the function of writing, whose role is to replace the thing with its absence, the object with its "vibratory disappearance." Literature's law is this movement toward *something else*, toward a *beyond* that yet escapes us because it cannot be, and of it we grasp only "the knowing lack" that "we have." It is this lack, this emptiness, this vacant space that is the purpose and true creation of language. (Surrealism, valuing the feeling of other presence, the primacy of the surreal, follows the same tendency.) Undoubtedly, certain positive values correspond to such a lack, as front to back: in the course of the work of the erosion it accomplishes, poetic language reaches a point at which things are transformed, transfigured, and, already invaded by emptiness, radiant "in solitary celebrations."

> Ainsi, quand des raisins j'ai sucé la clarté,
> Pour bannir un regret par ma feinte écarté,
> Rieur, j'élève au ciel d'été la grappe vide
> Et, soufflant dans ses peaux lumineuses, avide
> D'ivresse, jusqu'au soir je regarde au travers.

> So, when from grapes I have sucked their clarity,
> To banish by my sleight a distanced regret,
> Laughing, I raise to the summer sky the empty cluster
> And, breathing into its luminous skins, greedy
> From drunkenness, until evening I look through.

But this movement is surpassed by the strictness of language, it is toward absolute absence that it turns, it is silence that it calls. It is possible that what is for us only lack and nothingness "shines forth up there" or, as we read in "Little Air":

> Indomptablement a dû
> Comme mon espoir s'y lance
> Éclater là-haut perdu
> Avec furie et silence.

> Uncontrollably had
> As my hope throws itself there
> To burst forth up there lost
> With fury and silence.

But "up there" does not concern us: it is, on the contrary, the singularity and wonder of language to give creative value, a startling power to nothingness, to pure emptiness, to the nothingness it approaches, if it does not attain, as of its boundary and its conditions ("Equal to creating: the idea of an object, escaping, that is lacking").

Let us note that poetry, in this enterprise of detaching us from being, is trickery and play. It necessarily tricks us; bad faith and lies are its virtues. Like the hero of *Igitur*, it says, "I cannot do this seriously."

Its fate is tied to imposture. Why? Perhaps we would have an intimation of this if we reread the first sentence of our text. What is this "scattered trembling of a page" that, as expectation, suspense, or impatience, exists only in the future, always projected toward something else whose impossibility is its entire being? No doubt it is what Valéry calls a feeling, a thought of the dawning state or, more exactly, neither thought nor feeling but a birth, a hatching, an intention that seeks itself, a meaning that indicates itself, a still suspended meaning, of which we hold only the empty outline.

The poet marks thus the major privilege of language, which is not to express a meaning but to create it. Only this birth appears to be like a death and the approach of a final absence. From the fact that man speaks and, through speech, gives a new meaning to the world, one might say that man is already dead, or is, at least, awaiting death, and, by the silence that allows him to speak, tempted at each instant to fail himself and all things. He must, it is true, conduct the game to the end: to utter everything is his task, to utter everything and to reduce everything to silence, even silence. But silence, thanks to which we speak, leads us back to language, to a new language that is never the last. That is why the poet, like any man who speaks and writes, always dies before he has attained silence; and that is why, always, his death seems premature to us, the lie that crowns an edifice of lies.

It would be good to remember many striking points of these remarks on language. But the most remarkable of all is the impersonal character of language, the kind of independent and absolute existence that Mallarmé lends it. We have seen that this language does not imply anyone who expresses it, or anyone who hears it: it speaks *itself* and writes *itself*. That is the condition of its authority.

The book is the symbol of this autonomous subsistence; it surpasses us, we can do nothing beyond it, and we are nothing, almost
nothing, in what it is. If language isolates itself from man, as it
isolates man from everything, if it is never the act of someone who
is speaking in the presence of someone who hears him, we come to
understand that to one who contemplates it in this state of solitude,
it offers the spectacle of a singular and completely magical power. It
is a kind of awareness, without subject, that, separated from being,
is detachment, questioning, infinite ability to create emptiness and
to place itself within loss. But it is also an incarnate consciousness,
reduced to the material form of words, to their sonority, their life,
and giving us to believe that this reality opens up who knows what
path to us into the obscure heart of things. Perhaps that is an
imposture. But perhaps that trickery is the truth of every written
thing.

§ Mystery in Literature

"We readily speak of the mystery in poetry and Literature." It is curious that the first sentence of *The Flowers of Tarbes* [by Jean Paulhan] is to remind us of this mystery. Then the second makes us ashamed of it, and the third turns away from it: "To speak of the ineffable is to say exactly nothing. To speak of secrets is to confess nothing." "Those are not the problems."

Let us admit it, such a dismissal leaves us mistrustful. Perhaps it is the custom, when beginning a book, to speak of questions of which one does not speak. "There are a thousand of them." But when one is resigned to not knowing 999 of them, it is strange to advance the only one that is "pretentious and vain" to know. One would think it a matter, rather, of a problem so delicate that one could take it into consideration only by ignoring it, and could approach it only by approaching another. Perhaps there exists a *via negationis* for criticism, if problems exist in literature that one cannot evoke without making them disappear, problems that demand an explanation capable, by the very clarification it brings, of affirming the possibility of escaping all explanation. The mystery in literature is undoubtedly of such a nature that one degrades it if one respects it, and we drop it if we grasp it. If we honor it from afar, calling it secret and ineffable, it makes itself an object of disgust, something perfectly vulgar. And if we approach it to explain it, we encounter only that which conceals itself and we pursue only that which flees. The mystery might well be like those kinds of questions that are found to be solved when we decide not to employ all the method and rigor one should apply to consider them carefully.

The Flowers of Tarbes speaks about language. So do *Jacob Cow, Key to Poetry, Conversation on Various Subjects,* and up to *The Bridge Crossed.* They speak about it in the most precise manner, trying to see if language is subject to laws, and if these laws that concern expression can be expressed. Their starting point? An "obvious fact": language is made up of two distinct elements, one material— breath, sound, written or tactile image; and the second immaterial—thought, meaning, emotion. Content and form: it no doubt happens regularly in literature that this distinction is questioned, but it also happens regularly that the questioning takes an exactly opposite form. Some, who must be called Rhetorickers, reduce content to form (Paul Valéry: content is only impure form); while others, who have received the name of Terrorists, give thought precedence, and seek to reduce the word to it (Novalis: the letter is really a letter only through poetry).

So this is what ensues: literature, by avoiding all those who represent it, tends regularly to deny all division of language into two elements of equal importance; but the manner in which this denial is produced, sometimes oppressing one, sometimes destroying another, again regularly establishes the existence of these two factors whose assertion seemed at first, to some, purely academic and even naive. It is obvious that if half the writers acknowledge literature as form and the other half as content, there is a very troubling conflict there—very troubling, and very violent. For on the one hand, under the pretext of unity, it ends up constantly giving rebirth to the double aspect of language, which it would like to reduce. On the other hand, by its regularity, it seems to demonstrate something essential, a contradiction present in language itself and of which the opposing biases of critics and writers might only be the necessary expression.

The naiveté of Jean Paulhan, asserting that all language, all poetry, must be investigated starting from these two elements, sense and sound, ideas and words, is thus the least unthinking there is, if it is this naiveté that, its presence intact, is allowed to appear against them by all the theories of literature, themselves scarcely naive. Is there a stranger or more unreasonable dialogue than one in which we hear rigorously opposite assertions, which literature needs constantly to sustain against itself, answer each other? The writer who is most aware, most attentive to his art, is as if forced to have two opposing views on this art. Mallarmé: "The pure work involves the elocutionary disappearance of the poet, who yields the initiative to words." But: "Poetry consists of creating; one must take into one's soul states, gleamings of an absolute purity."

Every language can offer at each instant two opposite aspects, one verbal, one ideal. Every text can be appreciated from a double point of view: either as putting into play material phenomena—breath, sound, rhythm, and by *extension*, word, image, genre, form—or, according to meaning, emotions, ideas, the things it reveals. Goethe once showed Eckermann a manuscript covered with erasures. "So many words," said Eckermann. He was thinking of the resources, the wealth of speech. But Goethe replied, "Words! You do not see that there's not one left." And Berni, defending the poems of Michelangelo: "He says things, and you say words" (Jean Paulhan, *The Spectator's Program*). Yes, such an illusion is strange, not that it occurs but that it cannot not occur. Sometimes the same arrangement seems words, sometimes only thoughts, so that even to the one who exerts himself to grasp how it takes form, the illusion continues to impose itself, since in the *Key*, one can read "When one expresses the mystery without thinking it," which might lead one to suppose that there exists in the world of language at least one sentence that does not have a counterpart of thought, while the *Key* itself tries to teach us not only that there are no words without thought and no thought without verbal existence, but that in poetry thought and word are identical.

The provoking character of these remarks comes from their simplicity and from the impossibility, nevertheless, of going beyond them. Who will not say to himself, All right, that's understood, language is sign and sense, word and idea, we know that, we have always known it. But this is what happens: one is forced to stop knowing it. At each instant, it is natural for us to speak of the "power of words," of those words that are called great—liberty, justice, religion—because they are completely without thought, and seem, to us to exercise a dangerous power "over the mind and heart of men, *apart from their meaning.*" Apart from their meaning—what can be more singular? As if a word could lose its meaning, go outside of its meaning, all while remaining a word; as if it did not act then according to another meaning, forming with it a new indissoluble arrangement, having a word side and an idea side. When Lautréamont turns the proverbs upside down, "If Cleopatra's morals had been less short, the face of the earth would have changed: her nose would be no longer than that," he shocks us, because he upsets our belief that an order of words, to which a certain meaning corresponds, will not, if one reverses it, necessarily meet with another sensible meaning. But, for Lautréamont, "there is nothing incomprehensible" and every succession of words signifies something, every verbal arrangement has an aspect of thought.

The first volume of *The Flowers of Tarbes* is a long chain of proofs from which it follows that such writers are regularly mistaken on the nature of various expressions, commonplaces, for example. They see phrases in them that have lost their meaning, they find in them a dangerous excess of words, while others recognize in them, because of the banality that makes them invisible, an exceptional absence of phrases and a hypertrophy of thought. The Terrorist, completely enchanted with a dream of innocence in which things and emotions can appear to us in their original purity, without the words that constrain them and throw them to the common world, is obsessed by the linguistic aspect of language. One must wring the neck of eloquence, push away technique, be mistrustful of words, for words are only words. No ideal aspect for language the way Terror sees it: the star here eternally shows the frozen landscape of its extinguished volcanoes and its lifeless mountains.

Terror chases after the desperate dream of a language that would be nothing but meaning, and the fury with which it proscribes signs is a testimony of its fate to destroy, along with what it does not like, what it does like, and what it plans to save. But there another

discovery occurs. The author who disdains words must still, however, arrive at sentences. He must have rare forms, exceptional
figures of speech, words that, because of their newness, cease to be
words for him. In the end it is a matter of a language reduced to its
interior aspect, open to the inexpressible, new and almost innocent. But what an author has written, a reader reads. And this
reader not only does not undergo the illusion of the author who
thought he was dealing only with a thought without words, he
undergoes the opposite illusion of a language with a superabundance of words, one almost without thought. He sees only unusual
words at which he is embarrassed and because of which he believes
the writer to be precious and strange, when that same author had
aimed for the most spontaneous emotion; he speaks of literature,
when literature is banished. "Beautiful phrases, images," he thinks.
"The truest emotion, the thing itself," the writer feels.

If we lay aside the particular theories (which form another
treatise) on Terror and its drawbacks, if we do not search for
unchanging relationships between the one who writes and the one
who reads, we see clearly that these remarks answer to the simplest
and most mysterious experience. By analysis, we know to the point
of being tired of it that every spoken or written text is made of
words and ideas. We know it but we do not know it, and we
constantly become blind to one or the other of these aspects, either
to the word or to the meaning, until we deny the action and its
value. At rare moments, when it is a question of a piece of language
in transformation or in decay, with expressions that are at once
overused and usual, such as we use mechanically but that some stop
or snag makes suddenly visible to us, we come to discover *at the
same time* these two aspects of language: we perceive, in quick
succession or annoying simultaneity, this double face of the star, as
if, because of the disturbance, it had started to sway in front of us.
Or again, it is from an angle that we seem to glimpse the heads and
tails together, or by a quick fanning out that suddenly throws into
our presence, in a graspable display, the whole face of language,
whose two sides we otherwise see only as folded one over the other,
each hidden by the other.

Everyday language is such that we cannot see it at the same time, in its entirety, in its two aspects. If there (rightly) does not exist less of it, it is due to the fact that it is essentially a dialogue: it belongs to a couple, the speaking and the speaker, the author and the reader. The two relationships of language are displayed in their duplicity by this other duplicity, of the man who speaks and the man who listens: idea aspect, on one side, most often the speaking side, and word aspect, on the side of the spoken. "Author's thought, reader's words," said Jean Paulhan; "author's words, reader's thought."

But how these two functions of author and reader, of mouth and ear, are not assigned once for all, that each person is at the same time the two members of the couple, and writes sometimes as a reader and listens (more rarely) as if he were speaking—this confusion of tasks contributes to making habitual language into a language with only one side. One speaks but no one listens, one listens to what has not been spoken, or even no one speaks, no one listens: these situations are frequent.

Let us return to the writer. We can certainly claim that "this writer had certain *things* to say, certain *feelings* to express, that common language seemed incapable to him of rendering; that by dint of corrections, alterations, approximations, he finally succeeded in forming words so faithful to his ideas that they vanish in their presence and give him, when he uses them, the single feeling of a direct communion with his thought" (*The Spectator's Program*). We will say or think that his language is not *phrases, ways of speaking*, but the vision of things, meeting of emotions, and that the writer did not look for words but for words that render a thought. But let us see what happens. There is, if one realizes it, a singularity and almost a contradiction in the success we ascribe to this writer. Does he seek the phrase for its own sake? Yes; but the phrase is necessary to him, he cannot do without it, he constructed it in detail, giving it such a form, such a rhythm, such a color, etc. But, we are told, when he has it, it is so perfect that he believes he no longer holds this phrase but the thing, not a way of speaking but the emotion itself. It is possible, the event is even well established, but at the price of what paradox? This thing, in fact, does not really exist for him; insofar as it exists in reality, it exists (far from existing, it is absent, absence of itself, Mallarmé tells us) starting with words; words are what make us see it, what make it visible, at the instant they themselves vanish and are erased. They show it to us and yet they have disappeared; they no longer exist, but they always exist behind the thing that they make us see, and that is not the thing in itself but only the thing arising from words. Vanished though they may be, they still must remain very present, and we must feel them continually as that which disappears behind the thing, as that which makes it appear by disappearing. The writer's words have a triple existence: they exist to disappear, they exist to make the thing appear, and, once vanished, they continue to be and to disappear in order to maintain the thing as appearance and to prevent everything from sinking into nothingness. (Let us note that if we accept the observations of Mallarmé, for whom to write is not to evoke a thing but an absence of thing, we find ourselves confronting this situation: words vanish from the scene to make the thing enter, but since this thing is itself no more than an absence, that which is shown in the theater, it is an absence of words and an absence of thing, a simultaneous emptiness, nothing supported by nothing.)

Let us go on, now, to the side of the reader. Concerning such images as *milky way*, which we understand not as image but as the thing it shows, and which foreigners, on the other hand, discover and admire as picturesque words, the author of *Jacob Cow* writes: "We do not hear words directly, but following the meaning we form in them. The presence of the image in this sense reveals a delay, a rupture of understanding—like a short circuit of language. We judge writers in the same way." So it seems that the presence of the word or the image, under the reader's gaze, is illicit and the result of an accident or a false maneuver. And yet, it is indeed true that the word must be present in some way, if the meaning is also there; and undoubtedly the word is *understood* with the meaning it indicates, nor is this meaning separate from the expression that sights it, as could happen if the meaning were, in itself, the entire language. A short circuit occurs, we are told, that breaks the unity of speech and makes the word appear more or less fugitively in the meaning and the image next to the thing. A short circuit, but one with the most curious effects. For thanks to it, in language we see at once the image, the verbal aspect, as the essential and thought, the ideal aspect, as the only important thing. We discover at the same time that the word in itself, and the meaning in itself, make the language, and we see these two aspects as indispensable to each other, although each asserts itself as the fullness of everything and as disappearing so that the other can appear, both existing so that each can exist. Marvelous phenomenon, prodigious short circuit. But in truth it is perhaps not unknown to us; it is even familiar to us, for it bears, as its commonest and rarest name, the name of poetry.

We are now in a position to read the last page of *The Flowers of Tarbes* and to discover without surprise that it sends us back to the mystery. "Whoever directs his search in this sense (whoever applies the same methods that have unmasked and set right the Terror to Rhetoric, by reversing them) . . . must finally recognize in this metamorphosis and this reversal the exact face of the mystery, which common opinions, myths, poets had vaguely announced to him." Thus, at the last word there reappears what the first had removed, and that can scarcely surprise us if, when we were talking of language, we did not stop catching sight of what we could not speak of: this same mystery that disappears when it is explained, is degraded when it is venerated, and in which the division of all literature into two irreconcilable and inseparable halves, the fate of each of them to be correct only when seen from the other side, from the point opposite it, have led us to recognize the paradox inherent in language.

This paradox, too, can take different forms: that language is made up of two elements and yet is such that one must endlessly reduce these two elements to one alone, while continuing to reassert them both, is one of these forms. That the two sides of language—that cannot be seen at the same time, that can only be glimpsed together, from an angle and as in perspective, by the movement of the dialogue—tend, however, to be placed together, to unfurl gloriously in front of us, is another form of this paradox. Language wants to fulfill itself. It demands to be completely visible, without contenting itself with the subterfuge of perspective and the stratagem of dialogue. It aspires to an actual absolute. It aspires to it in the most complete way, and not only for itself, in its entirety, but for each of its parts, demanding to be completely words, completely meaning, and completely meaning and words, in a same and constant affirmation that cannot bear either that the parts that conflict with each other agree, or that the disagreement disturb the understanding, or that the understanding be the harmony of a conflict. This aspiration is the aspiration of poetry to existence. When the *Key* offers us this phrase, "It can happen that words and thought are undifferentiated in poetry," we understand that such a lack of difference expresses the possibility for language to be entirely each one of its parts, to be words and thought with the word, thought and words with the thought, and to be realized in this exchange independently of the logical terms that make it up.

Such a demand is no doubt formidable. But it only half surprises us if we remind ourselves we have already met it, in almost the same form, in Mallarmé's remarks on language. What did poetry demand under Mallarmé's name? Absolute being, one with a consciousness able to exist outside of any individual consciousness, self-realized, and capable, while expressing everything, of posing as the lack of everything. Particularly, poetry thought to be the act neither of an author nor of a reader: "Impersonified, the volume, so long as one separates oneself from it as author, does not ask the reader to approach. That is how it is; among its human accessories it takes place all alone: a deed, existing." Yet, we see clearly, it is exactly in the same form that the poetry of the *Key* shows itself. Between language's two terms, it is in search of a relationship such that it makes mystery and becomes unimaginable. This relationship, we have seen, is that the word becomes idea, the idea, word, "in such a way that each term of the relationship then loses the particular characteristics that define it." But how is this possible? By this simple act, in poetry the relationship preexists the terms; the terms exist only in this relationship, and what we know of isolated terms, from other experiences, has the same value only in the relationship that, strictly speaking, grounds them. In other words, in poetry, only the tension that unites the terms exists, and these terms are distinct only in appearance and from a subsequent point of view, from the point of view of ordinary language that has only formed itself starting from poetry.

Yet, if we remember well, of these two terms, one—thought—corresponds to the author, and the other—word—to the reader. To be most completely realized, language aspires to the existence in two parts offered it by the reunion of these two people, the confrontation of these two functions. But what if there are no more terms in poetry? If there is no longer idea on one side, word on the other, author here, reader there, but only a relationship? Doesn't everything happen as if poetry demanded not, certainly, the rather dubious mystical mingling of the one who writes and the one who reads (since neither one nor the other exists yet) but a fundamental unity, an awareness superior to the two poles, a kind of androgyny of language, starting from which, by a split, actually less decisive than the other, the two functions, originally united in one single relationship, began to exist apart, like two independent beings, most of the time forever strangers? We are told that everything should happen between author and reader as if there had been no language. But the fact is that, for original language, everything should happen as if there had been no author or reader, but one single, same power of saying and reading being substituted for sayer and listener. Only poetry exists at first. After which, the author and reader should indeed get mixed up in being.

Between the mystery of language and the mystery of poetry, there is thus similarity and opposition. The most elementary language carries in itself a light movement toward its complete realization, a minuscule need to make the two aspects that constitute it appear at the same time. In the *Key*, we see the mystery of language increased in poetry by the effort used to free itself from it. If this mystery is the metamorphosis of meaning in word and word in meaning, the poem, by fixing the word in a stricter substantiality and meaning in a stronger awareness, seems in fact an attempt to prevent the game of metamorphosis; it seems a challenge to the mystery, but one, produced as it is despite so many precautions and against the powerful machine made to annihilate it, that is only more striking and even more a mystery. Perhaps, in truth, the word "metamorphosis" brings only too close to us the strange anomaly represented by the claim of language to be completely achieved. For there is not only change, transformation of one element into another, but also the simultaneous maintaining of two opposite perspectives as if identical—as of an object that demands to be seen from one single point in all the aspects it presents from all the points from which one can see it—when, moreover, each aspect would be the entire object, and each aspect would assert itself in its sufficiency and its opposition to all the others, and yet all the aspects would have to show themselves in such a unity that the object *appeared* as stripped of aspects, without *appearances.*

When poetry seeks a more accomplished matter for itself and a meaning that is more sure, it is undoubtedly to disturb the change of one to the other, but it is also because the change can take place only starting from elements made irreconcilable. Let us not forget that each aspect asks to be seen fully, each asks to be given meaning, strengthened, made visible to the extreme, so that sound, rhythm, words, rules are given precedence, but the most elusive feeling, the thought that is farthest away, the truth that is most lost are also given precedence. At first only a conflict can result from this: we feel and sometimes regret that poetry, far from reconciling the elements of language, puts infinity between them, to the point where we have to believe that the words it uses have no meaning whatsoever, and the meaning it aims for remains beyond all words. And yet everything happens as if, starting with this dismemberment, fusion became possible, the distance of this infinite distance seemed nonexistent, and from this hostility the opposition stretched out in a simultaneous overlapping. Poetry, by the tearing apart it produces, by the unbearable tension it engenders, can only want the ruin of language; but this ruin is the only chance it has to be fulfilled, to become whole in broad daylight, in its two aspects, meaning and form, without which it is never anything but distant striving for itself.

One of the aims of the *Key* is to find a law whose legality is that of

the mystery, that is to say, that can be law applying even to that
which escapes the law and expression. It is the beginning of *The
Flowers of Tarbes* all over again. But this time, the problem is not
solved by silence; it is approached in the most open way. The
question is this: By definition, one cannot render the mystery, yet
there is no literature that is not accompanied by mystery, so how
can one open up a path, by literature and language, toward what
haunts language and lives in literature but cannot be expressed by
either? The answer is a mathematical formula.

The answer is important, but the question is no less so. Let us
read it: "I seek a law of which mystery is a part. To be more precise:
a law, such that this secret way of seeing, this kind of elusive but
easy thought, but one that plays at the lightest provocation that we
have named *mystery*, is necessarily set in motion by it and, forming
its tacit understanding, floods it with the clarity that it radiates. A
law, finally, that only arrives at meaning in its entirety by following
mystery." The gravity and purity of this text challenge the mind
and make it understand more than it would like to attain. Can
there be present in the mind and beneath it, not to disturb it but to
shed light on it, something that might be irreducible, and whose
nature it could in no way penetrate or approach? *Conversation on
Various Subjects* speaks of the folly without which our best thoughts
risk becoming ineffective. The study on Sade alludes to a mystery
without which one would not know how to explain anything: "And
as for me, I don't mean to say that a mystery can be an explanation.
I am only beginning to wonder if a valid explanation exists, one
that does not have to do with mystery. I simply see that, without
this connection with mystery (with mystery and with its hidden
demand, its returns in force), Sade would remain perfectly obscure
to us, vague, inconsistent." All the same, unreason, or a secret way
of seeing, or elusive thought, these terms are still traps that reason
intends for the part of itself that escapes it, and where it takes itself
at its true beginnings. Mystery is not non-meaning, since it is
foreign to meaning; it is not illogical, if logic has nothing to do with
it; it is not secret, for it is outside the genre of things that show
themselves or do not show themselves. What is it? Nothing, perhaps. But already such a question oversteps it in all respects.

"My aim is strictly logical." We might be able to find a reader who thinks the mystery here is gotten cheap. It is obvious, he would say, that language is not of the domain of pure thought, founded on traditional principles of similarity and non-contradiction. There is a sense other than intelligible sense, there is a meaning that is not yet either clear or distinct, that is not expressly thought, but that is, as it were, played or mimed or lived by every being capable of grasping and communicating a meaning. Yet it is exactly such a meaning that one first meets in speech, with which it is in such a close relationship that it finds in it its realization rather than its expression. To reserve the word "thought" for the single mode of conceptual thought and to throw to folly, to mystery, all that is outside of the conceptual, is to give more to mystery than it asks, and scarcely to understand it.

The same reader, we imagine, would complain at seeing language broken up into elements, separable in abstract analysis but in reality not distinct. To seek a law for poetry in which the relationships of meaning to sound could be reversed? That is to seek nothing mysterious, though, for it has always been understood that these elements sustain relationships of which explicit analysis cannot give an account. And then (he would add), let us pay attention to phrases like "Words and thought can be undifferentiated in poetry," and let us follow the work of analysis. The analysis begins by distinguishing material elements, like sound, breath, from elements of a different order, like meaning. These elements can be conceived separately (we know what a sound is, we have a vague idea of the word "meaning"), but they cannot exist apart (even breath, which we would say exists quite well outside of language, is not, like breathing, what it is as voicing of a letter), and their association is indispensable to the fact of speech: there can be no language in which sound is not united to a meaning, in which meaning does not exist without sound.

All that is certain enough. However, let us return to our phrase: there, it is no longer a question of sound or of meaning but of words and thought. This change is remarkable. The two elements that were at first only factors, isolated by analysis but not existing apart in reality, have now become autonomous parts of language:

breath is word, meaning is idea. In the form of real fragments of speech has now been realized what were hitherto only abstract constituents of this speech. But, starting from the moment the material side of language becomes an independent part of language, as a word is, we see that the passage from one side to the other and, even more, its indifference in this passage become a scandal or at least somewhat mysterious—exactly the mystery itself. As if an object had to take the place of another object and confuse itself with it in a perfectly inconceivable exchange. But suppose it were not a matter of an object, but of molecules, of atoms? And if, instead of object, it were a matter of components that one isolates momentarily for the purposes of analytic exposition, but that do not exist isolated outside of this analysis and that are thus justified in making themselves distinct only within the confines of analysis? Might the scandal actually not come from analysis itself that, on the one hand, uses its divisions, its method based on distinction and clarity, and, on the other hand, glancing back at real things and perceiving that what it has distinguished is still together, what it has separated is inseparable, then attributes to reality even its own impossibility? And, in the same way, does not the author of the *Key* meet the mystery, because he tries to express, in the language of grammatical legality and even of mathematical rigor, a relationship that has nothing to do with this legality or with this rigor, the mystery being here only in the choice of method and in the strangeness there is in applying it to an object that is not appropriate for it?

"My aim is strictly logical." But perhaps, frightened by the nearness of the mystery, our reader now distances himself from it too quickly. Perhaps he forgets the essential. We are not in search of just any mystery, but of the mystery in Literature, and not of any description of language, but of the description that literature implies. Literature is not solely language at rest, language definitively made, immobilized, and dead; it is more than that, and yet it is also solely that, for it aspires to the paradox of a language that, in the process of self-creation and as if being born, would prefer to be definitively made: to be perfect. The language of literature does not want to be separate from the freedom of the one who speaks and, at the same time, it wants to have the strength of an impersonal speech, the subsistence of *a language that speaks itself on its own*. It is a thing, a nature, and the awareness that ruins all that. One understands why "the aim is strictly logical." It is easy to conceal descriptions from precise demands, from the clearness of analysis—easy but insufficient. For literature wants a language that also accomplishes its logical function; it realizes itself and it is once and for all realized; it is constantly in the process of making itself and constantly perfect. By consequence the analysis that applies itself only to what is unmoving and always subject to its rules cannot be grasped, since it is not only at rest but also the perfection of rest.

In *Conversation on Various Subjects*, we learn to mistrust this argument—"business is business"—and these insults—"and so are you, you should look at yourself." Singular phrases. Let us look at the simplest: when a father tells his son who is spending too much of his allowance, "A penny is a penny," he does not seem to be persuading him of anything, yet he is coercing him with an annoying and almost irrefutable expression. But it is a phrase without any way around it: What makes it effective? Is it its obviousness, the logical nature of its content, a penny is a penny? Does it not have an understood part, a silent double that differs slightly from it, for example, something like "A penny is a lot more than a penny"? This second meaning is not expressed, and it comes to distort the logical exactness of the first meaning by forcing one to infer (without saying it) that a penny is not at all a penny.

Let us note that we have here an image of this mystery of which the *Key* spoke: it is indeed a matter of a secret way of seeing, of an understood part, that plays at the occasion of an expression and, remaining unformulated, gives it its meaning and its value.* And,

---

* That, at least, is what Nicole writes in his *Treatise on General Grace*: "One easily consents to this enthymematic line in Ovid's *Medea*: 'I could keep you, so I can lose you.' Many people, however, would have difficulty in finding the major premise. The majority of proverbs or sentential expressions to which wit has recourse are also based on confused views and reasons that one feels without working them out. . . . There is almost always a secret reason in these sentences,

certainly, one will say that the mystery is weak and the silence slight, since the least analysis discovers it and gives it its share of words. But perhaps that is because one seeks the mystery where it is not. What is troubling is not so much the mechanism of expression, and that it carries with it another expression, unveiled, as it is the fact that, even unmasked, it continues to act, it still troubles. As R.M., the interlocutor, says in *Conversation*, "Admit that there remains some kind of grave, almost tragic allure in logical argument, of which we have not been aware. As if some oracle were pronounced in it, that agitates the entire world." Such is the game of madness here: it looks just like reason each time analysis demonstrates it, then remakes itself as unreason each time verbal expression takes it up again. So that one yields to it as if one were ignorant of it. One restores it to silence, to ignorance, that permit it to act and destroy again. What momentarily chose identity as alibi assumes the role of contradiction again, and the role of negation that needs evidence to assert itself and reach us. Thus, the clearest language is often the most "mysterious."

Now it is possible that, all the while remaining troubled, we are deceived. And it would be surprising if we were not. Our deception is the proof (*preuve*) of the mystery, and our anxiety its ordeal (*épreuve*). In the law we are shown, it is mystery that makes us understand the law, but the mystery itself is inferred. It is as inferred, and as if behind the mind, that it accomplishes the understanding and incites the mind to the light. Let the mystery turn round, and assuredly it discovers something, something that

---

which causes this consenting of mind; and it is the same for almost all advice: one agrees only by virtue of this secret, unexpressed reason." Nicole adds this remark: "Books being only masses of thoughts, each book is in some way double, and imprints two kinds of ideas in the mind. For there is a mass of formed thoughts, expressed and conceived distinctly, imprinted in it; besides that, there is another compound imprinted in it, of indistinct views and thoughts, that one feels but would have difficulty expressing, and it is ordinarily in these views thus excited though unexpressed that the beauty of books and written works consists. Those that excite the most give more pleasure to the mind, because they are more lively and penetrating."

deceives it, because what it sees is itself, yet something uneasy, because, as soon as it turns away, it guesses again the presence and provocation of a strength unknown to it. Further, it sometimes decides to explain it by making it equivalent to what it knows of itself; sometimes it resigns itself to distancing it by abandoning to it the vaguest words, unsayable, ineffable, secret. What else can it do? Leave it in silence? But it is on the occasion of speech that the mystery plays, and it is perhaps like a part of non-language, like the part that in language itself would always be foreign to language; it is its contradiction and its end, but it is also starting from this end that language speaks best. The mystery is less in this non-language than in its relationship with speech, an indeterminable relationship, for it is in this relationship that the word is accomplished, and non-language, from its side, never *appears* except as a language simply differenced. Words must describe it to make us understand it, but that cannot be, since these very words need it to be founded in the relationship that constitutes them.

Certainly, silence is what we prefer for speaking of the mystery. Hölderlin:

> Denn Sterblichen geziemet die Schaam,
> . . .
> Muß zwischen Tag und Nacht
> Einsmals ein Wahres erscheinen.
> Dreifach umschreibe du es,
> Doch ungesprochen auch, wie es da ist,
> Unschuldige, muß es bleiben.

> For mortals modesty is suitable
> . . .
> If, in the twilight,
> Someday, a Truth should appear to you,
> In a triple metamorphosis transcribe it
> Although always unexpressed, as it is,
> O innocent, so it must remain.

And Goethe: "The fruits of the harvest must not be passed beneath the millstone. Words are good, but they are not the best. The best is not made clear by words." And Schiller: "If the soul

speaks, it is, alas, no longer the soul that speaks." And the author of
The Flowers of Tarbes, after the mystery he has just defined: "Let us
add . . . that I have said nothing." Strange privilege, a little
disconcerting, and one that seems naive, if this superiority of
silence is the superiority of one language over another, and that
seems usurped, if this silent language is only an approximation of
the real language, and that seems necessary, when one sees the word
send us endlessly back to an act of which it dreams as of the
moment when it could realize itself completely and at the same
time completely disappear. What is this act? Must one place it on
the side of this precise silence of which Brice Parain speaks, or of
the demonic silence of Kierkegaard? Silence by lack or silence by
excess? And why does the name of silence suit it better than the
name of language? The secret we seek is not one of those secrets
that "even when public must be respected by veiling them and
saying nothing." "I know," said Mallarmé, "one wants to limit the
mystery in music when the written aspires to it." And let us look at
these words of Paul Eluard: "Light and consciousness overwhelm
me with as many mysteries . . . as night and dreams." And again
("Uninterrupted Poetry"):

> Prendre forme dans l'informe
> Prendre empreinte dans le flou
> Prendre sens dans l'insensé
>
> Take form in the formless
> Take an imprint in the blur
> Take sense in the senseless

Is it not there, *appointed* in poetry itself, the form of the mystery
of poetry and of *Literature*, if, in whatever madness they claim, they
always make reason out of their madness and, to the utmost, lead
us in this transparent night where the dark is only inferred?

§ The Paradox of Aytré

William Saroyan is what one calls a spontaneous writer: he did not discover art through art, but "by hanging about in cities, eyes wide open." He thinks he draws his methods and ideas on literature from himself. "A story," he says, "has nothing to do with writing, it is not good English or good Latin or good Greek. It is rock, solid like rock, a solid rock. . . . A story is speech articulated from an ancient absence of speech. It is *now*, this speech, in this language that is neither English, nor Latin, nor Greek, but the language of stone which is the language of man, and fundamentally it is shaped and articulated silence." And again: "The best advice one can give is to draw one's language not from language itself, but from silence and oneself. It is the only possible advice. Do not write with words, write without words, write with silence."

This spontaneous writer takes back into account one of the most ancient wishes of literature: to write in order to reach silence. Certainly such a concern has, more than any other, found its theoreticians and its heroes since the nineteenth century. Everyone knows them. But it is Homer who said, "To speak about everything, to say everything, is the act of the silent man"; and Apollodorus of Athens: "Silence honors the gods by imitating their nature, which is to escape meaning"; and Æschylus: "The riddle is revealed to the one who knows how to keep silence in speech."

It is necessary, though, to see that Saroyan's advice is far from being clear and that the taste or superstition of silence surrounds all kinds of equivocations. When in *The Red and the Black*, after Mathilde's question about Mme. de Fervaques—"Has she made all the sacrifices for you that this fatal love has led me to make?"—Stendhal writes, "A gloomy silence was Julien's only response," it seems to us that this silence is only a hypocritical method of expression. But if we recall Bartleby the scrivener's words, setting against his master's every request this response, "I would prefer not to," we feel that speech here has the privilege of silence. To be quiet is not always the best way of being quiet. That is the reason that Pascal asserted that silence, also, is impure.

Silence is part of language: if we are quiet, that is a way of expressing ourselves. It has a meaning, like any gesture, any facial expression; and, moreover, it owes this meaning to the proximity of language, whose absence it manifests. If we are quiet when someone is waiting for a word from us, it is just as much the word that has not been said as our refusal to say it that shapes the silence and incorporates it in the dialogue that goes on. Everyone understands that a being gifted with language does not attain the same silence as a being without language. If he is mute by accident, he substitutes one language for another. If he is mute out of a refusal to speak, he can seem more silent than a mollusk or a stone would ever seem. But this excess of silence comes only from language, whose possibility it defies.

Still, even this taciturn speech has a way of making itself understood that is natural to it. My silence makes me take part entirely in the meaning I give it. I penetrate what I do not say, I weigh down on what is alleged about my speech, I slip more completely into my absence of response than into my response. And that is not only because, without talking, I have to speak with my entire body, with my presence asserted without phrases; for the silence of lips also demands the silence of face and of body: a power more stretched out than that of my separate and distinct organism is put into play in the absence by which I express myself. The entire universe that is mine is engaged in it and compromised, because this silence tends exactly to preserve of me only the boundary of the world with which I claim to merge.

In *The Bridge Crossed*, a dream is related to us in which the dreamer senses some flaw in his words that makes them transparent to noise. The dreamer concludes from this that it is not enough to invent his words; they also need a kind of tone to be heard. It is this tone that the timid lack: the orphan speaks in vain, says the proverb, whoever is nearby hears nothing. Silence within language is like an analogue of the word's power to intimidate, without which words are lost in noise. One could say that the word's accent, movement, attitude can separate themselves from the word and are more necessary to it than the verbal material itself. The man who keeps silent, to say no or to say yes, to promise or to threaten, is very far from holding on to a pure meaning still foreign to sentences; unlike the dreamer who is unable to communicate because he has forgotten to give a certain tone to his words, he can make himself understood by turning words away from their tone alone. And it is this tone that he supports momentarily with all his existence and with that of the world to which he is linked.

"Language has only one opposite, which is silence," Brice Parain says. If this assertion were imperative, the writer's condition would be simple: he would have to give up seeking, through speech, the end of speech. But literature claims to make an absolute out of language and to recognize in this absolute the equivalent of silence. If language can become complete, as poetry asks it to, if it can be completely realized, either by becoming an ability to say and hear previous to any sayer and any listener, or else by asserting itself as paradoxical object, capable of showing itself in one single aspect such as it would be seen from all points at the same time—that is, to appear in perspective in all its appearances and consequently as deprived of appearances—it must overtake language and, each instant expressing itself as totality, each instant be completely outside of language. Silence would then be attained starting from words and as the essential sign of their accomplishment.

This myth, we have seen, is, above all others, the myth of Mallarmé. But recall how he arrived at it. What is a word for him? In authentic language, a word is not the expression of a thing but the absence of this thing. "I say, 'a flower!' and this is already no more than 'the absent one of all flowers.'" The general quality there is in all speech is also what forms the basis for its poetic future. That which is its power of representation and signification creates a distance, an emptiness, between things and their name, and prepares the absence in which the creation takes shape. Naturally, the single word is nothing but the beginning of a shift, since, by its meaning, it makes present anew the signified object whose material reality it had removed. So it is necessary, if the absence is to be maintained, that another word be substituted for the word, one that distances it, and another for this word that flees from it, and for this last one the very movement of flight. That is how we enter the realm of images, and they are not solid, stable images but occur in an order in which every figure is passage, anxiety, transition, allusion, an act of an infinite trajectory. We are as if tracked down by this rule of absence that cannot do without a support and yet cannot tolerate the presence of what the support signifies; it goes so far that in the end we would no longer have to be in the presence of things or forms or images, but only of a poem, one that would rest on words in succession, their rhythm, their liaison, but as a whole, as totality, would not rest on anything; it would be the reciprocal suppression of every "term," of every point at which pure absence could stop and be formed, and, consequently, it would be the very absence of this language.

At first sight, such an attempt appears to be contradictory, unrealizable, and, as Mallarmé says, only a delusion. But it must be noted that real poetry is an effort toward this unrealizable, that (according to poets) it has as its foundation this impossibility and this contradiction that it tries vainly to realize. In short, it demands that language be achieved and affirmed—by way of an aspiration— as a paradox, and it gives us to understand that real language exists only when this paradox and, as they say, this mystery are outlined and stand out in current forms of speech. Again according to Mallarmé, the main forms of such a demand are the following. If the nature of poetry is to substitute an absence for the reality of "solid" and "preponderant" things, an absence at first determined and defined, then, gradually, the very absence of this absence, a movement toward "other thing," "a tacit flight of abstraction," "a virgin scattered absence," then there occurs a moment in which, everything having been uttered, poetry, being this everything, will itself be no more than the absence of everything, the "elocutory disappearance" of the universe, the container of nothing, a strange power balanced between nothing and everything. This is exactly the book of which the poet spoke—the Book, equivalent of the world, orphic explanation of the Earth—and which is not its summary in the manner of ancient alchemical formulas but its realization in a vanishing form, its gliding toward a mode of existence that is unable to be grasped.

But what happens? The closer poetry is to this boundary where "lacking everything, it replaces everything," the more the poem, to be capable of this operation of metamorphosis, must on its side have reality: the more it calls on sounds, rhythm, number, on all one calls the physics of language and that, in current speech, one ordinarily regards as useless. Thence the privilege granted to the written, to the book in its most material aspect: typographical composition, *mise en page*, "spaced sketch of commas and periods." Language must, the instant it allies itself to the movement of awareness, to its ability to be present to things by holding them infinitely at a distance, to its right to know by the nothingness of what it knows, ally itself also most to the opposite of awareness, to a thing, a solid, a pure and simple material presence. This is what Saroyan, with the calm of a spontaneous writer, claims to be rock, "solid rock," or something "like the sun," or simply "a thing." But Mallarmé, on his part, creates *A Throw of Dice*, which offers, in the simultaneous vision of the Page and the spectacle of a new sky, the movement and enigmatic scansion by which the word makes things disappear and imposes on us the feeling of a universal lack and even its own lack. Surely Mallarmé's claim is more subtle than that of the American writer, but it is only more contradictory than it, because what he wants to reveal to us as a thing—and a thing freed from chance—is the tension from which absence is born, the relentless pursuit by which words, thanks to their abstract value, destroy the materiality of things, then, thanks to their evident power of evocation, destroy their abstract value, and finally, by their mobility, their capacity for suspense, try to vanish into thin air, to extinguish themselves behind the reciprocity of their fires.

We now see why Mallarmé can think both that "everything, in the world, exists in order to result in a book" and that "silence, only luxury after rhymes," "is for the poet, roused by a challenge, to translate *it*." This is because he finds this silence starting from the simplest process of language: in this absence that every word consists of, and that is linked to its ability to give a meaning, to distance the thing in order to signify it ("so that there emanates from it," as he says in his vocabulary, "pure idea, without the annoyance of a near or concrete reminder"). In that way, silence is far from being the opposite of language; on the contrary, there is language only in silence, which is at once the condition, the intention, and the virtue of speech. I speak, but the moment that what I say creates around the thing I designate an emptiness that makes it absent, I am quiet; I also designate the distant absence in which everything will be submerged, even my speech. Thus are formed the hope and illusion of making words from silence and, as Mallarmé says, of holding on to "allusive words, reduced to equal silence" or even of arranging "under the understanding of the gaze an average string of words into definitive traits, with silence." It is a hope that, by managing to make the totality of language rise up, one can also restore to each of its parts the total absence it must signify, then be itself. But it is also an illusion, for the poem does not stop having an existence on two sides, of being a consciousness that destroys the world but also a thing that immobilizes it, a power of annihilation and an indestructible presence, its own negation, says Saroyan, and a reality of stone. And thus Mallarmé, just as he gives poetry a language of extreme physical density, sees himself finally tempted to attain silence by a simple material emblem, the white page, the white of the margin, "the space that isolates the stanzas," as if now silence were no longer in the power of poetry to deny the thing, but in its ambition to become thing itself, not in its dream of being completely unrealized by becoming completely real, but in its capacity of being a nature, and a nature withdrawn from all thought and all speech.

Then what remains of Mallarmé's attempt? First, that it is the poem's essence to implicate it, to begin it again, for the very reason of the failure and the impossibility it represents. Moreover, it discovers a complicity between silence and language whose nature it illuminates by inviting us to seek it in the capacity for absence and questioning that constitute any authentic speech. Writers and psychologists tend, in the beginning of language and at its source, to place a silence that might be like Paradise lost and whose nostalgia haunts our words. And it is useless to recall how many artists are tempted by regret and the presentiment of a silent night that they think is their mission to make visible to us. There again, Saroyan is a useful witness for us: "Any poem, story, novel or essay, no more or less than any thought, is a word come from this language that we have not yet translated, from this vast, mute wisdom of the night, from this vocabulary, without grammar or rules, of eternity." And let us remember that was the meaning of his first piece of advice: draw one's language from silence, write without words, write with silence.

In truth, this silence is not meant to surprise us. We read in Maurice Merleau-Ponty's *Phenomenology of Perception*: "We are losing awareness of the contingency there is in expression and communication, either with the child who is learning how to speak, or with the writer who says and thinks something for the first time, or finally with all those who transform a certain silence into speech." A little further on we read: "Our view of man will remain superficial so long as we do not return to this origin, so long as we do not find again, in the noise of words, primordial silence, so long as we do not describe the deed that breaks this silence." These quotations make it quite clear that the description here goes as far as the literary dream, that silence receives the same privileged place in it, prime and superior, that of seeming to be the guarantee of language that came from it. We know, too, that this silence is pointed out to us as the silence of awareness before it is stated in any explicit judgment and at the moment when the evidence of the *Cogito* has not yet been resumed in the affirmation that prolongs it and turns it away from its global meaning. It is this silent evidence that surrealism, for example, tries to carry faithfully into language through automatic writing. It is also what Pierre Emmanuel seeks when he recognizes in the image, "such as the moderns created it, a return to the original basis, to the primitive spontaneity of being."

These problems are important ones. But there is another we would now like to see better, for it is at once very naive and yet curiously implied by all writers and critics. This problem is: Where does literature begin?

It sometimes happens to a man that he feels an emptiness in himself, a defect, a lack of something decisive, whose absence becomes, little by little, unbearable. In a short story, "Aytré Who Loses the Habit," Jean Paulhan tells the tale of a soldier to whom this happens. Aytré is a sergeant and, with an adjutant who tells the story of the expedition, he leads a column of 300 Senegalese, along-side men of the Fourth Colonial, across Madagascar. Through the adjutant's laziness, Aytré is the one to whom the care of keeping the log of the journey falls. There is nothing extraordinary in this log: we arrive, we leave; chickens cost seven sous; we stock up on medicine; our wives receive magazines, etc. As the adjutant says, that smells of drudgery. But, starting from a certain day, after the arrival at Ambositra, the writing changes, slightly, no doubt, in appearance, but, on careful reading, in a surprising and over-whelming way. The explanations rendered become longer. Aytré begins to go into his ideas on colonization; he describes the wom-en's hairstyles, their locks joined together on each side of their ears like a snail; he speaks of strange landscapes; he goes on to the character of the Malagaches; and so on. In short, the log is useless. What has happened? Aytré has obviously lost the habit. It is as if the most natural things had suddenly begun to surprise him, as if a lack had been brought about in him that he sought to answer by unusual moves, an agitation of thoughts, words, images. And the adjutant is all the more ready to realize that he recognizes in his own uneasiness the trace of a similar predicament. The key to the enigma is easy to grasp. In Ambositra, Aytré met a Mme. Cha-linargues, whom he had known some months earlier and whom jealousy pushes him to kill; as for the adjutant, he prepares to keep a sum of money that the same person had handed over to him for her family. In both cases, for both men, something has begun to come undone; the events proceeding from the self have diminished in number: hair done up, judgments on colonization, strange landscapes, all these literary developments signify the same lack; because of it, now beings, behavior, even words can appear only in their insufficiency.

From this little story, it does not follow that literature must necessarily begin with crime or, failing that, with flight. But that it does imply a caving in, a kind of initial catastrophe, and the very emptiness that anxiety and care measure; yes, we can be tempted to believe that. But let us note that this catastrophe does not fall only on the world, the objects one handles, the things one sees; it extends also to language. That is the paradox of Aytré. In truth, it is easy, or something like easy, to imagine that Aytré, behind the act to which he was driven, found himself lacking and began to translate this lack by an excess of language that would try to fill it. Until then, he was enough for himself; now he is no longer enough, and he speaks to reestablish, by words and by a call to others, the adequacy whose disappearance he feels. Unfortunately, much worse must happen to him. For language is also struck: all the thick layering of words, the sedimentation of comfortable meanings that move off, detach themselves, become a slippery and dangerous slope. The threat spreads to anyone who allows himself to answer it. The writer does not always begin with the horror of a crime that makes him feel his precariousness in the world, but he can hardly think of beginning other than by a certain inability to speak and write, by a loss of words, by the very absence of the means of which he has an overabundance. Thus it is indispensable for him to feel at first that he has *nothing* to say.

In an excerpt we have cited, Kafka is amazed that man, at the height of unhappiness, can write, "I am unhappy." Where, he says, does this excess of strength come from, that allows me to communicate my exhaustion without making it false? But perhaps what Kafka calls overabundance or excess is really a reduction, a retreat before my natural being, an emptiness both in regard to my sorrowful state and in regard to words. Kafka is surprised that I can carry, by a brilliant development of words that signifies hope, affirmation, infinite possibility, an extreme unhappiness that is negation and impossibility. But Kafka's surprise is ambiguous: basically, what seems surprising to him is that an extreme unhappiness can still be the unhappiness of someone who feels it, who consequently remains capable of giving it a meaning and distancing it from himself in order to grasp it—under whatever form he likes. He seems to believe that this awareness of unhappiness is, with regard to unhappiness, a kind of increase, a surplus, a plus sign that might be a challenge to the minus that unhappiness implies. But why? How does the fact that the darkness torments me rise to a kind of transparency—could it be some kind of good, a remnant of luck? I recognize even more in that the first stirring of a fundamental deprivation and this destiny of mine of being always separated from myself, of not being able to hold on to anything and of having to let slip, between myself and what happens to me, the original silence, this silence of awareness by which the sense that dispossesses me of it falls at each of these moments. Thus, the "I am unhappy" explodes into a first emptiness that deprives me of it without alleviating me of it, emptiness that all language remembers and that it strives to find again, starting from the fullness and security of ordinary language.

What happens after that? The "I am unhappy" enters into literature and develops, to Kafka's surprise, with the flourishes and ornaments of a fine style. Flourishes aside, what is striking at first is that it occurs at all for whoever writes (and for whoever reads), like an emptiness in the world of ordinary words, surely not a total devastation but a threat that does make its usage problematic, difficult, and rare. For example, while a colloquial phrase can, without inconvenience, be exchanged for a thousand others with the same meaning, original language, on the contrary, "poetry," does not allow exchange or change; this is so not only because of the necessity that the text not suffer any alteration, but also because of a kind of poverty that makes it untranslatable, intransmissible in another form, as if the privation were such that, outside of the words touched by the poet, all had stopped being available, as if a new world really were beginning, a new field of language in the ruin forever used up by everyday language. One can certainly wonder at this beginning, this intention in its dawning state, and believe it possible only by an excess of strength, but this beginning is first an end. From one of its sides, poetry makes sense, but from another it unmakes it. It distances the word, and if it does give us the word, it is from a distance. It dangerously connects the possibility of speaking with an impossibility that becomes almost its condition. It allows us to write "I am unhappy," but this *first* expression of unhappiness, by taking away from us thoughts already formed, frequented, and certain, exposes us to an experience full of risk, and more than that, to a silent faltering, a stammering that its perfection does not prevent us from recognizing as a lack.

When Aytré writes, "The Malagaches who lead the canoes make the sky vibrate with their incomprehensible songs, which do, however, have their style. That makes life seem gay to us," who would be surprised to discover the effects of a terrible suffering in this gaiety and the expression of this gaiety? One sees clearly how the world that is opened and undone can become the world of a happy life and how a language in the process of destruction expresses, because of that, unhappiness, but also happiness and beauty and human generosity. If one says, perhaps to reproach him, that Aytré's words, far from threatening ruin, become, to the degree that he "loses the habit," more chosen, more thought out, more *happy*, this would be only naiveté, since, for this sergeant, recourse to the most literary or beautiful language signifies only the irreparable loss of the only language that was certain for him, that in which it was enough for him to write, "We are doing twenty kilometers a day." So instead of experiencing a feeling of satisfaction and creation when he finds words like "The strangeness of the things in Madagascar answers to that of the men. At every turn, there are landscapes of a lunatic originality," he feels, on the contrary, the embarrassment and distraction of someone who feels himself deprived of words, for whom their handling becomes the most deceptive proof and, as it were, the exploration of his own emptiness. That Valéry reproached Pascal for *this distress that writes so well* remains the sign of a very strange misunderstanding, as if Pascal had necessarily had the feeling of writing well, as if this admirable language we lend him had not been for him as dull, as stripped of future, as stifling as the misery whose extent it caused him to discover. What Valéry attributes to Pascal is his own reaction in the face of Pascal's style, but Pascal, when he was writing, did not feel himself the author of Pascal's style and, quite the contrary, he saw in the *Pensées* the weak elements of a forever absent book, a confusion that did not become ordered, and the very "shipwreck" of which Valéry wanted to recognize only the eternal debris, too well made to be saved.

It is in *Jacob Cow* that we read "The lot of poets is that the simplest acts are difficult for them—for example: there is something like a lack of spirit in them that metaphors translate." If a lack of this kind is enough for names to become undone and images born, one can also, under the name of figure of speech, understand why language is haunted by its own impossibility, if it is necessarily related to feelings of anxiety and absence in which the possibility of language is almost nonexistent. In Aytré, speech comes to answer to a fundamental lack, but speech is itself attained by this lack, sent back to its beginning (or, just as well, condemned to end) and thus made possible by that which makes it impossible. In this paradox, the role of deception is obvious, and it is especially large because of the literary game, which, the instant language is closest to the blank existence of consciousness, aims at a subsistence that disengages from it, at an autonomy that announces its future, its historically enduring value of experience. From that comes this effort of poetry to become the realization of a complete unrealization, such that when achieved, the primal absence would be asserted in it (in the manner of a thing, stone, block, sun, regarded as symbols of anything deprived of meaning) on which all our deeds, our acts, and the very possibility of our words rise up, the absence in which poetry itself would disappear by the fact that it achieved it. That is why we can readily see in the search for silence one of poetry's most obsessive concerns; yet it must be noted that this name of silence is scarcely suitable here: properly speaking, there is silence only in daily life, in what Merleau-Ponty calls "the spoken word," when we are so immersed in words that words become useless. On the contrary, the silence of creative language, this silence that makes us speak, is not only an absence of speech but simply an absence, this distance that we put between things and us, and in ourselves, and in words, and that makes the fullest language also the most porous, the most transparent, the most nonexistent, as if it wanted to let the very hollow it encloses flee infinitely away, a kind of small urn* of emptiness.

* *Alcarazas*, an unglazed vase that keeps water cool by evaporation. — TRANS.

§ The Language of Fiction

It is generally acknowledged that the words of a poem do not play the same role or maintain the same relationships as those of ordinary language. But a narrative written in the simplest prose already suggests an important change in the nature of language. This change is implied in the smallest sentence. When I find, at the office where I work, these words, written by my secretary, in my memo book, "The head clerk called," my relationship with the words will be completely other than if I read this same sentence in *The Castle*. The words are the same, I give them roughly the same meaning. In both cases, I do not stop at the words. I pass over them, and they open up to a knowledge linked with them, so that I grasp from my book directly, instead of the words written there, the connection I must make with the supervisor whose subordinate I am, while in the novel, the still obscure existence (we are in the first pages of the book) of a regional administration with which relations seem uneasy.

And yet, from the reading of my memo book to that of the novel, the difference is great. As an employee, I know who my supervisor is, I know his office, I know many things having to do with who he is, what he says, what others say about him, what he wants, the difficult nature of our hierarchical relationships, the intolerable sense of hierarchy for me, etc.; my knowledge is, in a way, infinite. As new as I may be, I am pressed on all sides by reality, and I attain it and meet it everywhere. On the other hand, as a reader of the first pages of a story, I am not only infinitely ignorant of all that is happening in the world being evoked, but this ignorance is part of the nature of that world, from the moment when, as an object of a narrative, it is presented as an unreal world, with which I come into contact by reading, not by my ability to live. There is nothing poorer than such a universe. What is this head clerk? Even if he were described to me in detail, as he is later, even if I entered perfectly into the whole mechanism of the Castle's administration, I would still be more or less aware of the little that I know, for this poverty is the essence of fiction, which is to make present to me that which makes it unreal; it is accessible to reading alone, inaccessible to my existence. No richness of imagination, no preciseness of observation could correct such destitution, if it is always implied by fiction and always put down and taken up by it through the thickest content or the one closest to the real that it is willing to receive.

To return to our sentence. Although read from my own book and articulated with the most present reality, it brings me to the feeling of the event that it signifies and of the act to be accomplished that will result from it, but without the knowledge it carries in itself being in any way expressed. This knowledge will normally remain that of an empty awareness that could be filled, but is not filled; as a reader aware of words that mean something, I have present in my mind neither the words that I read and that the meaning makes disappear, nor this meaning that no defined image presents, but only an ensemble of connections and intentions, an opening onto a complexity yet to come. In daily life, to read and hear implies that language, far from giving us the fullness of things in which we live, is cut off from them, for it is a language of signs, whose nature is not to be filled with what it aims for but to be empty of it. Its nature is not to give us what it wants to have us attain, but to make it useless to us by replacing it, and thus to distance things from us by taking their place, and taking the place of things not by filling itself with them but by abstaining from them. The value and dignity of everyday words is to be as close as possible to nothing. Invisible, not letting anything be seen, always beyond themselves, always on this side of things, a pure awareness crosses them, so discreetly that it itself can sometimes be lacking. Everything then is nullity. And yet, understanding does not stop occurring; it even seems that it attains its point of perfection. What could be richer than this extreme destitution?

In the novel, the act of reading is not changed, but the attitude of the one who reads makes it different. "The head clerk himself called," the janitor's son says in *The Castle*, "that is what is so annoying to me." Undoubtedly these words, too, are signs and act as signs. But here, we do not depart from a reality given with our own. It is a question, on the one hand, of a word that has yet to wake up, and on the other hand, of an imagined ensemble that cannot stop being unreal. For this double reason, the meaning of words suffers a primordial lack and, instead of pushing away all concrete reference to what it designates, as in day-to-day relationships, it tends to demand verification, to revive an object or a precise knowledge that confirms its contents. It does not follow that images necessarily play a large role in novel reading; we know quite well that imaginary narratives speak little to the imagination, and that the interest and value of a novel are not a function of the abundance of images it produces. But a more subtle phenomenon occurs. To the extent that their meaning is less guaranteed, less determined, that the unreality of fiction holds them apart from things and places them at the border of a world forever separated, words can no longer be content with their pure value as sign (as if reality and the presence of objects and beings were all necessary to authorize this wonder of abstract nullity that is everyday talk), and at the same time take on importance like verbal gear and make evident, materialize what they signify. The *head clerk* first of all comes into existence from this name, a name that is not lost in the meaning of a label that evaporates as soon as it is spoken; it exists as a verbal entity, and all that I can know of it from now on will be impregnated with the self-nature of these words, will show it to me particularized, drawn by them. This does not mean that, in a novel, the method of writing counts more than what is described, but that the events, characters, acts, and dialogues of the unreal world that is the novel tend to be evoked, grasped, and realized in words that, to signify them, need to represent them, to have them immediately seen and understood in their own verbal reality.

The sentence in the story and the sentence in daily life both have the role of a paradox. To speak without words, to make oneself understood without saying anything, to reduce the heaviness of things to the agility of signs, the materiality of signs to the movement of their signification—it is this ideal of a pure communication that is at the heart of universal talk, of this way of speaking that is so prodigious, in which, while people speak without knowing what they say and understand what they do not listen to, words in their anonymous usage are no more than ghosts, absences of words, and by that itself, in the midst of the most deafening noise, empower a silence that is probably the only one in which man can rest, as long as he lives. The language of real existence wants to unite these two opposing characteristics: for as long as it is given us, a real thing among things, which we arrange like an experience and which we do not need to make ours in order to use, it is also an act tending to go into thin air before it is accomplished, supported only by the emptiness of a possible intention, as near as one can imagine to non-existence. A sign of the superabundance of beings, to be itself as a trace and sediment of the world, of society, and of culture, it is pure only if it is nothing. On the other hand, the sentence in the story puts us in contact with the unreality that is the essence of fiction and, as such, it aspires to become more real, to be made up of a language that is physically and formally valid, not to become the *sign* of beings and objects already absent (since imagined), but rather to *present* them to us, to make us feel them and live them through the consistency of words, the luminous opacity of things.

It goes without saying that these two languages have thousands of intermediaries that bring them closer and mix them together. In our everyday sentences, the image can come to fill up the gap that is the meaning of the word; knowledge can be actualized in it by animating this meaning. Often, as beings capable of imagining and producing fiction, we go toward things that are not there and whose evocation demands to be supported by the complicity of a language less freed from itself, more realized. The example we have used is only the example of an embryo of a story; thus we must think of it with all its appropriate breadth and complexity. We will see then that, as prosaic as prose is and as close to banal life as the story is, language undergoes in it a radical transformation, because it invites the reader to realize from the words themselves the understanding of what happens in the world offered him, and whose entire reality is to be the object of a story. We like to say of a reading that it *holds* us; the expression answers to this transformation: the reader is in fact held by the things of fiction that he grasps, given by the words; like their own characteristics, he holds on to them, with the feeling of being enclosed, captive, feverishly withdrawn from the world, to the point of experiencing language as the key to a universe of bewitchment and fascination where nothing of what he lives is found.

But it happens that in a story, language, instead of being the abstract meaning that gives us concrete things (the aim of everyday speech), seeks to revive a world of concrete things appropriate to represent a pure meaning. We arrive at allegory, myth, and symbol. Allegory introduces the ideal of daily prose into fiction: "the story" sends us back to an idea of which it is the *sign*, in the presence of which it tends to disappear, and which, once set down, is enough to express and affirm itself. Myth, on the contrary, implies an actual *presence* between the beings of fiction and their meaning, not the relationships of sign to signified. By its involving us in mythic story, we begin to live its meaning; we are impregnated with it, we really "think" it, and in its purity, for its pure truth can be grasped only in things in which it is realized as action and feeling. Myth, behind the meaning it makes appear, endlessly reconstitutes itself. It is like the manifestation of a primitive state in which man would not know of the ability to think apart from things, would reflect only by incarnating as objects the very movement of his thoughts and thus, far from impoverishing what he thinks, would penetrate into the richest, most important thought, the one most worthy of being thought. Thus literature can create an experience that, illusory or not, appears as a means of discovery and an effort not to express what one knows but to experience what one does not know.

It is understood that symbol is not allegory. Its task is not to signify a particular idea by a determined fiction: the symbolic meaning can only be a global meaning, which is not the meaning of such an object or such an action taken in isolation but that of the world in its entirety, and of human existence in its entirety.

It is in this movement that imagination becomes symbolic. The image it seeks, the figure not of such-and-such a thought but of the tension of the entire being to which we carry each thought, is as if immersed in the totality of the imaginary world: it implies an absolute absence, a counterworld that would be like the realization, in its entirety, of the fact of being outside reality. There is no symbol in such a demand, and this demand, operative behind all the movements of the story, prevents it, by its continuously active negation, from receiving a determined meaning, from becoming only significative. The symbol signifies nothing, it is not even the imaged meaning of a truth that would otherwise be inaccessible; it always surpasses every truth and every meaning, and it presents us with this very surpassing that it grasps and makes evident in a fiction whose theme is the impossible effort of fiction to be realized as fictive.

The aim of every symbol is always more or less its own possibility. It is a story that is enough for itself and it is the lack that makes this story insufficient; it makes out of the lack of its story the subject of its story, it tries to realize in it this lack that always infinitely surpasses it. The symbol is a narrative, the negation of this narrative, the narrative of this negation; the negation itself appears sometimes as the condition of all the activity of art and of fiction and, consequently, as the condition of this narrative, sometimes as the sentence that pronounces its failure and its impossibility, for it does not accept being realized in a particular act of imagination, in the singular form of a finished narrative.

In the symbol is thus manifested, at the highest point, the pressure of a paradoxical demand that is more or less evident in all its forms of language. On one hand, it is made of events, details, gestures: it shows faces, the smiles on faces, a hand that takes a spoon and carries it to the mouth, crumbs of plaster that fall from the wall when someone climbs it. These are insignificant details, and the reader does not have to seek or receive meaning from them. They are nothing but particularities, worthless moments, dust of words. But on the other hand, the symbol announces something, something that surpasses all these details taken one by one and all these details taken together, something that surpasses itself, that refuses what it claims to announce and discredits it and reduces it to nothing. It is its own emptiness, the infinite distance that it cannot interpret or touch, a lacunar immensity that excludes the boundaries from which the symbol endeavors to make this infinite distance appear. And yet, the symbol is not unformulated either, and if it rids itself of concrete traits to end up at the formless, it is completely lost. It is nothing but circumstances, circumstances borrowed from ordinary life, only those, inseparable from them, yet it is out of reach. That is why one readily thinks it is outside of time, and tries to reduce it to the nontemporal language of thought. But it is not outside of time, it is not abstract: it is outside of reality, first in this sense that it confuses itself with imagined events, grasped in their absence as present, then in this other sense that it wants to grasp again not only such-and-such imagined event but also the very possibility of the imaginary, the totality of the imaginary, and, behind each unreal thing, the unreality that could reveal itself in itself and for itself.

This attempt is rigorously contradictory. It cannot come about. And all the same, it is valuable only in its impossibility, it is possible only as impossible effort. Hegel says of symbolic art that its principal fault is *Unangemessenheit*: the exteriority of the image and its spiritual content do not succeed in coinciding fully, the symbol remains inadequate.* Undoubtedly, but this *fault* is the essence of the symbol, and its role is to send us endlessly back to the lack that is one of the ways by which it would like to make us experience lack

---

* The symbol, it is true, is only the beginning of art for Hegel.

in general, emptiness in its entirety. The symbol is always an experience of nothingness, the search for a negative absolute, but it is a search that does not succeed, an experience that fails, without this failure being able to acquire a positive value. A writer who expresses himself in symbol, whatever the theme of his meditations is, can finally express only the demand of the symbol, and measure himself by the misfortune of a contradictory negation that seeks to surpass all particular negation and assert itself as universal negation, not as an abstract universal but as a concrete emptiness, a realized universal emptiness. Likewise, every writer who grapples with the experience of death as transcendence can only fall into the ordeal of the symbol, an ordeal he can neither master nor refuse.

Kafka's example is present in everyone's mind. Too many interpreters tell us too clearly what Kafka wanted, what he was, what he sought in his existence and his writings, so that one does not wish to return to silence a work that wished only for silence and with which the commentary of fame, as profound and ingenious as it may be, can only be in disagreement. This very disagreement, this disturbance in the triumph that crowns an infinitely miserable life, the almost unlimited survival that posterity promises him, this failure in success, this lie of misery that leads only to the brilliance of fame—such an ironic contradiction is part of the sense of the work and was felt beforehand in his search.

Kafka, probably under the influence of Eastern traditions, seems to have recognized in the impossibility of dying the extreme curse of man. Man cannot escape unhappiness, because he cannot escape existence, and it is in vain that he heads toward death, that he confronts the anguish and the injustice of it; he dies only to survive. He leaves existence, but only to enter into the cycle of metamorphoses, to accept the degradation of vermin, and if he dies like vermin, his disappearance becomes synonymous, according to others, with renewal, with a call to life, an awakening of voluptuousness. There is no actual death in Kafka, or, more exactly, there is never an end. Most of his heroes are engaged in an intermediate moment between life and death, and what they seek is death, and what they miss is life, in such a way that one does not know how to characterize their hopes, if they place their hope in the possibility of losing all hope, and how to appreciate their regrets, if these regrets eternalize the condemnation they undergo.

In "The Hunter Gracchus" and in "The Guest from the Dead," Kafka expressed directly the strange condition of the dead who do not die. But these little stories are parables; they make us touch what they mean to say, and since their meaning is connected to the undefined power of negation that reveals death, there is a contradiction between the nature of the story that is achieved and precise, and its content that demands the absolute ambiguity of negation. On the other hand, the story of *The Castle* is symbolic. One can certainly interpret the odyssey of K. One can recognize in him the being who left his homeland, as one leaves existence, and who, with the very means that he used to live, tries to get himself accepted by death. K. was called, and it is quite true that death seems a call; but it is also true that to answer this call is to betray it, to make something real and true of death. All his efforts to reach the Castle are marked with this contradiction: if he strives, struggles, desires, he reveals always more existence; while if he remains passive, he misses what he aims for, death being death only when one makes it one's own and it stops being the death of no matter whom, any death whatsoever.

We also see K. uniting ignorance with cunning, extreme awareness with extreme non-awareness, rejecting the help that is offered him, for he knows that no one else can replace him in this task; he struggles to obtain what this struggle prevents him from attaining, for while struggling, he can do nothing else: all that remains to him to save himself is to work endlessly at his curse. Moreover, what is the aim? Who can claim here to have touched it? The village? But the village people represent the most miserable stage between existence and non-existence. Frieda floats between disappointment, desire, and indifference; she does not know what the assistants are; she undergoes their attraction, she is ashamed of that attraction, she resists it, she succumbs to it; pitiful failure, existence of reflection, light of refusal. The functionaries? We suspect they are more powerless than anyone: feeble, frightened, they are incapable of supporting the existence of below, and yet they haunt it, they desire it, they call for it, they miss it. Where is death's rest? O Death, where is thy victory?

Kafka experienced very deeply the relationships of transcendence and death. And that is why, in his work, sometimes it is death that appears to beings as that which they cannot attain, sometimes it is that which surpasses beings that appears in the unworking and misery of death. Sometimes death appears as transcendence, sometimes transcendence appears dead. This reversal already shows how dangerous it is to claim to fix, in an explicit form, the interpretation of a story in which negation is at work and shows itself just as well as the nothing that prevents the absolute from being accomplished except as nothingness that measures absolute accomplishment. The passage from yes to no, from no to yes, is the rule here, and all interpretation that avoids this (including that which hypostasizes this alternation) contradicts the movement that makes it possible. To see in K.'s story the image of the unhappinesses of existence that cannot be grasped as existence because it cannot be found as the end of existence, remaining unreal, self-negating, insofar as it is not capable of being really non-existence, profundity of that which is beyond life, assertion of nothingness without memory—it is clear that such an interpretation vainly contains the ambiguity of a proposition in which assertion and negation are in continuous threat of reciprocity. As long as it rests in the well-determined form of an abstract thought, it escapes the verdict it renders and it fundamentally disobeys the symbol, losing all its meaning the moment it isolates this meaning and makes it discernible.

So one must plunge the interpretation back into the heart of the story, lose it there and lose it from view, and grasp again the movement of fiction whose details assert only themselves. The inn, the peasants with their stubborn, frustrated faces, the iced light of the snow, Klamm's pince-nez, the pools of beer in which Frieda and K. roll—that is what matters, that is what one must experience to enter into the life of the symbol. There is nothing else to look for, nothing more to understand. And yet, one cannot be content with that either. Bury oneself in the story? But the story itself rejects you. Each episode contains a question about itself, and this question is also the profound life of fiction; it is the story, it shows itself face to face, it asserts itself, it converses. Where is the symbol? Where it appears, where it hides? Where there are only calm, firm appearances, where appearances grate and are torn apart? Where things are present with their natural obscurity, where behind things their emptiness emerges, behind the story the absence of story, behind the profundity of symbol the impossibility that erodes the work and forbids its accomplishment? It is these very questions, and it dies from these questions. In this sense, every symbol that does not ruin the work in which it develops is ruined in the commentaries it provokes, that it cannot prevent itself from provoking. It must, to subsist, be unaware of itself in fiction, and those who make it known, make it sterile by declaring it.

Such is its last ambiguity: it vanishes if it awakens; it perishes if it comes to light. Its condition is to be *buried alive*, and in that it is indeed its own symbol, symbolized by what it symbolizes: death that is life, that is death as soon as it survives.

§ Reflections on Surrealism

In an article in *Horizon*, Philip Toynbee remarked, "It is striking that we are always ready to be reminded of the number of French writers who were surrealists or were under the influence of surrealism. In England, the influence was negligible, and perhaps it was not necessary. But it seems that nothing was more profitable than a sojourn in this school." Perhaps surrealism's situation is ambiguous. We readily recognize—even more readily than before the war—the deciding role it played in French literature. Does that mean that surrealism has become historical? There is no longer a school, but a state of mind survives. No one belongs to this movement anymore, and everyone feels he could have been part of it. In every person who writes there is a surrealist calling that is admitted, that miscarries, seems sometimes usurped, but that, even when false, expresses a sincere effort and need. Has surrealism vanished? It is no longer here or there: it is everywhere. It is a ghost, a brilliant obsession. In its turn, as an earned metamorphosis, it has become surreal.

One can approach surrealism from many different ways. One can look for what it was in itself and the date its influence began. One can try to understand it in the light of preoccupations that have developed since. We may be wrong to neglect what was its central discovery, the automatic message. It is true that on this point the failure of the attempt seems sometimes irredeemable. But the fact that Breton always stayed with it, with an indefatigable perseverance, that he sought to save it from all the shipwrecks and even from his own doubts ("The history of automatic writing in surrealism would be, I'm not afraid of saying it, that of a continued misfortune"), is enough to show that this method was not an artificial invention and that it fulfilled one of literature's principal aspirations.

Automatic writing is a weapon against reflection and language. It is supposed to humiliate human pride, particularly in the form that traditional culture has given it. But in reality, it is itself a proud aspiration toward a way of knowledge, and opens a new unlimited belief in words. Surrealism was haunted by the idea that there is, there must be, in man's constitution a moment in which all difficulties are removed, in which antinomies no longer have any meaning, in which knowledge completely takes hold of things, in which language is not speech but reality itself, yet without ceasing to be the proper reality of language; in this moment, finally, man touches the absolute. Surrealists seemed to their contemporaries to be destroyers. Dada's heritage is there for something. And the character of nonconformist violence was naturally the most striking. Today, what strikes us is how much surrealism affirms more than it denies. There is a wonderful strength in it, a drunken and powerful youthfulness. In a way, it needs to make a clean slate, but above all it seeks its *Cogito*.

But what does it find? Curiously, it finds that it is an exact replica of Cartesian experience. One can say that surrealism had the presentiment of rediscoveries that at about the same time and for many years were in the process of turning German philosophy upside down. What Breton sought (or what he discovered in a kind of nocturnal hallucination) is an immediate relationship with himself, "immediate life," forming a connection with his true existence without any intermediation. This relationship is not to be sought in exceptional states, in unitary experiences of mystical form: it is at hand, everyone is addicted to it all day and all night long. I think, I suffer, I have the feeling of thinking, of suffering, this feeling is real, it is immediately linked to what I think, to what I suffer, it is an "absolute." But, at this time, Breton had a singular illusion (favored, moreover, by contemporary scientific tendencies): it seemed to him that this feeling could become an immediate language, become language without any sort of words intervening between him and this feeling. If I say, or better if I write, "I suffer," these words, provided they were written outside the control of my consciousness, not only express exactly my awareness of suffering but are at heart this very awareness. The effectiveness and importance of automatic writing is that it reveals the prodigious continuity between my suffering, my feeling of suffering, and the writing of the feeling of this suffering. With it the opaqueness of words is established, their presence as things is lessened. They are all that I am at this very instant. By raising the constraints of reflection, I allow my immediate consciousness to burst into language, I allow this emptiness to be filled and this silence to be expressed.

Neither Breton nor his friends worried about securing the foundations of their method. There was quite a bit too much of the casual in their procedures, they lacked enough seriousness (and this lack of seriousness was itself something rather serious) to arrive at actual justifications. However, Breton, in the first manifesto, wrote this, which can only be an allusion to the *Cogito*: "I believe more and more in the infallibility of my thinking about myself, and it's too right. . . . By definition, thought is strong, and incapable of seeing itself at fault." And he added: "All the same, in this writing down of thought, where one is at the mercy of the first exterior distraction, 'bubblings' can be produced. . . . It is on account of suggestions that come to one from without that one must make these weaknesses evident." For a rigorous analysis, these remarks are perhaps a little confused, but at bottom nothing is clearer: awareness of my thought "infallibly" reflects my thought; the writing down of the thought also infallibly reflects this thought; only suggestions from without intervene and reestablish an interval between me and me speaking. An exterior complication that does not call into question either the fact or the nature of language.

Surrealists have extracted the most brilliant literary consequences from this "discovery" and, for language, the most ambiguous and varied effects. In this domain, they still seem, above all, destroyers. They loose their fury on discourse; they take away from it any right usefully to mean something; fiercely they break discourse as a means for social relationships, for precise designation. Language seems not only sacrificed but humiliated. Yet it is a question of something else: language disappears as an instrument, but only because it has become subject. Thanks to automatic writing, it benefits from the highest promotion. It is confused now with man's "thought," it is linked to the only real spontaneity: it is human freedom acting and manifesting itself. That rational constructions are rejected, that universal significations vanish, is to say that language does not have to be *used*, that it does not have to serve to express something, that it is free, freedom itself. When surrealists speak of "freeing" words, of treating them other than as little servants, it is a veritable social revindication they have in view. There are men and a class of men that others think of as instruments and elements of exchange: in both cases, freedom, the possibility for man to be the subject, is called directly into question.

But this emancipation of words can occur only in a double sense. On one hand, in automatic writing, it is not, strictly speaking, the word that becomes free; rather, the word and my freedom are now no more than one. I slide into the word, it keeps my imprint, and it is my imprinted reality; it adheres to my non-adherence. But on another side, this freedom of words means that words become free for themselves: they no longer depend exclusively on things that they express, they act on their own account, they play, and, as Breton says, "they make love." Surrealists became well aware—and they made use of it admirably—of the strange nature of words: they saw that words have their own spontaneity. For a long time, language had laid claim to a kind of particular existence: it refused simple transparency, it was not just a gaze, an empty means of seeing; it existed, it was a concrete thing and even a colored thing. Surrealists understand, moreover, that language is not an inert thing: it has a life of its own, and a latent power that escapes us. Alain wrote that one must always verify where ideas are—they do not stay in their place, that is why they cannot be on their guard. It is the same for words: they move, they have their demand, they dominate us. That is in part what Brice Parain called the transcendence of language. Breton contents himself with speaking "of this little uncompromising world over which we can sustain only a very insufficient surveillance and in which, here and there, we rectify some flagrant offenses." Language becomes a weird life, without innocence, something lingering and sometimes tremendously quick, like lightning. We know that surrealism is very much attached to the magical aspect of things; but it had already observed this magical power in language, which embodies it and wonderfully illustrates it.

Having left this double meaning, it is quite clear that Breton and his friends are exposed as contradicting themselves in the strangest and, probably, the most fortunate way. With automatic writing, it is my freedom that triumphs, it is the most immediate relationship, the only authentic one, of man to himself, found and manifested. From this angle, one can say that the poetry of Éluard was essentially poetry of surrealism, poetry of that immediate life that surrealism felt and glorified, not transparent poetry but poetry of transparency, as incomprehensible and obscure for the beings who live in a conventional world as the most absolute hermeticism. This poetry, which seems never to have been very much in line with automatic writing, expressed, however, better than any other the moment, previous to language, that automatic writing tries to touch, in which I have the pure feeling of what I feel. It is a veritable poetry of the *Cogito*. But surrealism is also the freedom of words: Dada's heritage, "words set free," sentences decomposed, rags of advertising texts set end to end? Perhaps, or especially, the succession of a long and immense poetic work whose causes are spread out over the course of centuries. The result is that these free words become centers of magical activity and, more than that, things as impenetrable and opaque as any human object withdrawn from utilitarian signification. We are far now from the category of the immediate. Language no longer has anything to do with the subject: it is an object that leads us and can lose us; it has a value beyond our value. We can be taken in a storm or in a swamp of words. It is rhetoric become matter.

We see to what ambiguity, literally, this double point of view leads us. If language is linked to the silence of my immediate thought and is authentic only when it *realizes* it, we must say good-bye to literature. The furious thrusts against the ideas of work, art, talent come in part from the postulate of *writing from thought.* "Surrealism's characteristic is to have proclaimed the complete equality of all normal human beings [this word 'normal' marks, it is true, a rather strange reserve] before the subliminal message, and to have constantly maintained that this message constitutes a common heritage; it tries to vindicate each one's right to share in what must at all costs soon stop being thought of as the exclusive privilege of the few." Outdated, then, the point of view of the originality of artistic talent, of verbal research for itself. Yet it is a fact: surrealism appears to us as an aesthetic more than anything, and seems to us occupied first with words. Is it an inconsistency, a shameful weakness of writers of literature to be what they are? Rather, it is fidelity to their conception of language. Words are free, and perhaps they can free us; one has only to follow them, to abandon oneself to them, to place all the resources of invention and memory at their service. If rhetoric consists, as Jean Paulhan says, of maintaining that thought comes from words, then it is certain that surrealism is rhetoric. And Breton, the first, affirms it for us: "Still (after the attempts of Ducasse, of *A Throw of Dice*, of *Calligrammes*), we were not sure that words already lived their own life, we did not dare see them too much as creators of energy. We had emptied them of their thought and we waited without believing too much that they commanded thought. Today, it is an accomplished thing: now they have what we expected of them." We remember that the first journal of those who were going to become surrealists was called *Literature.* Nor was this ironic.

The characteristic of Breton is to have held irreconcilable tendencies firmly together. No more literature, and yet an effort at literary research, a care for figured alchemy, a constant attention given to procedures and images, to criticism and technique. Writing is not what counts ("I think that poetry . . . emanates more from the life of men, writers or not, than from what they have written or from what we suppose they could have written." And we recall the famous *Literature* survey that asked, "Why do you write?" and the only answers, gathered with a certain care, were that of Valéry: "I write out of weakness," and that of Knut Hamsun: "I write to while away the time"). Still, writing counts; writing is a means of authentic experience, an altogether valid effort to give man awareness of the meaning of his condition. The same Breton reserved his most solemn and lofty statements for such a subject, and perhaps the most persuasive. "Once again, all we know is that we are gifted to a certain degree with speech and that, through it, something grand and obscure tends imperiously to express itself through us. . . . It is an order that we have received once for all and that we have never had the leisure to discuss. . . . To write, and I mean to write so difficultly, and not to seduce, and not, in the sense one ordinarily understands it, to live, but, it seems, all the more to be morally self-sufficient, and, short of being able to remain deaf to a singular and untiring call, to write is thus not to play or cheat, so that I might know."

This very beautiful "setting the record straight" forms part of the text *Legitimate Defense*, one of the first published by Breton to clarify his position in the face of communism. It is common practice to treat this avatar of the surrealists lightly. Their declaration of Marxist beliefs has not always seemed very serious. Jules Monnerot asserts that in any case Marxists could not take them seriously. "The right to be exceptional recognized in the poet," this tendency to believe that "poetry communicates with revolution," that "revolutionary grace could be obtained by poetry," the will to pursue, cost what it may, the experiences of inner life, *and that, of course, without outer control, even Marxist*—these ambitions could only lead them to throw themselves at communism "like a college degree at a discipline" (*Modern Poetry and the Sacred*). That may be, but the fact remains that the phase was neither fortuitous nor arbitrary, and it remains very significant as an example of the profound engagements that literature cannot prevent itself from forming as soon as it becomes aware of its greatest freedom. Surrealism did not always push literature away, but it always pushed away literature that was taken as the art "of embellishing, even a little, the leisure of others." If there were in this group, across all the metamorphoses and dissidences, a permanent conviction, it is that poetry is related to the condition of man in his entirety, that it is not any activity whatsoever but an activity that concerns man as a whole. To that conviction this other one came to be added: the reality of man is not of the nature of things that are. It is not given, it must be conquered; it is always outside of itself. Poetry that is at once the awareness of this endless surpassing, its means, and this surpassing itself, is never given: poetry has nothing to do with the world in which we live, which is, at least in appearance, a world of things completely made. Thence the primacy of the imaginary, the call for the marvelous, the invocation of the surreal. Poetry and life are "elsewhere" (Monnerot indicates very well that, by its taste for the unusual, the surrealist has particularly in view an experiment in search of the something else, a feeling of other-presence), but "elsewhere" does not designate a spiritual or temporal region: elsewhere is nowhere; it is not the beyond; it signifies that existence is never where it is. Surrealism is one of those attempts by which man claims to discover himself as totality: incomplete totality, he is yet capable, at a privileged instant (or by the single fact of seeing himself incomplete), of grasping himself as a whole. As it is at once an inspired movement and a critical one, it mixes all kinds of views, postulates, aware and confused researches, but the main intention is clear: surrealism is in search of a kind of existence that is not that of the "given," of things as they are. (It does not know very well if this "other" existence can be attained by analysis, by investigative experiences, like that of the subconscious, of the dream, of abnormal states, by a call to a secret knowledge fled away into history, or if it must be realized by a collective effort to change life and the course of things.) And at the same time it is in search of an absolute event, in which man manifests himself with all his possibilities, that is to say, as the entirety that surpasses them. It is an absolute event, the revelation of the *real* functioning of thought by automatic writing. It is an absolute event in which *everything* is *realized*, the discovery of a "certain point of mind in which life and death, the real and the imaginary, past and future, the communicable and the incommunicable, high and low, cease being perceived as contradictory." (And Breton adds, in the *Second Manifesto*, "Yet one could seek in vain in surrealist activity for a motive other than the hope to determine this point.") The signs are countless that this supreme effort, by which man tries to turn round on himself and seize a gaze that is no longer his own, has always been the dream and resource of surrealism. And what does René Char tell us? "In poetry, it is only starting from communication and the free placement of the totality of things among themselves across us that we find ourselves committed and defined, in a position to obtain our original form and our preliminary properties." And again: "Imagination consists in expelling from reality many incomplete people, in order, by contributing the magical and subversive powers of desire, to obtain their return in the form of a completely satisfactory presence. That is, then, the inextinguishable uncreated reality."

In what way, then, did the support of Breton and some of his friends for Marxism make them believe that the realization of this dream would be furthered? To assert that one writes not for amusement or for love of art but because the fate of man is engaged in this activity in the end leaves us somewhat uneasy. Purely interior engagement often seems illusory. One is never sure of not "playing" and of not "cheating." The engagement wants to become more serious, to conclude itself, to be a weighty thing, something that must be accepted, which can be put out of one's mind only by making it one's own at each instant. Breton said this, with his habitual sangfroid: he and his friends were at first in search of something to do in common. "One will search and I suppose one will find vital reasons that, initially, would have made some of us prefer to act together rather than singly; yet that would have ended up with the creation of various papers that did not, in reality, have the approval of any of us. Something at least, I already think I can say it, will thus have happened with a will that might otherwise have remained indecisive. This minimum of dependence freely accepted will also have had the effect of relegating to the back-

ground of our preoccupations what was nothing but a brilliant
accessory, since it belonged more particularly only to this one or
that one of us. For lack of the discipline of class, a discipline"
(*Communicating Vases*). Perhaps it is a law that all art that disengages itself from the inner elements that enslave it (rejection of
imitation, refusal of words as instruments of exchange, refusal of
art considered amusement), tends to be engaged in an exterior
action that weighs it down. The more useless it becomes, the more
it needs an end to make something useful out of this uselessness. It
is its gratuitousness that makes its placement "in the service of the
revolution" inevitable.

But it is still clear that if Breton and Éluard and Aragon met with
Marxism rather than any other political activity, it is not by chance.
If René Char wrote this admirable song of refusal, *Beginning of the
Partisan*, "The poet has returned for long years to the nothingness
of the father. Do not call him, all you who love him. If it seems to
you that the swallow's wing no longer has a mirror on earth, forget
this happiness. He who made bread from suffering is not visible in
his glowing lethargy. Ah! beauty and truth make it so that you are
present, numerous, in the volleys of release!" one must imagine that
this refusal was not without reason or without value. In truth, it is
glaringly obvious that historical dialectic offers to all those haunted
by the ideas of a perfected man, of a limit of the human condition,
a chance of the first order: complete man is not to be sought, now,
in the rifts and disorders of capitalist society, it is not to be known,
it is to be done. (Marx's famous sentence, "Men have, until now,
only interpreted the world in different ways; now it is a question of
changing it," was turned and turned again in all its angles by the
surrealists.) When dialectic is at its end, then consciousness will be
completely present to itself; with society classless, it will be realized
and seen in its totality. "At the end of our phase of history, Marxists
see the *complete man*, Spinoza's man, renewed and incomparably
more magnificent. Only materialists do not believe that this end
will be attained because it is conceived. They have an ideal without
idealism" (Guterman and Lefebvre, *Consciousness Mystified*). Undoubtedly, Breton is not altogether skeptical when he envisages

such an ideal, but he is aware enough that there is perhaps a play of words in this use of the word "perfected," or in any case he speaks of it with a certain indifference, as if, in all ways, the absolute realized by history could not change the actual structure of awareness, and as if it always needed nonhistorical problems to achieve this change. Thus he writes, as early as 1926, "There are gaps in us that all the hope we place in the triumph of Communism does not overcome; is not man implacably an enemy to man, will boredom end only when the world does? Is not all assurance of life and honor vain, etc.?" And in 1932, in an even firmer manner, "I will not tire of setting against the present imperious necessity, which is to change the far too faltering and worm-eaten social foundations of the old world, this other necessity, no less imperious, which is not to see an end to the coming Revolution, which obviously would be at the same time the end of history. The *end* would be for me only the knowledge of the eternal destination of man, of man in general, whose destiny could be fulfilled only by the Revolution" (*Communicating Vases*).

This last assertion shows the reasons for which the surrealists turned to Marxism. In the present state of society, all problems are distorted, poetic problems along with the others, and poetic problems before all the others, since poetry is knowledge and manifestation of the fate of man in his entirety. By the fault of the capitalist state, man is not only oppressed and limited, but he sees himself as other than he is, he takes as essential questions problems created by societal tensions: for example, he is aware of his anguish and his tearing apart, but he does not realize that tearing apart and anguish are disguised by the disarray proper to a society that is collapsing. Likewise, as long as the problem of freedom for the collectivity of men is not concretely settled, the metaphysical problem of freedom cannot be legitimately posed. It is when man's freedom has no longer to be *made*, when it is given in deeds, realized in all its conditions, it is then that freedom will become aware of itself as that which always transcends these conditions, that which is never realized, never given or done. Man will be free because, as Breton says, "the artificial precariousness of man's social condition will no

longer veil from him the real precariousness of his human condition," that is to say, because, in a free society in which he can
choose only to be free, he will still have to choose for himself,
without being able to unload this care on anyone or ever to be
"freed" from it. Thus, the service that surrealism expects from
Marxism is to prepare for it a society in which everyone could be
surrealist, but especially in which the aims of surrealism would be
led to good, in all their purity, without misrepresentation or falsi-
fication. How could poetry cease being involved in social revolution? It is this task of the revolution that, far from masking its own,
"hands over its perspective to poetry," for thanks to the revolution,
poetry understands that neither poetry nor poetic values really exist
except at the moment when man, having nothing more to do,
because everything is done, discovers the meaning and value of this
nothing, the proper object of poetry and freedom both. (Francis
Ponge notes, for example, that his poems are written as if on the
day after the revolution.)

Let us now see around what themes surrealism takes form.
Literature is banished, but language mixes with the pure moment
of awareness: words are ideas. Art disappears as an end, nothing but
life and the deepening of life matter; yet one gives the greatest
possible attention to technical researches, formal effects, artistic
falsehoods (the "attempts at simulation"). Finally, the poet demands an absolute freedom: he pushes away all control, he is
master of his means, and just as free with respect to the literary
tradition as he is indifferent to the demands of moral standards,
religion, and even reading. Yet this freedom ends here: "Surrealism
in the service of the Revolution." If one unites two by two, by a
very significant bipolarity, these themes that call to each other by
opposing each other, one will see that the writer for whom writing
has the meaning of an essential questioning does not lose interest
for all that in the effort of technical invention and formal creation,
and on the contrary endlessly associates his verbal research and his
inner research, as if the authenticity of his experience were linked
to its literary value ("A perfect sentence is at the highest point of the
greatest life experience," wrote Léon-Paul Fargue). And we will also

see that the most uncommitted literature is at the same time the most committed, because it knows that to claim to be free in a society that is not free is to accept responsibility for the constraints of that society and especially to accept the mystifications of the word "freedom" by which society hides its intentions.

In summation, literature must have an efficacy and meaning that are extraliterary, that is, it must not renounce its literary means, and literature must be free, that is, committed. Perhaps, considering the force of these paradoxes, we will understand why surrealism is always of our time.

§ René Char

We like Georges Mounin's book *Have You Read Char?* because it approaches René Char with the method and seriousness, the ardent patience and spirit of measurement to which the university resorts when studying the consecrated celebrities of poetry. The essence of Char's celebrity cannot but remain foreign to a consecration. But why couldn't the traditional means of literary history serve to speak to us about texts for which every other manner of explanation would be faulty? The need to understand and interpret, the many *that is to say's* that the reading of poems requires, according to this surprising and almost fatal impulse that believes poetry is more accessible if analogous words are substituted that destroy it, these naivetés, often corrected, moreover, by strong scruples, detract nothing from Mounin's admiration, itself admirable for his certainty and penetration, and for the intimacy of his connections to the strongest poetic movement. His experience as a reader deserves every respect, for it is that of a man quite fortunate for having known, thanks to an absolute confidence, how to read the poet who could give the most sense and the most dignity to this reading.

The relationships between a poem and a reader are always of the most complex kind. It is not true that poetry can do without being read, and that the poem must haughtily ignore the reader; yet previous to any reader, it is exactly the role of the poem to prepare, to put into the world the one who has to read it, to force him to exist starting from this still half-blind, half-composite that is the stammering reader involved in habitual relationships or formed by the reading of other poetic works. It is the same for the reader as for the poet. Both poet and reader of this poem take their existence from it, and are strongly aware of depending, in their existence, on this song to come, this reader to become. That is one of the mysterious demands of poetry's power. The poet is born by the poem he creates; he is second to what he makes; he is subsequent to the world he has brought to life and concerning which his ties of dependency reproduce all the contradictions expressed in this paradox: the poem is his work, the truest impulse of his existence, but the poem is what causes him to be, what must exist without him and before him, in a superior consciousness wherein are united both the obscurity of the depths of the earth and the clarity of a universal power to establish and justify.

Thence arise the debates about the inspiration and creative activity of the poet. One of Georges Mounin's mistakes is to waste his time reproducing them through traditional analysis. "Inspiration" and "reflection" are terms of an illegitimate analysis, stemming from one of the most unimaginative of all dichotomies. One can put the most possible distance between these two operations, the most unequal sharing of privileges; one can see in them, on one side, an excess of awareness, on the other, a fruit of unawareness, the happiness of passivity and the grace of work. But these differences are only the awkward sketches of a difference of a kind completely other than more or less aware activity measures. *Inspiration* means nothing other than the anteriority of the poem in relation to the poet, the fact that the poet feels himself, in his life and his work, yet to come, still absent in face of the poetic work that is itself all future and all absence. This dependence is irreducible. The poet exists only after the poem. Inspiration is not the gift of a secret or a word granted to someone already present; it is the gift of existence to someone who does not yet exist.

As for *work*, it signifies, before the anteriority of poetry and its claim of forming an absolute awareness, the unrealizable and impossible nature of this claim: the deception this represents for all

those who hold to the conditions of the fact of the poem; the
necessity of leaving a language already given and a dominating
existence infinitely present; finally, the preoccupation with replacing, by an increase of individual awareness, the impossible absolute
awareness that should make up the poem in itself. We have not yet
seen clearly that the primacy of conscious work in Valéry is only a
degraded reminiscence, an indirect and bitter homage to the Mal-
larméan concept of an absolute poetic awareness, superior to any
author and any reader and alone capable of authorizing these two
functions of art and language.

One of the greatnesses of René Char, one that is unequaled in
our time, is that his poetry is a revelation of poetry, poetry of
poetry, and, as Heidegger almost says of Hölderlin, poem of the
essence of poem. As much in the *Marteau sans maître* (Hammer
without a master) as in *Alone They Remain*, poetic expression is
poetry faced with itself and made visible, in its essence, through
words that seek it. *Leaves of Hypnos*, "these notes" of a "partisan,"
thrown into the day-to-day difficulties of action and the obsession
with events, contain the strongest and simplest poetic words that
poetry has used to clarify and recognize itself. It is in these pages
that the supremacy of the poem is best revealed, not only over the
poet but over poetry itself. "The poem is furious ascension; poetry,
the game of arid riverbanks." "I am a man of riverbanks—excava-
tion and inflammation—not always able to be torrent." But *The
First Mill* had already asserted it:

> Aptitude: porteur d'alluvions en flamme.
> Audace d'être un instant soi-même la forme accomplie du poème.
> Bien-être d'avoir entrevu scintiller la matière-émotion instantanément
> reine.

> Aptitude: carrier of alluvium in flame.
> Boldness of being for an instant oneself the accomplished form of
> the poem. Well-being of having glimpsed the sparkle of matter-
> emotion instantly queen.

Language speaks wrongly of poetry in general; this word, "poetry," refers poetic works to a form, ideal or abstract, that might

surpass them to explain and judge them. But the poem does not look to poetry as to a power that might be anterior to it and from which it should await its justification or its existence: it is not the reflection lit up by a star; it is not even the momentary manifestation of an ability always superior to its works. To understand that the poem is creator and prime is to understand that it is always in this order: what is general depends on what is unique.

But it is also to understand why the poem is division, vexation, torment. It does not come from a higher reality, capable of guaranteeing it; it does not refer to a truth that would last longer than it; it is not rest, for it does not rest on anything, and the poet receives only the anxiety of a movement without beginning or end from it. "Magician of insecurity," says Char, "the poet has nothing but adopted satisfactions. Ash always unfinished." A poem is

> La tristesse des illettrés dans les ténèbres des bouteilles
> L'inquiétude imperceptible des charrons
> Les pièces de monnaie dans la vase profonde

> Sadness of the illiterate in the darkness of bottles
> Imperceptible anxiety of wheelwrights
> Pieces of change in the deep mud

Sun singers:

> Les disparitions inexplicables
> Les accidents imprévisibles . . .
> Les cerveaux incultes . . .
> La pariétaire des prisons
> Le figuier allaiteur de ruines

> Inexplicable disappearances
> Unforeseeable accidents . . .
> Uneducated brains . . .
> Wallflower of prisons
> Suckling fig tree of ruins

"All that separates itself convulsively from the unity of the world . . . and lands on us at full speed," the "figures vanished as soon as composed," "nonsubmissive intelligence," the seismic treasure of famines," the despair that "backs down . . . from the question only in order to admit despair," all that is refusal in us, questioning, disturbance, marks the provocation of poetry, the call addressed to the poet by the poem, this fragile and anxious part of each of us that lives on poetry ("And as fragility and anxiety feed on poetry"). So one must understand that poetry refuses to accept all the forces of submission and immobility, that it cannot content itself with sleep whose *ease* is dangerous, that it seeks surreality insofar as the domain is its *irreconcilability*, and that finally the "honest, eager, impressionable, and bold poet will be careful not to sympathize with undertakings that alienate the prodigy of freedom in poetry, that is, of intelligence in life."

This exalted meeting of opposites, this orgasm of "for and against animated by an equal and murderous violence" (of which Artine speaks in *Le Marteau sans maître*)—what is the sense of it for the poem? First, the poem does not belong to the easy world of used things, of words already spoken. It is "inseparable from the foreseeable, but not yet formulated," it rouses the poet, causes him to be born by making him contemporary with what is first ("The poem is a moving assembly of original determining values in contemporary relationships with *someone whom this circumstance makes first*"). Everything carries us back to the sources, invites us to join their retinue. We are as if called outside of ourselves to hear not speech, but that which is before speech, silence, "the speech of the highest silence":

> La vie inexprimable
> La seule en fin de compte à laquelle tu acceptes de t'unir
> Celle qui t'est refusée chaque jour par les êtres et par les
>   choses
> Dont tu obtiens péniblement de-ci de-là quelques
>   fragments décharnés
> Au bout de combats sans merci
> Hors d'elle tout n'est qu'agonie soumise fin grossière.
>
> Inexpressible life
> The only one in the final analysis to which you consent to
>   unite yourself

The one that is refused to you every day by beings and by
  things
From which you obtain with difficulty here and there a
  few bare fragments
At the end of merciless fights
Outside of it all is but submissive agony crude end.

The poem is never present. It is always just short of presence, or
just beyond.

It escapes us because it is our absence rather than our presence
and because it begins by making emptiness, and takes things from
themselves, and substitutes endlessly what cannot be shown for
what it shows, what cannot be said for what it says. It designates
either as "the great unformulated distance," or as "the fascinating
impossible," or as the rule of the imaginary, that horizon of obvious
facts, silence, and nothingness without which we could not live,
speak, or be free. It is "the unfathomable chasm of darkness in
constant movement," it is "the Angel, our primordial care," it is
"the black color that encloses the living impossible," "anguish . . .
mistress of speech."

And similarly, if Char's poet seems so often capable of the future,
and his poetry of surpassing time, prophetic existence, it is because
the essence of the poem is to be in expectation of itself and to be
able, like "Love":

Être
Le premier venu.

To be
The first to arrive.

It is, in a way, because the poem exists that the future is possible.
The poem is this movement toward what is not and, even more, the
enjoyment of what has not been granted, the appropriation, in the
most substantial presence of This is not yet there, This will be there
only if I myself have disappeared. ("It happens that the poet in the
course of his researches runs aground on a shore where he was
expected only much later, after his annihilation.") One feels that
the horizon of absence and unreality that surrounds the poem, and

the indulgence of the imaginary and the marvelous, signify only one of the terms of fundamental poetic contradiction: the poem goes toward absence, but it is to reconstruct total reality with it; it is striving toward the imaginary, but it aims for "the productive knowledge of Reality." The search for totality, in all its forms, is the poetic claim par excellence, a claim in which the impossibility of being accomplished is included as its condition, so that if it ever happens to be accomplished, it is only as something not possible, because the poem claims to include its impossibility and its non-realization in its very existence.

When Char writes in *The Formal Share (Alone They Remain)*, "Imagination consists of expelling from reality many incomplete persons, making use of the magical and subversive powers of desire, to obtain their return in the form of a completely satisfying presence. This, then, is the inextinguishable, uncreated reality," we see clearly how poetic imagination distances itself from reality in order to join this very movement of self-distancing to this reality, to make inside of what is, that which is not, and take that as its principle, an absence that makes presence desirable, irreality that allows the poet to possess the real, to have a "productive knowledge" of it. Poetic imagination does not attach itself to things and people such as they are given, but to their lack, to what there is in them of the other, to the ignorance that makes them infinite ("A being whom one does not know is an infinite being"): thus they are "expelled," they cease to be what is present, what one has in order to become what one would like to have, what one desires. But having become desire, imagination, in this absence it has brought to life, recognizes not the absence of nothing but the absence of something, the movement toward something whose realization it demands and whose "return" it obtains without renouncing the distancing this return permits. Now, it takes pleasure in things that are, as if they were not granted it; it receives from their presence the irreality that makes this presence possible, and realizes the imaginary by rediscovering the imaginary in the real. Such is the supreme paradox of the poem, if it is "the realized love of desire that has remained desire."

Every poem presents itself to the poet as a whole in which he sees himself involved, an ensemble that he dominates although he is only a part of it, a compound that defines and constitutes him although he is the master of it. For some, like Mallarmé, this totality is that of language, all of whose elements, exchanging themselves freely each for the other, realize the complete equivalence of speech and silence. For others, the poem leads them to assert the totality of things and the free communication among them through the poet, and the possibility for the poet to ground himself, to create himself starting from this totality that he himself creates. "In poetry," says Char, "it is only starting from communication and free placement of the totality of things among them through us that we find ourselves engaged and defined, able to obtain our original form and our probative qualities." The ambiguity of this relationship explains that the poem anticipates the poet in whom it nonetheless has its origins, for it is in the poem that the complete and completely free presence of beings and things is realized, starting from which the poet manages to become what he is. The poem is the truth of the poet, the poet is the possibility of the poem; and yet the poem stays unjustified; even realized, it remains impossible: it is "the mystery that enthrones" (*Alone They Remain*), "the meaning that does not question itself" (*Leaves of Hypnos*). In it are united, in an inexpressible and incomprehensible connection, the obscure depths of being and the transparency of awareness that grounds, the "exquisite, horrible, moving earth" and the "heterogeneous human condition"; for this exalted meeting, in which each "grasps the other and qualifies the other," precedes all qualification, escapes all determination, and signifies only its own impossibility.

In certain eras, "the poet will complete the meaning of his message by the refusal of self, then will join the party of those who, having stripped its mask of legitimacy from suffering, assure the eternal return of the stubborn stevedore, ferryman of justice" (*Alone They Remain*). The poem in which the totality of existing and sensed things is brought together, as their justifying principle, cannot be considered rid of words. It also puts us in contact with all that is sovereignty in the world, in opposition to all that is fait

accompli, weightiness of fate, fossilization of man. That Char's
poetry, the closest to the essence of poetry, has led him to the
struggle of the partisan in the world, that it has continued to
express itself in this action, to be this very action without losing
anything of the purity of its essence, that is what "verifies" it as the
ability to "overflow the economy of creation, to enlarge the blood
of acts." What Georges Mounin writes about Char the partisan
seems strictly true to us; and still he has not been able to speak of
Leaves of Hypnos, "these notes" that, a short preamble says, "were
written in tension, anger, fear, emulation, disgust, ruse, furtive
recollection, illusion of the future, friendship, love." Perhaps, as
Char says, they are affected by the event. But it is the ephemeral
nature of the event that finds what it can use in them to become
lasting; even were they to seem "nothingness" compared with such
pathetic circumstances, they would seem impersonal, since they
express only general movements, the self-protective "mimicry" of a
community, yet whatever quality of pathos and strength they have
kept increases by not being spent "in view of tortured blood";
written by no one, they are such that they could be found only by
someone alone.

In *Leaves of Hypnos,* the few precise notes where we find certain
events of secret combat described are scattered among poems,
reflections without dates, images risen from the depths of the
timeless world; that these notes of detail and actuality seem each
time, in this collection, necessary and as if inevitable, shows better
than any other proof how, for a poetic existence, poetry is revealed
to itself, not only when it reflects itself but also when it decides
itself and can thus speak of everything, exactly because it is itself in
everything, the presence of everything, the search for totality, that
it alone has the ability and right to speak of everything, to say
everything.

Such a language in which we feel ourselves completely involved
and whose fullness is so large that it seems to demand our participation, so that we understand it mentally as far as we understand
physically, a language capable of expressing ourselves—that is what
Char proposes to the reader to unite him with the poem. This

language is the most present that can be. It is impossible to subtract from it. The sovereignty of its tone is extreme. It is like Heraclitus's style, a style of aphorism in which the conciseness of the expressions and the authority of images express the energy of an extraordinary and even oracular awareness. And it is true in Char's work that the aphoristic form is frequent; starting with *Alone They Remain* especially, language stays almost always grave, it asserts itself slowly, with a certain solemnity, seeking in the weight of abstract terms a hammer's density. But what makes this grave slowness so powerful is that the most lively succession of figures also presents itself in it: the smallest possible unit of time contains the strongest reality of images, the most brilliant sparkling of "matter–emotion instantly queen." Alliance of a lasting language, with a plenum of things felt, lived, possessed "instantly," slowness of a flat rhythm and a stable syntax serving to transmit the most distinct moments, the most varied contacts, the greatest number of presences, and, as it were, a simultaneous infinity of successive impressions, emblem of the totality of metamorphoses—it is from this contradiction that arises in part whatever power of enchantment and summation there is in such a form.

There is nothing more removed from speech. And yet it admits its resources, it collects the articulations of the sentence, interrogation, apostrophe, invocation, by which the logical changes reproduce various motions of the heart; but these relationships with the outside, expressing the part of common language, are reconquered by the relationships of inside in which burns, in extreme condensation, the experience of the least communicable intimacy, or in any case the one closest to the incommunicable. There is neither disequilibrium in that, nor disagreement, and solitude becomes a spreading fire, *branch of the first sun* shining without shade until evening. "Under the harmonious authority of a wonder common to all, the particular destiny is accomplished all the way to solitude, all the way to the oracle." (The oracle, solitude of the future.)

Images in a poem are in no way a designation or illustration of things or beings. Neither are they the expression of a completely

personal memory, of a completely subjective association of elements put together. For example, seeing on tiles some rounds of
light resembling the ocelli in birds' plumage, I say, "The sun is a
peacock on the roof"; but it is a question only of a metaphor here,
an exterior indication, quite foreign to poetic values; it will be
possible for me, speaking of the sun, to speak of the peacock or of
the tile broken by the sun or of any other detail noticed in the
course of this scene, and the obscurity of the allusion will not stop
increasing, but as long as it depends on the single accidental nature
of a memory, it will be linked to a language to which one can have
the key; it will bring nothing more than a useless arbitrariness,
without power and without justification.

The image in a poem is not the designation of a thing but the
way in which the possession of this thing, or its destruction, is
accomplished, the means found by the poet to live with it, on it,
and against it, to come into substantial and material contact with it
and to touch it in a unity of sympathy or a unity of disgust. The
image is first an image, for it is the absence of what it gives us and it
makes us attain it as the presence of an absence, calling, there inside
us, for the most animated movement to possess it (that is the desire
of which Char speaks). But, at the same time, the poetic image, in
this very absence of thing, claims to restore the foundation of its
presence to us, not its form (what one sees) but the underside (what
one penetrates), its reality of earth, its "matter–emotion." In this
new presence, the thing loses its individuality of object closed by
use, it strives to be metamorphosed into a completely other thing
and into all things, in such a way that the first image is also led to
change and, carried away in the cycle of metamorphoses, becomes
endlessly stronger and more complex in its ability to transform the
world into a whole by the appropriation of desire.

The images of the poem are thus infinitely various, and yet they
obey a fundamental tendency, they reproduce a call that is the first
intention under which the poet feels himself drawn into the intimacy of things and their total presence. This obstinacy of a first
figure is the proof of the authenticity of all the others, while it is at
the same time the source of their efficacy, the fountain that the poet

"torments with his unappraisable secrets." The contortion of images is very great in Char's poems; Mounin has marked those that
come from space, from light, and especially from this *river* that
hollows out its mirror solitude in words. But more even than the
repetition of similar images, the identical material meaning of
images ostensibly different is striking. The river, "this giant river
that goes forth . . . hollowing out its bed in its passage," is not only
the infinite force of a movement without matter and reduced, as it
were, to its transparency: it has something solid, it has the hardness
of ice that it can become "fluvial necropolis," "carnivorous landscape," that, in an instant, has the unbreakable force of crystal
planes. The river, "furious rising, torrent," is also "the arid play of
banks"; in that, we have seen, it is poem and poetry. And the first
works are *First Alluviums*, and when the young Char, biting into an
apple, puts a dead man's head in his teeth, it is "under the *streaming*
and equally ambiguous traits of the poem" that this first object
of transmutations appears. But another image, no less constant,
makes out of the poem a hammer, the *Marteau sans maître*, of the
poet, "the imperceptible anxiety of wheelwrights," the one who
lives "in the nacelles of the anvil" or "on the anvil of the white fury"
of day, the one who "surrounds his head with a blacksmith's
apron," or again "the mice of the anvil." "This image," says Hypnos, "would have seemed charming to me, at another time. It
suggests a swarm of sparks decimated into a bolt of lightning (the
anvil is cold, the iron not red, the imagination devastated)." Thus
from the spurting hammer, at the intersection of the double solidity of bronze, arises the most lively madness, the one most glowing
with movement and with light, the very lightning of metamorphoses, and that is why "this hard-to-see river, this radiant and
enigmatic river" where we recognize poetry can also be "baptized
Marteau sans maître."

This image in which are united this undamageable nature of
solid things and the stream of becoming, the thickness of presence
and the scintillation of absence, expands in its turn in other forms,
but without losing its material ambivalence. The poet is "the great
wheelbarrow of marshes," "the tipcart of reeds that burn"; metallic

names impose the presence of iron, of stone; he is "the grass of lead," "the grass of cinder," "the red bird of metals," "brother, faithful flint," "the gold of wind," all hard things, but things that movement does not stop skimming. And when the universe uncovers itself, it opens onto the same admirable figure:

> Le silex frissonnait sur les sarments de l'espace.

> The flint trembled on the twining stems of space.

This badgering of the same images comes from an obsession with their profound nature, and this in its turn answers to the essence of poetry, expresses the obsessive fear of its fundamental contradiction: "this exact middle of rock and sand, of water and fire, of cries and silence" that endlessly wants to reveal it to us. The image is neither an ornament nor a detail of the poem, nor some product of man's sensibility: it is the poem manifested starting with things, the movement of things and beings trying to unite the heaviness of the depths of the earth and dazzling transparency, the line of flight and stability of a stature immovably placed. It is the whole poem, just as the poem is the whole of things, a struggle toward this everything, as language, by the contrast we have found between the gravity of the sentence and the flight of images, is another form of the same movement to wake up—and to reestablish antagonisms.

From the poem the poet is born. It is born before us and in front of us, as our own future, as the unexpected that torments and fascinates us. At each instant, we owe it our life, and even more than life, that which, in our life, but unknown to it, *holds courage and silence awakened*: its truth.

§ The "Sacred" Speech of Hölderlin

Heidegger's important commentary on Hölderlin's hymn, "As on a holiday . . ." poses a certain number of questions that concern Heidegger himself. We will put those aside. There are others we must also neglect—this, for instance: Heidegger's commentary follows the poem word by word, as careful and as detailed as a commentary could be, conducted according to the methods of didactic erudition. Is such an explanation legitimate? In what way is it? That is what the commentator did not care to let us know, less uneasy in that than Gundolf, who, studying the great elegy "Archipelago," took care to ruin his study from the beginning by recalling that a poem is a whole and that the contents of thought that we impose on this whole have in themselves no reality whatsoever. Still, Gundolf contented himself with questioning the poem in its entirety. Heidegger's questioning interrogates each word, each comma, and demands from all the isolated elements, taken one after the other, a full answer, itself isolable. The impression is often quite strange. When all is said and done, however, there is in it more of appearance than of reality; for if the question has indeed the exorbitant aspect of a question that asks each fragment of the poem its account of itself and forces it to justify itself analytically, Heidegger's analysis, progressing according to the circular procedure that is so characteristic of him, finally ends up not by piecing back together the general meaning, starting from all the particular meanings it specifies, but by finding again in each instant the passage of the poem's totality in the shape of which the poem has momentarily settled and paused.

One could also wonder if a meeting is possible between the vocabulary of an autonomous philosophic reflection and a poetic language that came into our world almost a century and a half ago. But, on this point, the poem has answered: a poem is not without a date, but despite its date it is always yet to come, it speaks in a "now" that does not answer to historical indicators. It is presentiment, and designates itself as that which does not yet exist, demanding the same presentiment from the reader to make an existence for it, one that has not yet come into being. It is the same for poems as for gods: a god, says Hölderlin, is always greater than his field of action:

> Wenn aber die Stunde schlägt
> Wie der Meister tritt er, aus der Werkstatt,
> Und ander Gewand nicht, denn
> Ein festliches ziehet er an
> Zum Zeichen, daß noch anderes auch
> Im Werk ihm übrig gewesen.

> When the hour sounds,
> As the master leaves the workshop
> And the clothing he wears then
> Is festive clothing,
> As a sign of the work
> That still remains for him to accomplish.

This clothing of celebration is the one the poem dons for the reader; it is capable of seeing and being ahead of itself, and of distinguishing, underneath the word that has worked, the word that shines there, reserved for what has not yet been expressed.

It is, moreover, very quickly apparent how much Heidegger's commentary tries to answer faithfully to the poem's intentions. Even the vocabulary he uses, although in appearance his own, is also the vocabulary of the poet. The word "Open" that belongs to the terminology of his recent works and that serves him here to sketch out an interpretation of Nature in Hölderlin (nature not being a particular reality, or even only the whole of reality, but "the Open," the movement of opening that allows all that appears to appear) is a word that Hölderlin himself met and recognized exactly in this sense: in the elegy "To Landauer," for instance, "Und dem offenen Blick offen der Leuchtende sei" (And may the shining light open to the opened glance").

The double repetition of the word *offen,* "open," answers exactly to the double movement that "the Open" signifies: to open up to that which opens up; *der Leuchtende,* the illuminating ability of that which illuminates, is given here clearly as subsequent to the movement of lighting up and opening out (*des Himmels Blüte,* the preceding line says) that makes it possible. *Das Offene* returns many times in the poems, and it undoubtedly retains the meaning that roughly answers to our expression "open air, to go out into the open air." But when we read *dass wir das Offene schauen,* the meaning turns into this: the being who wants to see must first meet *das Offene.* One can see only in the freedom of that which is open, in this light that is also opening, lighting up. "Your divine work, Light, who make all things unfurl," Empedocles says in the first version of *The Death of Empedocles*; this unfurling is divine work because it is also the divine role of light, the divine movement by which light can illuminate, and which it receives with a clarity previous to it, as it is previous to everything.

So we do not have to fear that the commentary adds to the text. We can say that anything lent to it had been borrowed from it. That is another remark we might be tempted to make, thinking of the correspondences between language that interprets and language as object of interpretation: we know that the language of Hölderlin is poor in appearance, poor in words, poor in themes, monotonous, the humblest, yet the most exalted that has ever been written, for its movement elevates it above all the others. But the language of Heidegger is, on the contrary, of an incomparable richness and virtuosity (as Rovan's translation also attests). More than ever, it seems, this is made possible by the resources with which the German language is infinitely rich, this dangerous power that words draw from the play of their structure, from inflections of meaning provoked by the untiring dance of prefixes and suffixes around an etymologically transparent verbal body. The confidence Heidegger has in the words of his language, the value he gives to their more or less secret interconnectedness, constitute a remarkable phenomenon. Words seem to carry in themselves a hidden truth that a well-conducted interrogation can cause to appear. After having analyzed etymologically the term *physis*, he adds: "But Hölderlin was unaware of the signifying force of this fundamental and primal word that even today we are scarcely beginning to assess." So certain words have a meaning that goes past us, one we manage only slowly to discover (and quite obviously it is not only a question of archaeological meaning, such as a scholarly investigation could reveal). Heidegger's striking observation, once again, reveals the vigilant presence of the pre-Socratics behind him. It is true indeed that Hölderlin was unaware of this interior play of words, this brilliant virtuosity that is his commentator's, and that so contrasts with the modesty of his own language. Let us add that the unparalleled soaring of this language, this rhythm that is its superior truth, this surge upward are in their turn ignored by the commentary that attends only to the development and prosaic composition of the poem.

Hölderlin's themes are poor. But since the poem has no other object than itself, poetry, more strongly than anywhere else, is real and true there, with the truth that gives it the right to make use of all the rest and, to begin with, of everything. When we want to find out what the fact that the poem, the song exists really signifies, and if we claim to question this fact from without, this questioning must lead to Hölderlin, because, for him and from within, such a question made the poem be born. To question Hölderlin is to question a poetic existence so strong that, once its essence is unveiled, it was able to make itself the proof that it was an impossibility, and to extend itself out into nothingness and emptiness, without ceasing to accomplish itself.

The poet is the mediator; he connects the near to the far. The merchant who also brings close and unites, the river that is nothing but movement and passage—one is considered the poet's equal ("The Archipelago"), the other as language itself ("The Ister"). But it is again a question of an image that is completely exterior to the poetic calling. Not only is poetry supposed to accomplish this mediation and, by accomplishing it, accomplish itself, but it must first make the mediation possible. It is not simply the instrument that elements and men make use of to meet each other; it expresses and forms the very possibility of this meeting, and this meeting is the basis and the truth of what meets. Thus is sketched out the theme that all poetry, whatever its forms may be, always ends up finding again: essentially, poetry relates to existence in its totality; wherever poetry asserts itself, existence, considered as All, also begins to assert itself. The idea of All, we know, haunts Hölderlin's theoretical reflections at the same time and just as deeply as those of Hegel. That is why, among all the names the hymn gives to Nature, Heidegger's commentary immediately gives precedence to the word *allgegenwärtig*; Nature is the all-present, is present as All. What poetry has connections with, what, undoubtedly, allows it to be connection itself, is not nature (as plant, people, or sky, or nature as ensemble of real things) but what Empedocles calls *boundless totality*: this means both a totality that neither the real nor the unreal can limit, and also an All in which this freedom of not being bounded by anything is yet integrated and included.

"Oh sacred All! You inner, living, complete whole!" says Panthea, conveying Empedocles's message. It is toward this All that poetry heads, and it is by answering the call of this "complete whole" that he "educated himself" (according to the word in the hymn) and takes shape: "For full of a high meaning, / With a silent strength, great Nature / Embraces the one / Who foresees, so he can take shape."

But how can such a call be made? And how can this All of nature surround, embrace "the one who foresees"? (*Umfangen*, "embrace," is a term one finds frequently in the poems of Hölderlin, who seems to have borrowed it from the "Ardinghello" of his friend Heinze. In a general way, the same words tend to pass again and again from one poem to another with Hölderlin, and often with a rather persistent meaning: thus *Umfangen* always designates, it seems to us, the movement of confident and conciliatory approach by which the sacred elements make felt whatever accessible qualities they have, in opposition to the agitation and blazing that form other ways of announcing themselves to the poet. It is this return and this constancy of words and themes that make any commentary on the poet enticing, possible, and infinitely perilous.)

We see that this All in which poetry now finds itself involved also involves it in an extreme intensity of mysteries, questionings, and oppositions. In appearance, it seems simple for the poet to wake up and open out into nature's embrace. But the question is this: Where will he find this nature everywhere present, everywhere near present? Where will he find it as the presence of All, as movement passing from ether to abyss, from gods to chaos, from height of day to extreme night? It is itself presence as All only if the poet calls it, and alas! he cannot call it, for to be capable of this calling, to exist as a poet, he needs exactly this miraculous omnipresence that he still lacks. It is well known that Hölderlin profoundly linked god and man, each needing the other, with only poetic existence assuring the truth of their union. Undoubtedly, the gods are not what is highest in the world; and nature, as their mother, soars above them. But let the sacred Father himself, summit of light, be abandoned to solitude, deprived of truth and life; let man on his side become a mute, isolated shadow, without the heat of true existence which is that of the heart: nature would lose its essence of all-presence and the world would no longer be the Universe. And this is what would happen if the world lacked the poem:

> Denn wenn er schon der Zeichen genug
> Und Fluthen in seiner Macht und Wetterflammen
> Wie Gedanken hat der heilige Vater, unaussprechlich wär
>   er wohl
> Und nirgend fänd er wahr sich unter den Lebenden
>   wieder
> Wenn zum Gesange nicht hätt ein Herz die Gemeinde.

And deprived of words, solitary,
Vain existence in his darkness, he that still
In his power, like so many thoughts,
Has enough signs, bolts of lightning
And waves, he would not be able to find his way
    anywhere,
The sacred Father, true among the living
If song did not rise up from the united heart of the
    community.

But, on his side, the poet, the one who gives voice to the song,
can come to the world only if the world is the Universe, reconciled
and pacified, capable of surrounding him, embracing him, "edu-
cating" him poetically, that is to say, a universe in which the poet,
already present, accomplishes his work, in which men are a community, in which the song of this community is gathered into one
alone and in which the gods themselves find their truth and their
place among the living.

Naturally, this is not a logical difficulty. This contradiction is the
heart of poetic existence, it is its essence and its law; there would be
no poet if he did not have to live out this very impossibility,
endlessly present. But let us look more closely at what this impossibility means. This, it seems, is fundamental: that the poet must
exist as a presentiment of himself, as the future of his existence. He
does not exist, but he has to be already what he will be later, in a
"not yet" that constitutes the essential part of his grief, his misery,
and also his great wealth. Historically, this situation is one that
Hölderlin experienced and sang of in the deepest grief: he had been
born in a time when poetry was in a bad way, *in dürftiger Zeit*, in a
present that was null, confined in this nullity by the double absence
of the gods, those who had vanished and those who had not yet
appeared. Thus, companionless, having nothing to say and nothing to do except this very nothing, he was deeply aware of existing
only in waiting, in movement held above its nothingness: *ich harre,
ich harrte*, this word returns endlessly to express the anguish and
sterility of waiting, as the word *ahnen* indicates its value and

fertility, since it is this always-to-come existence of the poet that makes all the future possible, and firmly maintains history in the perspective of "tomorrow" that is richer with meaning, *deutungs-voller*, and for which one must strive in the emptiness of the lived day.

> Sie scheinen allein zu seyn, doch ahnen sie immer,
> Denn ahnend ruhet sie selbst auch.

> They [poets] seem alone, but they always foresee,
> For this foreseeing is also its [nature's] rest.

These two lines from the hymn "As on a holiday . . . " mark the parallel situation of the All, which the poet's existence lacks, and of the poet, who, in his solitude, has not yet received the strength from the All to call it. Both, in their reciprocal implication and because of the reciprocity of their absence, are already carried toward each other, and by this movement overtake their solitude and their sleep. The poet's solitude is only apparent, for it is presentiment, presentiment of solitude, and already affirmation of something that is beyond itself, of a "later" that is enough to break the boundary of isolation and to open up communication. In the same way, nature's rest belongs in appearance only to an empty presence, empty of poetic existence, in which it rests; it rests, undoubtedly, because it still lacks the movement of communications, but by this very rest, by this emptiness full of presentiment that is, in it, the actual form of the poet's existence, it already escapes rest and soars up, foreseeing its all-presence, its presence as All.

The poet exists only if he foresees the time of the poem; he is second to the poem, of which he is nonetheless the creative power. This, it seems, is the second meaning of the opposition and the impossibility that are at the heart of poetry. Why does the poet foresee, why can he live in this way of foreseeing? It is because the poem is previous to the poet, and exactly this *ahnen* is the way for the poet to feel that he exists before himself and, *free as he may be, free as the swallow*, in the dependence on this very freedom, his response may be free but it is a response to this freedom. Hölderlin's entire work bears witness to the awareness of an anterior power surpassing the gods as well as men, the very one that prepares the universe to be "completely whole." Heidegger, whose commentary on this point is particularly *ahnend*, calls it, along with Hölderlin, the Sacred, *das Heilige.*

Und was ich sah, das Heilige sei mein Wort.

And what I saw, may the Sacred be my speech.

If this term "the Sacred," designating gods, nature, the day, is constant in the poems, it remains very rare as a fundamental word, condensed and collected into itself: Hölderlin sometimes recognizes the Sacred in his work, not the realized and revealed work but one that is close to his heart, that is the foundation of his heart, that corresponds nearly to the *eternal heart* of the hymn "As on a holiday . . ." a phrase that designates not only the interiority of the Sacred, as Heidegger interprets it, but also the interiority of the Sacred inside the interiority of the poet, in his heart, his mediating force insofar as it is love.

The Sacred is the shining power that opens to the sacred all that its shining attains. One of its underground ways is made up of nature's sleep and the poet's foreseeing. That nature, this mother of the gods, "divinely present," owes to the Sacred its most essential qualities, its divine all-presence—this is what the lines of "At the Source of the Danube" assert, lines that, although subsequently crossed out, were nevertheless expressed by it:

Wir nennen dich, heiliggenöthiget, nennen,
Natur! dich wir . . .

We name You, urged by the Sacred, name you
Nature, we you . . .

The language and rhythm of the verse do not come through in translation. But the verse lets us understand at once that nature is Nature only after the naming it receives from the poet, since, if the speech that establishes nature comes from him, he is only answering the exigent call of the Sacred. By answering it, he himself becomes the sacred necessity he obeys, and finally, once named, nature is then intimately close to the poet; from then on, the "you" of Nature and the poetic "us" cease to be separated. What is the Sacred? It is the immediate, Heidegger says, taking his inspiration from a prose fragment of Hölderlin, the immediate that is never communicated but is the principle of all possibility of communicating. A little further on, Heidegger adds, "Chaos is the Sacred in the self."

On this point, it seems that the commentator was more sensitive to tradition than to Hölderlin's experience. Chaos, assuredly, opens up in a profound way in the poems and hymns: it is given a very strange name: *das freudigschauernde Chaos*, chaos in which trembling is made into joy. But to seek in this an experience of chaos as such an experience of night might completely distort the poet's experience. Neither chaos nor night lets itself be felt in it in such an absolute way. On the contrary, night and chaos always end up by testifying to the law and form of light. Nothing could be further from a Novalis, even though movement of certain themes comes close, there is nothing nocturnal in Hölderlin's poems, nothing funereal. Even in the elegy "Bread and Wine," whose words are poured by the night, it is asserted of the poem that

> Weil den Irrenden sie geheiliget ist und den Todten,
> Selber aber besteht, ewig, in freiestem Geist.

> Consecrated as it is to the lost and the dead,
> It itself remains eternally within the freest mind.

Further, we read

> Fest bleibt Eins; es sei um Mittag oder es gehe
> Bis in die Mitternacht, immer bestehet ein Maas,
> Allen gemein

> This firmly abides, whether it is noon
> Or nearing midnight, a measure always endures
> Common to all

The Sacred is the day: not the day as it contrasts with the night, or the light as it shines from above, or the flame that Empedocles goes to seek below. It is the day, but anterior to the day, and always anterior to itself; it is a before-day, a clarity before clarity to which we are closest when we grasp the dawning, the distance infinitely remote from daybreak, which is also what is the most intimate to us, more interior than all interiority.

> Göttliches Feuer auch treibet, bei Tag und bei Nacht,
> Aufzubrechen. So komm! daß wir das Offene schauen
>
> The divine fire, by day and by night, pushes us
> To break away and soar up. So come! Let us see the Open.

Das Offene, that which opens up, and by opening up is a call for all the rest to open up, to be lit up, to come to light. This feeling of *es tagt*, "the day is breaking," that makes night possible as well as day, chaos as well as the gods, this feeling itself shines mysteriously across all Hölderlin's work, drawing it dizzily upward. Moreover, it is explicitly recognized in many forms: not only by so many words that in each thing associate the fact of appearing, its appearance, with the light, but in a more secret way, by the strange condition of the Immortals, who, closer than we are to the purity of pure shining, are, because of that, at least the greatest, in a place beyond light that yet is clarity and nothing but clarity.

> Und noch höher hinauf wohnt über dem Lichte der reine
> Seelige Gott vom Spiel heiliger Stralen erfreut.
> Stille wohnt er allein und hell erscheinet sein Antliz.
>
> And even higher, above the light, the pure
> Blessed God finds his joy in the play of sacred rays.
> In silence he lives alone, and clarity is the appearance of
> his face.

Clarity that is original, unsurpassable, and not born of the gods, for in the innocent sleep that is the pure gaze of the gods eternally shines its transparence:

> Schiksaallos, wie der schlafende
>   Säugling, athmen die Himmlischen;
> Keusch bewahrt
>   In bescheidener Knospe,
>   Blühet ewig
>   Ihnen der Geist,
>   Und die seeligen Augen
>   Bliken in stiller
>   Ewiger Klarheit.

> Without destiny, like the infant
>   Who sleeps, breathe Those of the sky;
> Chastely enclosed
>   In a flower's hope,
>   Blossoming for eternity
>   Is their mind,
>   And their blessed eyes
>   Look into the peaceful
>   Eternal clarity.

Shining power whose outpouring is the law, principle of appearance of what appears, origin of all ability to communicate—if such is the Sacred, we understand that by "foreseeing" it, the poet already places himself in the bosom of the all-presence, and that the approach of the Sacred is, for him, the approach of existence. But now the enigma takes a different form. In the beginning, there was no poet yet, because he needed the All to exist and the All needed his mediation to be the All. Now, existing as "not yet," he has grasped, foreseen the arrival of the Sacred, which is the principle of this very arrival, which is arrival anterior to any "something is coming" and by which "all" comes, the All comes. But then the question must be posed: If there is a Universe in which everything communicates, what good is the poet, what remains for him to accomplish? And doesn't the dignity of his essence escape him, the dignity of being the quintessential mediation and also the co-present, contemporary of the All? Hölderlin experienced this other form of the poetic impossibility: "Nature, divinely present, / Has no need of speech," says Empedocles. And in one of the last hymns,

"The Only One," in which poetic thought is concentrated in the most dangerous way, it is said, "Always is this valid, that, at every moment, the Universe is in its entirety." *At every moment, alltag*: if the law, anterior to all, assures the coming of the All to itself at all times, this "at every moment" also makes it so that there is no more "moment" for poetic existence. However, what is the universe always worth (*es gilt*) in its entirety, when it exists by the pure affirmation of the pure law? Two other excerpts from the same hymn let us glimpse it. First this, which immediately follows the text cited above:

> Immerdar
> Bleibt dies, daß immergekettet alltag ganz ist
> Die Welt. Oft aber scheint
> Ein großer nicht zusammenzutaugen
> Zu Großem. Alle Tage stehn die aber, als an einem
> Abgrund einer
> Neben dem andern.

> Always
> Is this valid, that, at every moment, the universe is
> complete.
> But often
> The Great do not assert themselves in union
> With the Great. Always, as on the edge of the abyss, they
> stand
> Side by side

And a few lines before:

> Nämlich immer jauchzet die Welt
> Hinweg von dieser Erde, daß sie die
> Entblößet; wo das Menschliche sie nicht hält. Es bleibet
> aber eine Spur
> Doch eines Wortes; die ein Mann erhaschet.

> For always the exultation of the
> Universe
> Tends to distance it from earth and leave it

Bare; if the human does not hold it back. But there
  remains
The trace of a word; that a man can grasp.

We foresee that by such texts, the pure universe, formed by the
pure law of which Ottmar speaks in the song "To Mother Earth,"
calls the human, that is to say, the poet; it calls him so that it will
not lose itself in the expansive infinity of its origins that it holds: as
it is, it is indeed limitless totality, and must be, but this "limitless"
must also become its limit, be integrated in the totality—and that is
why the poem must come. One can say this again: the possibility of
communicating, such as it emanates from the law, is too large to be
truly communication; it is "absolute mediatedness," says Hölderlin; it needs to be mediated, so that the side by side is not closeness
to the abyss but actual understanding, a real community of values
(*Zusammentaugen*). Speech will devote itself to that: speech whose
essence is to *remain*, even as a trace, to be foundation of what
remains, to establish "between day and night something true." The
language of the gods is change and becoming ("Archipelago"), but
mortal language is persistence, assertion of a duration that lasts,
unity of time torn apart. That is why the Immortals need mortals,
need finiteness: that is what establishes them in the world and gives
them being in the awareness of being. Their light, too close to
original unfurling, needs to become thicker to light them up truly,
to become clarity upon them. Before the poem, the day is the
darkest there is. Origin of transparency, pure beginning of what is
going to pour forth, it is the most profound mystery—and also the
most frightening: it is the unjustified, starting from which it must
take its justification, the incommunicable and the undiscovered
that is also what opens up and, by the solidness of poetic speech,
will again become what discovers itself in the end.

In the hymns, particularly those last poems in which Hölderlin
himself feels carried away by the flight, the jubilant expansion
toward the boundless, Hölderlin endlessly repeats tragically: There
is still much left to say, to hold back, to contain, *Vieles aber ist zu
behalten*. The poem is in fact that which holds together, that which

gathers together into an unfounded unity the open unity of the principle, that which in the fissure of illumination finds a firm enough foundation so that something can manifest, and so that what does appear can maintain itself in a shaky but lasting agreement. It is said again in "Patmos," a hymn uttered already under the veil of madness:

> der Vater aber liebt,
> Der über allen waltet,
> Am meisten, daß gepfleget werde
> Der veste Buchstab, und bestehendes gut
> Gedeutet. Dem folgt deutscher Gesang.

> The Father
> Who reigns over every thing
> Loves above all else that one strives
> For the firm letter and that the persistent
> Be well signified. To that answers German song.

The poem is not the simple ability to give a meaning, later, to what, already said, might survive, might be something persistent (*Bestehendes*); it is the very ability, by the meaning it gives, to lead to persistence, thus to allow the stream of becoming to survive, language of the gods, trembling of things in the beginning of the day. That is why the poet is *weltlich*, he is of the world, he must keep to the world; and that is also why the line is true that Heidegger clarified so perfectly in his 1936 lecture:

> Was bleibat aber, stiften die Dichter.

> But what lasts, the poets establish.

Thus the possibility of poetic existence is restored. It is undoubtedly restored, but only to hurtle toward a greater impossibility that is its fundamental trial. The poem must exist, because without it the day would be there but it would not light up; without it everything would communicate, but this communication would also be at every moment the destruction of everything, lost into an always open infinity, refusing to return

to its infinity. The poem, through speech, makes what is unfounded become foundation, makes the abyss of day become the
day that constructs and brings forth. *Das Heilige sei mein Wort*, it
makes it so that the Sacred is speech and speech is sacred. But how
can that be? How can the Sacred, which is "unexpressed," "unknown," which is what opens provided only that it is not discovered, which reveals because unrevealed—how can it fall into
speech, let itself be alienated into becoming, itself pure interiority,
the exteriority of song? In truth, that cannot really be, that is the
impossible. And the poet is nothing but the existence of this
impossibility, just as the language of the poem is nothing but the
retention, the transmission of its own impossibility. It is the reminder that all worldly language, this speech that takes place and
goes on in the domain of radical ease, has as its origin an event that
cannot take place; it is linked to an "I speak, but speaking is not
possible," from which nevertheless emerges the little sense that
remains to words.

Heidegger, in his commentary, insists, in a manner unique to
him, on silence: it is silence that could lead the Sacred to speech
without rupture. The Sacred cannot be grasped right away, even
less can it become speech; yet by the silence of the poet, it can let
itself be pacified, transformed, and finally transported into the
speech of the song. Silence is the only real communication, it is the
authentic language: in such assertions one recognizes a well-known
theme of Heideggerian thought. What has become of the problem?
It has taken another form, but it still remains a problem; or, rather,
there is now a double enigma: why and how can "the agitation of
chaos, which offers no resting place or stopping place, the terror of
the Immediate that foils every direct grasp, the Sacred" let itself be
transformed and joined with silence? And then, why and how can
silence let itself be joined with speech?

The theme of silence is not foreign to Hölderlin: "I learned to
worship the divine in silence," he says in a poem of the Diotima
cycle, addressing the Sun that, "sacred," has risen "in rest and in
silence above those who do not know rest." The word "still" is, with

one or two exceptions, the only word Hölderlin uses to allude to something that resembles silence. In reality, it does not have to do with language but designates a much larger sphere, all that words, pacification, tranquil profundity, calm interiority, can suggest.* "Still" has, moreover, an ambiguous value in the poems: sometimes it signifies blessing, peace, and gentleness; sometimes it is the adversity of aridity, the cursed retreat of life and speech. In a poem to hope:

> Wo bist du? wenig lebt'ich; doch athmet kalt
>> Mein Abend schon. Und stille, den Schatten gleich,
>>> Bin ich schon heir; und schon gesanglos
>>>> Schlummert das schaudernde Herz im Busen.

> Where are you? I have lived little, and though already
>> frozen I breathe;
>> In me evening, and silent [still], like the shadows,
>>> Already I am here, and already deprived of song
>>>> My heart, asleep, trembles.

"Still" is not the fullness of silence here, but the emptiness of the absence of speech, the darkness and coldness of an existence in which silence no longer makes itself a poem. That is because silence is marked by the same contradiction and the same tearing apart as language: if it is a way to approach the unapproachable, to belong to what is not said, it is "sacred" only insofar as it makes communication of the incommunicable possible and arrives at language. To be quiet is not a superiority. "May the Sacred be my speech," that is the poet's call, and those are words that are "sanctuaries," temples of the Sacred, not silence. It is necessary to speak, that is the only thing that is appropriate. And yet it is impossible to speak:

> Und nenne, was vor Augen dir ist,
> Nicht länger darf Geheimniß mehr
> Das Ungesprochene bleiben,

---

* As these lines from a poem to the gods show: "Peaceful ether (*stiller Aether*), you who keep my soul beautiful in grief." Peace does not pacify grief, but, uniting it to its opposite, summons the moment of reconciliation that is beauty.

Nachdem es lange verhüllt ist;
Denn Sterblichen geziemet die Schaam,
Und so zu reden die meiste Zeit,
Ist weise auch von Göttern.
Wo aber überflüssiger, denn lautere Quellen
Das Gold und ernst geworden ist der Zorn an dem
      Himmel,
Muß zwischen Tag und Nacht
Einsmals ein Wahres erscheinen.
Dreifach umschreibe du es,
Doch ungesprochen auch, wie es da ist,
Unschuldige, muß es bleiben.

Name what is in front of your eyes,
No longer need the unexpressed remain mystery,
That has been so long veiled;
For it behooves mortals
To speak with restraint of the gods,
This also is wisdom.
But if more abundantly than pure springs
Gold runs streaming and when to the sky anger mounts,
Between day and night
One time a truth must appear.
In a triple metamorphosis transcribe it,
Though always unexpressed, as it is,
Innocent, so it must remain.

    Into this line a double contrary movement thrusts itself in an extreme way, one that does not succeed either at conciliating itself, or pushing itself back, or penetrating itself; it is a double prohibition, a double demand rigorously contradictory. The unexpressed must be unveiled—it must, that is a duty—and yet it is an act that is not appropriate. But despite the inappropriateness, and because of the very wrath of heaven, of the burning of the day grown more severe, demanding ever more imperiously the mediation of speech and of the true, the necessity to name and transcribe now becomes absolute. Necessity that is of the law, necessity that will obey all conciliatory precautions, that will make a call to all mediators: three times, the unsayable will be transposed before being said. And yet, despite demand and despite mediation, the ineffable remains always unexpressed, for that is also the law.

The poet must speak. This speech is already implicit in the farthest beginning of the point of day, it is simultaneous with the absolute anteriority of the Sacred. Further, it is demanded by the advent of the Universe as common mind, the common community of values. Yet when he speaks, he speaks but does not speak, he leaves what he has to say unexpressed and leaves unmanifested what he shows. And this is what happens to him—having spoken, because the gods ask him to speak, now:

> jedoch ihr Gericht
> Ist, daß sein eigenes Haus
> Zerbreche der und das Liebste
> Wie den Feind schelt' und sich Vater und Kind
> Begrabe unter den Trümmern

> Their judgment
> Is that his own house
> He destroy and what is dearest to him,
> He treat as an enemy and father and child,
> He bury under rubble.

We feel it strongly, that this judgment is not the simple punishment of language's excessiveness. Language and expiation are the same: the poet destroys himself, and he destroys his language that he lives, and no longer possessing a before or an after, he is suspended in emptiness itself. Ruin, dispute, pure division, really *jedem offen*, he writes, open to all, because it is now no more than absence and destruction; it is as such that he speaks, it is then that he is the day, that he has the transparence of day, *denkender Tag*, the day become thought.

Hölderlin did not take pleasure in celebrating suffering and unhappiness. Just as he was called by the day and not by the night, so it is harmony and joy he seeks, and if he happens to pray, it is to obtain a moment, a short moment of rest, so light will not consume him too soon, so it will not shake him right away down into its depths. But he could do nothing. He was not at liberty to reject his freedom; not only did he never shy away from this freedom of poetic existence that condemns him at once to the distress of an existence purely to come and to the terrible trial of being the place of extreme opposition, but he embodied it as no other did. He transformed himself into it, he became it and it alone, and no one has done so with such pure modesty, with such accomplished greatness. To support the fullness of the day, to load this weight of logs that is the sky onto his shoulder, he knew what it cost, and what it cost him, not because suffering is in itself sacred, worthy of being suffered, but because whoever wants to be a mediator must first be torn apart. Whoever wants to take on the ability to communicate must lose himself in what he transmits, yet feel himself incommunicable.* Finally the one who, seized by the exultation of the mind (*Begeisterung*), becomes the way of the mind, must dangerously take on himself the unjustifiable origin, the obscure beginning of universal burgeoning. "When the gods truly show themselves," says Hölderlin, "when that which reveals itself remains under his gaze, man is thus made, he does not recognize it or see it. To endure, to suffer, that is what he must do, and then a name comes to him for what is dearest to him, then words become flowers in him." And in the "Grund zum Empedokles": in personality, in the midst of the greatest passion, the meeting of extremes is accomplished, but this passion is only a moment that disappears along with the one who endures it. Thus, by death, extremes will be

---

* Such is the other form of opposition that the poet meets, the speech of the people, song of the heart united with the community, whose voice rises to the highest, to infinity, but that as collectivity cannot sing. For song, in order to manifest what is common to all, needs the voice of solitude that alone can open up to the secret ("Song of Ottmar and Hom"). Likewise, the poet is love; it is his love that gradually makes the gods come down toward men, that gives everything to all, but at the same time love makes all mediation impossible, for *it attaches itself only to the Only One* ("The Only One").

reconciled in a higher way, and "the passion of the moment that has gone by finally emerges more universal, more contained, more lucid, clearer."

Death was the temptation of Empedocles. But for Hölderlin, for the poet, death is the poem. It is in the poem that he must attain the extreme moment of opposition, the moment in which he is carried away to disappear and, disappearing, to carry to the highest the meaning of what can be accomplished only by this disappearance. Impossible, the reconciliation of the Sacred with speech demanded that the poet's existence come nearest to nonexistence. That is when, for one moment, it itself seemed possible, when, before foundering, it agreed to assert itself in song, come from an already silent body, uttered by a dead voice, so that the only hymn worthy of the essence of day rose from the depths of the vanished day, so that the mind also was glorified by that distraction—not because the highest is darkness, or because in the end the mind must be tied to its loss, but because the All made itself language to say it: whoever wants to meet the dark must seek in the day, look at the day, become day for himself: "Enigma is the pure gushing of what gushes out / Profundity that shakes everything, the coming of the day."

Such is the "sacred" speech of Hölderlin.

§ Baudelaire's Failure

In his long study published as a preface to the *Personal Writings*, Sartre draws an unforgiving portrait of Baudelaire. Baudelaire once evoked, speaking of Poe, an unfortunate whose forehead bore this tattoo: No Luck. One could also say of Baudelaire that fate struck him with an unusual anathema. But Sartre shows that he deserved his constant misfortune: from the shameful judicial verdict, the torture of an unending affair, and the pain of being unrecognized, up to his final decline, he is the one who made his misfortune; he called it, he sought it, and he did not stop until he found it.

Sartre's demonstration is very impressive and, as a whole, quite fair. It is true, then: Baudelaire had the life he deserved, a sordid life without refinement, conformist in his revolts, liar in the frankness that elevated him, a life faked and failed; all these judgments demand few reservations. But if we accept them, as we must, we must accept another, which Sartre neglects: it is that Baudelaire also deserved *Les Fleurs du Mal*, that the life responsible for his "bad luck" (*guignon*) is responsible for this signal good fortune, one of the greatest of the century.

This is certainly strange. And Sartre's gap underlines this strangeness. Baudelaire's life, as he proves, is nothing but the history of his failure. Yet this life is also a complete success. Not an accidental success but one premeditated, and one that does not add to the failure but that finds its reason for being in this failure; one that glorifies this failure, makes impotence incredibly fertile, draws out the most shining truth from a fundamental imposture.

Why was Baudelaire a great poet? How could poetic greatness, which is perhaps the greatest of all, be made with this lack of greatness, of effectiveness, of truth, and, an even more remarkable fact, with this absence of creative intention that led the poet to so much compromise and neglect? For it goes without saying that to explain the fortunes of Baudelaire, one would no more invoke his genius than Sartre would explain his miserable life by some fatal flaw in his character. And it is again obvious that the same choice that explains his failed existence explains his fulfilled existence, that the same premeditation that drove him to be neither truly free nor truly rebellious drove him to enact one of the greatest gestures of poetic liberation that has ever been seen, as if wherever man fails, literature takes flight; wherever existence takes fright, poetry becomes fearless.

Let us note at the start: in these judgments, it is not a question of taking into account values in the name of which we could define what was failed and what was not, ignoring the ideal that Baudelaire gave himself. It was not only in relation to the pharisaical wisdom of his time that this marginal man failed and weakened. Certainly, for Villemain, even for Sainte-Beuve, just as for Ancelle or his mother, he was nothing but a failure, a half-maniac, dishonored by his debaucheries and justly punished by his horrible end. But he failed more profoundly, for he failed in front of himself. His existence was not unfortunate because it featured a ridiculous failure in front of the Academy, under the supervision of people whom he despised, and poverty, indifference, and sterility, but much more for having desired academic fame, having drawn pride from the false praises of a Sainte-Beuve and having sought the world's protection, in face of which he claimed to assert himself in the solitude of an uncompromising independence.

It was not the morality of "fortunate men" that condemned him, it was his effort to free himself from this morality, an effort that, far from freeing him of it, made him party to it, so that, by glorifying himself for not having any part in this shameful happiness, he also did all he could to attain it and to share the same without having been appeased by it. Baudelaire's failure is that of a man who had the revelation of his freedom and whom this freedom frightened. That is why he is unfortunate, feeling as a disgrace failures that are such only in the eyes of a narrow-minded world: he kept calling them, seeking them out at once to punish himself with them, defy them, and succumb to them without even having had the merit always to suffer from them.

The Napoleonic code condemned *Les Fleurs du Mal,* but *Les Fleurs du Mal* condemned Baudelaire, whom this code impressed and who, in his heart, accepted its principles. Even more: he acted as if he should never have written them, but, at the very most, he could have managed to keep the dream of them, to glimpse them, in the half-torpor of his lazy life, as the lucid loss crowning the dishonor of that life. Baudelaire's failure is final. He wanted to live poetically, but he recoiled before the consequences of that decision, which would have deprived him of the daily comfort and support of an unwavering morality. So he also accepted living outside of poetry, living to succeed. But if he welcomed the hope of a social success, he welcomed it only to have the possibility of losing it, to give himself a sure, precise ideal, which gave him the right to apprehend and experience his powerlessness to attain it.

Half disloyal to poetry—to which there is no half-loyalty—half enemy of the world that recognized enemies only in those who exclude it completely, he gave to poetry a life already compromised and to the world's success a mind in search of failure. On the side of poetry, there was failure because there was acquiescence to a non-poetic certainty. And on the side of the world, the failure is called misery, mistake, decline.

Baudelaire's poetic fortune had its origin in its loss, and not a loss with respect to the values that poetry questions but in a retreat from poetry, in a lack of poetry. Is this not strange? And is it not even stranger that precisely with this Baudelaire whose life is so seriously tainted with poetic infidelity, poetry is not content with asserting itself in written poems, work enclosed in the purity of a book, but as experience and the very movement of life? In short, everything happens as if poetry needed to fall short and fall short of itself, as if it were pure and profound only by reason of its own shortcoming, a shortcoming that it encloses like the void that deepens it, purifies it, and endlessly prevents it from being, saves it from being and, because of that, unrealizes it, and by unrealizing it, makes it at once both possible and impossible, possible because it does not yet exist, if it realizes itself starting from what makes it fail, and impossible because it is not even capable of the complete ruin that alone could support its reality.

This paradox demands to be studied more closely. According to Sartre, Baudelaire is the man who, being deeply aware of the unmotivated, unjustified, unjustifiable nature of his existence, of the abyss that free existence represents, did not agree to look straight at this freedom. Instead, he sometimes limits it by establishing it in an ordered and hierarchical universe, sometimes embodies it in a distinct object, valid for others and unquestionable for himself (his poems, for example), sometimes cunningly uses it, vowing himself to Evil out of hate for Good, but, in the damnation on which he prided himself, recognizing implicitly the sovereignty of what damns him, and allowing himself the hope of a salvation possible with the proud satisfaction of pushing away this salvation.

In a word, Baudelaire retreats before what he calls the abyss and what Sartre calls existence, and he seeks guarantees on the side of a truth or of an objective, moral, social, or religious authority, what Sartre and Baudelaire both call being. This is a debate that we would not dream of excusing, for he himself described it in a poem that anticipates Sartre's analyses in the most precise way. This poem is "The Chasm":

> Pascal avait son gouffre, avec lui se mouvant,
> —Hélas! tout est abîme,—action, désir, rêve,
> Parole! et sur mon poil qui tout droit se relève
> Mainte fois de la Peur je sens passer le vent.
>
> En haut, en bas, partout, la profondeur, la grève,
> Le silence, l'espace affreux et captivant . . .
> Sur le fond de mes nuits Dieu de son doigt savant
> Dessine un cauchemar multiforme et sans trêve.

J'ai peur du sommeil comme on a peur d'un grand trou,
Tout plein de vague horreur, menant on ne sait où;
Je ne vois qu'infini par toutes les fenêtres,

Et mon esprit, toujours du vertige hanté,
Jalouse du néant l'insensibilité.
—Ah! ne jamais sortir des Nombres et des Êtres!

Pascal had his chasm, moved with it,
—Alas! all is abyss,—action, desire, dream,
Language! and in my hair which stands straight up
So many times from Fear I feel the wind pass.

Above, below, everywhere, the deeps, the shore,
Silence, terrifying and captivating space . . .
On the ground of my nights God with his knowing finger
Draws a nightmare of many shapes, unremitting.

I am afraid of sleep as one fears some great pit,
All full of vague horror, leading no one knows where;
I see nothing but infinity from every window,

And my mind, haunted always by vertigo,
Numbness jealous of nothingness.
—Ah! never to go from Numbers and Beings!

We cite this well-known text to show how the philosophical terminology of the commentary reveals nothing new about the attitude it discusses, and consequently is not able to betray it. In this poem, we recognize most of the movements starting from which the life and work of Baudelaire can be understood. Feeling of the abyss, awareness that the abyss is all, and exactly that all, the All, is precisely the abyss—this all that poetry seeks and can assert and find only in the abyss. Awareness that existence, made unbearable by the chasm, will not fail to elude itself, that it will find two exits, one leading to the objective assurance of being, the other ending up at nothingness and all its substitutes, indifference of the skeptic, detachment of the dandy, all the forms of salvation by impotence and sterility. And even more obscure, awareness that the abyss tries to make itself visible by making itself pass for the knowing work of a God and the illusion of a bad dream. Awareness, finally, of the ambiguity of the abyss, "terrifying and captivating": "Alas! All is abyss—action, desire, dream, / Language!"

That language can be abyss, that is what opens the way of poetic creation to Baudelaire. To write poems answering to an original aesthetic ideal, to write stories, novels, plays, as is fitting for a true man of letters—he wanted this, it was his goal. But in this same Baudelaire, gratified if he reached the fame of a Gautier, lives also the revelation that all is abyss and that "all is abyss" is the foundation of speech, the movement starting from which this can truly speak. How is that possible? What meaning can such a revelation take with a man whose main activity was writing and who, despite all the distinction of his mind attentive to rare works, did not pretend to write in vain?

We do not say that this question finds in Baudelaire a mind most apt to clarify it, for this mind is precisely too attached to the aesthetic, too capable of clarifying art by deepening it theoretically rather than in relation to it. Such a problem cannot lead in the awareness of a creator to the aid of general answers. It can only be temporarily and superficially the object of critical considerations. It is this problem itself that is the critique, that writes the critique of its creator.

It is certain that Baudelaire always had a high idea of art, but he also always considered the exercise of art as a normal activity, accomplished following the rules and not necessarily giving place to insurmountable debates. Gautier, perfect man of letters, master in matters of language and style, seemed to him the poet above all others. For the same reason, he had confidence in rhetoric, in which he saw not only arbitrary constraints but also providential rules in agreement with profound poetic movement. "It is obvious that rhetorics and prosodies are not tyrannies invented arbitrarily, but a collection of rules called for by the very organization of spiritual being. And prosodies and rhetorics never prevented originality from manifesting distinctly. The opposite, to realize that they helped the hatching of originality, would be infinitely truer" (*Salon of 1859*). In such faith in rhetoric, Sartre would recognize the need for an authority disguised as reason, this same need that drove Aupick's nephew to wish to live as an eternal child under the care of an unquestionable Father. But let us look more closely.

Baudelaire's poetics is well known. It rests on a certain idea of imagination. Baudelairean imagination is a very complex power, essentially destined to surpass that which is, to begin an infinite movement and, at the same time, one capable of returning to an ordered reality, that of language, in which it represents and embodies this movement. Following the customs of his century, Baudelaire speaks of imagination as of a faculty, but this expression does not mean that man finds in it an instrument already fashioned that it is enough for him to set in motion. When man imagines, he is completely imagination. When he imagines, he is not even imagining, he is undergoing imagination, in the effort and tension to imagine.

Imagination for Baudelaire is, in all its forms, equilibrium and constant disequilibrium. Endless movement of surpassing, it is always beyond what it indicates, daydream that does not rest. Moreover, if it always wants something else, if nothing that is nature can satisfy it, that is because it is trying to attain nature *in its entirety*, in which both the world foreign to the artist and the artist who sees the world and sees himself through the world are found, he who tries by a magical act to make arise, from himself and his art, by imagination, the unsurpassable totality of the universe that contains him.

Baudelaire expressed this in the clearest way: "What is pure art according to modern perception? It is to create a suggestive magic containing object and subject at the same time, the world exterior to the artist and the artist himself." When he criticizes naturalism, he criticizes it because this theory claims to reduce art to the transcription of a natural fact ("Poetry's destiny is great. . . . It endlessly contradicts fact, to the point of almost ceasing to be"; Pierre Dupont, in *Romantic Art*), but especially because it thinks it attains nature, when one truly attains it only if one attains it in its entirety, if one "knows *all* nature."

Baudelaire, like all those for whom the word "poetry" has a

meaning, knows that poetry is an experience lived by means of existence and language, experience that tends to cause the meaning of all things together to be born, so that starting from this meaning, each thing is changed, appears as it is, in its own reality and in the reality of the whole. Speaking of Delacroix, he writes: "Edgar Poe said, I don't know where, that the result of opium for the senses is to endow all of nature with a supernatural interest that gives to each object a more profound meaning, more willful, more despotic." Poetry and art want to realize this illusion of opium. Each word attests this: it is *all of nature* that is transformed and, because of that, it *interests* us, it matters to us as no longer being nature, but nature surpassed, realized in its surpassing, the *supernatural*; this interest, however, is not a movement into emptiness, foreign to reality. It sends us back, on the contrary, to *each object* that appears thus in the light of the movement that surpasses it and, far from losing itself in a dissolving subjectivity, asserts itself as it is, with the *despotic* meaning—stubborn, Sartre would say—of things that are in themselves and do not change.

Such is the true meaning of the word "supernaturalism" that Baudelaire made his own and that has been repeated haphazardly. Supernaturalism does not aim for a region above reality, even less for an actual world different from the world in which men exist, but it concerns reality in its entirety, the *whole* world, that is to say, the possibility for things to be completely present to each other, each in its complete existence. It is a possibility that changes them by showing them as they are, a presence that is imagination itself.

We know what role Baudelaire made the theory of correspondences, of universal analogy, play. We will not linger to show how such a role is obviously implied in this idea of imagination. If analogy and metaphors are the essential resources of the being who imagines, it is because in metaphors and images he finds at once this movement of surpassing that carries him toward something else ("For those privileged ones—artists and children—an image represents *something else." Years in Brussels*) and also the true meaning of each object as it sends back to him the experience of everything. Undoubtedly, Baudelaire is strongly tempted to recognize in this theory of correspondences a key to the world and in universal analogy the sign of a superior order, mysterious certainly, but true and definitive. This temptation answers to his need "not to go from Numbers and Beings"; it also answers to his taste for general ideas and aesthetic problems, a tendency that expresses the same care to argue the abyss, to make it bearable by making it the object of a problem. For Baudelaire, the image is perhaps an explanatory theory, but first of all it is passion. The remark in *My Heart Laid Bare* has an obvious truth: images are for him his *great*, his *only*, his *primitive passion*. And he pursues them, lives them as one lives a passion, because they represent to him the accessible way to an inaccessible end.

Further, Baudelaire says of Delacroix: "He is the infinite in the finite." So there is not enough contradictory effort in which this "sharp peak that is the infinite" pushes us. Carrying contradiction to a higher point, we must, with this always unfinished movement, excluding any limit, any rest, nevertheless realize a finite, finished, perfect object. We know that for Baudelaire, irregularity is the main part of beauty, but we also know that beauty cannot do without a harmoniously ruled form. Beauty is the unexpected and it is the expectation of rhythm; something vague, that can never be grasped, something absent and as if deprived of itself—and also something that is the most exact, the just agreement of a rigorously accomplished project ("The poet's greatest happiness: to accomplish justly what he aimed to do"). To recall that Baudelaire made of coldness, of the stone's dream, the ideal whose cult he proposed, is only to recall one of the terms of the logic of opposites, with which, he says about Poe, "creation is at work." Coldness but in passion, passion without limits but within the firmest boundaries, the greatest madness of sensitivity asserting itself by lucidity, reflection, criticism, irony. For imagination to announce itself, the meeting of these two extreme signs "that mark the most solid geniuses" is necessary: *to be passionately in love with passion, and coldly determined to seek the means to express passion in the most visible way.*

If poetry let the contradictions that it implies appear clearly, the experience of its impossibility could not occur, and poetic torment would be without value. But it is in ambiguity that poetry becomes creation. And when we see nothing in it but destruction and contradictory passion, at that instant, the instant of the greatest difficulty, we also discover the ease that reconciles everything. Thus, Baudelaire's *finite*, which is first the infinite's principle of questioning, the agonizing work by which dream must be surmounted, transformed, in order to become real yet without losing its spontaneity, the finite becomes the certainty of written language, the rules that fix it, the happiness of a rigorous order traditionally accepted.

So the movement of endless tension toward a forever unachieved totality seems like a tragic effort, thus also like the benevolence of inspiration, the providence of sleep. And *the infinite in the finite*—undoubtedly that is something easy; but to hold these two movements together, to compose them, to realize one by the other, if that implies a great effort, the work of art finds exactly there the most precious resources, and one sees in the end that the unexpected, far from opposing the expectation of rhythm, is perceptible only in this expectation, that vagueness agrees with the most exact language, just as the obscurity of dream, to express itself, finds all that is necessary in language's transparency. It becomes natural to Baudelaire to praise the poetry of Poe in these terms: "It is something profound and glittering like dream, mysterious and perfect like crystal."

Language is certainly an abyss, but the abyss, in order to speak to us, needs *numbers*. A rather remarkable ability and, for that reason, a little annoying. But did it annoy Baudelaire? We can think, along with Sartre, that this way of feeling himself loyal to the abyss while leaning on the solidity of the banks suited him very well, and that, if his choice attached him so purely to poetic creation, it is precisely because poetic creation is pure only in the equivocal. Every poet has bad faith in his game: he can do nothing against it, but with it he can do everything and even save his good faith, be lost and yet succeed.

But it still must be seen on what conditions.

Poetry is a means of putting oneself in danger without running any risk, a mode of suicide, destruction of self, that comfortably leaves space for the surest affirmation of self. It is right to recall it, because this criticism is demanded by literature itself and because in truth this has meaning and value only as passion lived by the writer, in the imposture to which he feels himself an accomplice. But when we begin to underline the poet's ambiguity, we also lose the right to stop this movement, to stabilize it in one of its points, to qualify it. It is the nature of ambiguity to escape arrest and qualification. While bad faith is being accomplished, it is just as much the advance of a good faith, too good ever to accept itself, as the irresponsible game of imposture that refuses to be engaged and take real risks.

In this sense, Baudelaire's bad faith, so well analyzed by Sartre, is also the poet's superior morality, this morality that leads him to travesty, to the superficial fakery of dandyism. In this new subterfuge, he undoubtedly seeks another solution to poetic impossibility, but at the same time he uses it to denounce this other, too satisfying subterfuge that is language. Dandyism hardly counts in his story, and no one judged better than he the weak import of this *cult* in which he saw himself with too many of his contemporaries to have really appreciated it, he who, when it came to social class, would have liked only one in which he would have been alone. "What is this, then," he said, "this passion that, become doctrine, has made ruling adepts, this unwritten institution that has formed such a high class? It is above all the ardent need to make an originality for oneself, contained in the outer boundaries of propriety" (*The Painter of Modern Life*). This judgment shows that if he really counted on such a way to assert his freedom, he had no illusion about the sincerity of this little game of revolt.

The "gaps" of life had for Baudelaire the importance of an ordeal, trifling in its nature but major in its effects, essential especially because it helped him, indirectly and without his even knowing it, to experience the value of work. Dandyism as a means of emancipation is the poorest of alibis, and he was not fooled by it. No more was he fooled by his "free" life. We know that "the artist commonplace in demeanor and conduct" always seemed despicable to him. "I would like a neologism to be created, a word made destined to condemn this kind of cliché. . . . Have you not often noticed that nothing is more like the perfect bourgeois than the artist of concentrated genius?" ("Some Foreign Caricaturists"). Misconduct, laziness, the life of disorder that he led (or thought he led) did not stop weighing on him, far from seeming an aesthetic ideal or admirable moral to him. Because of his secret conformism? Perhaps. But this is what actually happens: into this existence that he dreads, he sinks down more and more, this life of lost time, wasted work, fatal to his literary activity; the more it overwhelms him and holds him prisoner, the more it finds him compliant and makes him feel the approach of the *abyss* in which he fears he will be lost.

It is not because it shocks the editors of the *Siècle* that this life, from so many sides so contrary to itself, constitutes a major hardship. It is that it makes the consolation of artistic creation always more difficult for him, a consolation that, because it suited him perfectly, because he placed it above everything, involved him in indulgences dangerous to poetic ambiguity itself. It must be pointed out that the dogma of sterility that the name of Baudelaire attaches to the ideal of art is imposed by Baudelaire's example after his death, but he himself wanted nothing so much as the great fertile creators, the Balzacs, the Delacroix, the Gautiers. His dream was not to write some deathless verses, but an infinitely varied body of work, with many novels, plays, an immense body of work by a man of letters. There were so many unrealized projects that he dragged after him, images of tranquil hopes of long ago, that little by little haunted him like the sign of distress from which he could no longer escape.

If he had liked nothing but dreaming, if, from the start, aware that language is abyss, he had believed that silence is closer to authenticity than the most beautiful poems, he would have managed very well with his laziness and his impotence. But—thanks perhaps to his conformist weakness—it was precisely the finite he could not do without. Poetic demand always remained for him the demand for a ruled, ordered, studied, thought-out language, one that was as lucid as possible; pure dream never succeeded in concealing from his eyes the fault that made it possible or the illusion it represented.

Let us recall "The Double Room": "A room that resembles a daydream, a truly *spiritual* room." This room is poetic purity realized: "On the walls, no artistic abomination. Compared to pure dream, to unanalyzed impression, definite, positive art is a blasphemy. Here, everything has the sufficient clarity and delicious obscurity of harmony." Yes, it is the absolute, poetic sufficiency: time is stopped, eternity reigns. But all of a sudden, there is a knock on the door. "A terrible, heavy knock sounded . . . and, as in infernal dreams, it seemed to me that I was being hit in the stomach by a pickax." The Spiritual Room is then revealed as it is, a dump, an ugly, narrow world, where eternity is now only time that asserts, "I am Life, unbearable, implacable Life. . . . Live, then, damned." So pure dream is nothing but impurity. Its twin is banality, always present, concealed only by illusion. What does it matter, the compliant poet will say, if I delude myself with this false eternity that is nothing but the forgetting of time? Yes, but poetic condition wants it: scarcely has satisfaction begun than the knock, demanding awakening, is struck, and it is poetry itself that strikes this *heavy, terrible* blow, which shows what dream is: hypocrisy, nothingness.

We will not follow all the forms this debate takes with Baudelaire: a very long study would be necessary. We would simply like to note that questioning, if it goes from subterfuge to subterfuge with him, from compromise to compromise, because it never stops, also never allows us to denounce these compromises and these subterfuges—and this movement, moreover, far from being a skillful way of transforming disequilibrium into a resource of equilibrium, prepares him for a fall whose seriousness he enters deeply without enjoying it.

It is difficult to forget this: the writer who attributes a great deal of poetic value to work is also the one who, not managing to work, discovers a form of activity more profound than work, from which his body of work came in part, and to which it bears witness. We have the habit of seeing in Baudelaire only the theorist of the *finite* that strangely limits the role of inspiration. And yet it is he who declares, "In art, it is something not noted enough, that the part left to man's will is quite a bit less great than we think." It is again Baudelaire who recommends writing without repenting, without deletion, and is the first to seek automatism: "I am not a partisan of deletion, it troubles the mirror of thought. . . . If very clear execution is necessary, it is so that the language of dream is very clearly translated; if it is very fast, it is so that nothing will be lost of the extraordinary impression that accompanied its conception." And undoubtedly, to the degree that the impossibility of working asserts itself, he multiplies his calls to work to find inspiration again. "The more one works, the better one works, and the more one wants to work. . . . Work *six* days without *respite*." But, standing before work as before another abyss, one must return to one's "I am reasoning too much," "start writing right away," by which he tries to make contact with immediate life and the revelations characteristic of this life (see, for example, the letter to Asselineau, in which he so admirably transcribes one of his dreams, one of the most "surrealist" experienced before that word was coined).

Thanks to the disquiet that carried him to solutions that were both impracticable and fertile, routine work and absolute passivity, he arrived at desperate moments whose poetic signification is great. He discovered the mysterious, unknown impulses that carry the horror of action over into action. "It is a kind of energy that sparkles with boredom and daydream," an energy by which, he says again, man becomes capable of provoking, of tempting fate, experiencing the extremity of life while risking it and playing with it. It is experience in the most profound sense of the word, that, because of its character, not systematic but spontaneous, with a man little capable of spontaneity, has perhaps as much value as all the experiences of Rimbaud's derangement (*dérèglement*). "The Bad Glazier" foretells the *Notes from Underground*.

When Baudelaire writes, "One must always be drunk. Everything is there: it is the only question," we should recognize the literary nature of this recommendation: drunkenness is there for words' effects. "You have to get drunk without respite . . . on what? On wine, poetry or virtue, as you please." But this drunkenness, proposed with bad faith like a superior goal for poetry (with bad faith, since finally with this *get drunk* he makes nothing more than a poem), this indifference in drunkenness, when taken to language, makes the poetic drunkenness that leads to lucid works more and more difficult. At that instant, disgrace can well seem to be the punishment he secretly wanted, wanted while hoping to extract himself from it and pull out [of the game]; but, from the instant it reaches him, comes near, becoming more menacing every day, it also has this remarkable double result: to reassert the value of the poetry of speech, a consolation that is now no more than a perpetual torment; to discredit the poetry of silence, the poetry of living with the flow, to which it would be too easy for him to abandon himself. That is why "Rockets" (in which Sartre sees a reassessment of thoughts without freshness and without profundity) take on an incredible importance and become, for the poetry of the future, a tragic signal, on which many eyes will come to rest. What does he write of it? "Morally as well as physically, I have always had the sensation of the abyss, not only of the abyss of sleep but of the abyss of action, dream, memory, desire, regret, remorse, beauty, number, etc. I have cultivated my hysteria with pleasure and terror. Now I always have vertigo, and today, 23 January 1862, I have undergone a singular warning: I have felt the wind of imbecility's wing pass through me."

We will note that Baudelaire no longer speaks here of language as the abyss. A dramatic omission. At the time when language becomes for him the void that he first recognized in it, when, experienced as a vertigo, it is lost in the absence it reveals, it is at this instant that he avoids denouncing it. It is as if he wanted to keep this refuge for himself, as if the poem, become impossible in him, were waiting and demanding to be created starting from the impossibility in which he cornered it. For, it must be made clear, imbecility, this evil worse than Evil, in no way offers him the end where it would be pleasant and commendable for him, after so many annoyances, to find rest, no more than it shows itself to him, now that it is there, quite close and, so to speak, at his mercy, as the supreme avatar of poetic intelligence. At many times in his life, death, suicide, nothingness were his temptation, a temptation that often lacked seriousness, with which he played; we are right to see in it a prudent way of symbolically satisfying his disgust with living. If he can write to Jules Janin, *the fortunate man*, "What! you have never wanted to get out, just to change the view! I have very serious reason to pity one who does not love death," then we must pity him also, for not keeping silence on a desire that he never pacifies and that leads only to the letter of 30 June 1845 and its strange confession: "I kill myself because I believe I am immortal, and I hope." Strange confession. What does he hope? And what is the sense of this immortality that invites him to die? Nothing, undoubtedly, that resembles the immortality of his former religious faith; nothing, either, that can seem like an ultimate blasphemy, a challenge carried in the name of Evil, beyond death, against Good, one last time offended.

It is striking that Baudelaire never trusted nothingness. He has the very profound feeling that the horror of living cannot be consoled by death, that it does not encounter an emptiness that exhausts it, that this horror of existing that is existence has as its main signification this feeling that one does not stop existing, one never leaves existence, one exists and one always will exist, which is revealed by this very horror. What does "The Skeleton Worker" teach him?

> Voulez-vous (d'un destin trop dur
> Épouvantable et clair emblème)
> Montrer que dans la fosse même
> Le sommeil promis n'est pas sûr;
>
> Qu'envers nous le Néant est traître;
> Que tout, même la Mort, nous ment,
> Et que sempiternellement,
> Hélas! il nous faudra peut-être
>
> Dans quelque pays inconnu
> Écorcher la terre revêche

Et pousser une lourde bêche
Sous notre pied sanglant et nu?

Do you want (terrible, clear
Emblem of a fate too hard)
To show that even in the grave
The promised sleep is far from certain;

That to us Nothingness is traitor;
That everything, even Death, lies to us,
And that eternally,
Alas! we will have perhaps

In some unknown country
To scrape the sour earth
And push a heavy spade
Beneath our bleeding, naked foot?

And in darkness what does he discover? Darkness? Emptiness?
Blackness? No, but the eternally recurrent sense, starting from the
vanished being, of a being to whom disappearance itself restores
both meaning and existence.

Comme tu me plairais, ô Nuit! sans ces étoiles
Dont la lumière parle un langage connu!
Car je cherche le vide, et le noir, et le nu!

Mais les ténèbres sont elles-mêmes des toiles
Où vivent, jaillissant de mon œil par milliers,
Des êtres disparus aux regards familiers!

How you please me, oh Night! without those stars
Whose light speaks a known language!
For I seek emptiness, and blackness, and nakedness!

But darkness itself is a canvas
Where live, spurting from my eye by the thousands,
Vanished beings with familiar looks!

So nothingness cannot be counted on to end anything, since,
when one has entered into existence, one has entered a situation
that has as its essential nature the fact that one is never finished

with it. Heidegger's "being-for-death," far from characterizing authentic possibility, would thus represent for Baudelaire only one more imposture. We do not have death in front of us, but existence that, as far as I go forward, is always in front, and, as low as I sink, is always lower, and, as unreally as I assert myself (in art, for example), infests this unreality with an absence of reality that is still existence.

> —Mais pourquoi pleure-t-elle? Elle, beauté parfaite
> Qui mettrait à ses pieds le genre humain vaincu.
> Quel mal mystérieux ronge son flanc d'athlète?

> —Elle pleure, insensé, parce qu'elle a vécu!
> Et parce qu'elle vit! Mais ce qu'elle déplore
> Surtout, ce qui la fait frémir jusqu'aux genoux,
> C'est que demain, hélas! il faudra vivre encore!
> Demain, après-demain et toujours!—comme nous!

> —But why is she weeping? She, perfect beauty
> Who could put at her feet conquered humankind.
> What mysterious evil gnaws at her shapely side?

> —She weeps, madman, because she has lived!
> And because she lives! But what she is lamenting
> Above all, what makes her tremble to her knees,
> Is that tomorrow, alas! she will have to live again!
> Tomorrow, the day after tomorrow and forever!—like us!

Thus, art and the work of art (that the statue of Christopher represents in these verses) assert, behind the hope of surviving, the despair of existing endlessly, in the dissolution of all form and all existence, a dissolution that, by still being form and existence, continues, beyond all life, the ambiguity and imposture that have driven our life.

It is this experience that makes the word *atrocious* authentic; it is a word with which Baudelaire qualified his poems, and it is this experience that gives all its importance to the image, banal as it is, of the abyss. For, even more than the idea of freedom (from which one can at least draw the reassuring principle of a new ladder of

values) could have done, it involved him in an endless questioning
and did not even leave him the hope of rest in death or nothingness. By the abyss, the horror of existing discovers in existence what
is already below death, beyond its own end, and in "the numbness
of nothingness" a pseudo idea and false hope. The *I hope* of
25 January 1845 answers to this feeling that one does not leave
existence by death, but *I hope* answers always to that movement of
escape and flight from which the dogma of immortality arose: by
this dogma, the horror of always being dissolved into existence has
become the hope of always *being*, and the beyond of life that is life,
the being of the beyond.

Baudelaire did not kill himself on that day that he hoped for
death. And he saw that death lied, that nothingness was a traitor.
He approached imbecility, though without recognizing in this
decline the victory of the infinite over the finite or a satisfying
means of surmounting calm, rational abilities. Soon he loses the
use of words. His disgrace is complete. Yet what happens to him?
One can easily assert with Sartre that he merited this end, and *merit*
clearly implies that the end is not meritorious, which accords with
Baudelaire's own viewpoint, as with that of Villemain, for whom
the spectacle of a silent, destroyed man on a hospital bed could
appear sublime. But then we must recognize this: if this end judges
Baudelaire for establishing a catastrophe for which he is responsible, it finds him not guilty of having played without risk, of having
chosen to fall without downfall, and even of having loved misfortune without being able to suffer from it. At least on this point,
imposture stops being attributable to him. Mystification is in truth
achieved, and the symbolic ruin that his poems depict becomes real
enough to impose its seriousness.

Naturally, one can claim that Baudelaire did not want that, that
he planned this shabby end only through aims of life that hid their
awful nature from him. Undoubtedly. But that hardly matters, and
from the instant one makes him responsible for this disaster that he
did not prepare, one must also, in the thousand decisions of bad
faith that led him to pluck misfortune, find again the implacable
seriousness of final tragedy. We know there is nothing fortuitous in

an existence. If Baudelaire died in scandal and the destruction of his devastated genius, it is because, in his life, he did not content himself with brushing against scandal and suffering in the course of gratuitous or symbolic excesses; instead, he consented to involve himself deeply in them, if only for a day, if only by a gesture.

Thus poetic truth decided it. Baudelaire's debacle, his struggle in the last months with words that tricked him, all the anguish that thousands of unknown sick people, afflicted with the same disease, share with him without affecting literary history, seems the heroic end of the questioning in which, for a few seconds, the *all is abyss* of language and the sure, calm, and beautiful poems that carried it are united; it is the final sacrifice by which the poet, who knows nothing of it, is led to lose himself in order to realize and make present poetry always to come, always to do.

And the strangest thing happens then: it is that the works written in full shelter from this drama, that participate neither in its gravity nor in its seriousness, that are striking by artifice or formal assurance, all that he wrote, dreamed of writing, failed to write, all that he did, his concessions to the world, his timid man's revolts, his sad academic aims, all that is transformed by the tragedy of the last moment and accepts from it the meaning of an accomplished fate, because questioning the end did not fail him. Is this just? That is not the question. Now that Baudelaire is dead in the glory of final shame, his least papers, the least acts of his life are lit up with a new light that changes them, and everyone learns to read them backward, to decipher them behind the silence that stretched upon them a definitive effacement.

Thus, the *veritable* failure of the last hour flows back on an entire life that was perhaps false, transforming it into a life poetically *true*. It is through this failure that the ambiguity of an existence that could have borne very bad names declares itself instead as a successful experiment because pushed to the extreme, where even failures have their value, where poetry profits from betrayals and infidelities. From then on, death will enchant Baudelaire. It gives him more than he ever had, more than his life: an interminable life. Having lost very much, he won everything. Literarily, at least. For someone who, all the while loving art, saw a curse in the unreal eternity of the work of art, those comings and goings of posterity, those brilliant vicissitudes that mix him with our times, represent perhaps a side of nightmare that he glimpsed and feared. In this sense, if he was responsible for the failure of his life, he is also responsible for the success of his survival. A man who would have liked *to be great only for himself* does not succeed in being great for others without some grave defects. And when this fame has as much brilliance as that of Baudelaire, one must indeed recognize him as guilty of it, and discover in him all that he lacked to remain obscure.

§ The Sleep of Rimbaud

The *Complete Works* of Rimbaud, published in the Pléiade series, give us all the satisfactions one could expect from this kind of edition. For a long time, these works, so slender, were not less mistreated by the editors than by their author. Hypocrisy, excessive zeal, facetiousness, all contributed to making them dubious. For some years, however, particularly since the labors of Bouillane de Lacoste, the most beautiful texts have become definitive. Rolland de Renéville—with Mouquet—continued this work of setting the record straight. The *Complete Works* give us a better version of the *Illuminations*. They consecrate the authenticity of *The Zutiste Album* (enriched with two previously unpublished works, "The Drunken Coachman" and "The Wicked Little Angel") that had long been considered doubtful. They also definitively attribute to Rimbaud "A Heart Beneath a Cassock," published twenty years ago by André Breton and Louis Aragon. They make public the three sonnets of the "Stupra." Finally, they reunite for the first time the greater part of the letters in a corrected and finished version. All these texts are clarified by philological annotations; only interpretations and poetic commentaries are lacking. But this very gap guarantees the quality of the edition.

In their short preface, the editors note that misunderstandings went hand in hand with the fame of Rimbaud. Dr. Jean Fretet's study, often well informed, often thoughtless, does not seem able to diminish these misunderstandings. There is certainly no harm in giving a psychopathological interpretation to Rimbaud's story and adventure. But Dr. Fretet does not content himself with interpreting; he wants to explain—to explain all the aspects of an existence by only one of its aspects, and one on which the information is conjectural and discovers its value only by undergoing all possible interpretations. That is the fault of Fretet's study, *Poetic Alienation: Rimbaud, Mallarmé, Proust* (and it is even more obvious when it discusses Mallarmé).

Of Rimbaud, we surely know just about all we will ever know. From time to time thousands of verses are sent to us from Abyssinia, lines that vanished on the way. Even Renéville could not lay hands on "The Spiritual Hunt," which he asserts was written in the course of the first half of 1872 and which he distinguishes from the *Illuminations*. We don't say What does it matter? But it is probable that we know as much and more about Rimbaud than he knew about himself.

We will not recall that his fame was divided between the poems that he wrote and those that he did not deign to write, between poetry that he affirmed and poetry that he rejected. Since the time of his death, the silence he kept for twenty years has seemed a bewitching enigma: while still alive, he had poetry cut out of him, said Mallarmé with a dread in which there is some envy. Twenty minds, and some of the greatest, have endeavored to find the key to this enigma. Why? That is perhaps what is strange. Why does it seem so surprising that a mind with a gift for letters all of a sudden turns its back on literature and completely loses interest in an activity in which it excelled? That there is, in such a refusal, scandal for everyone shows what immeasurable value everyone attaches to the exercise of poetry.

Rimbaud's scandal took many forms: first he writes masterpieces, then renounces writing others while he appears capable of producing many. To renounce writing, when one has proven to be a great writer, certainly does not occur without mystery. This mystery increases when one discovers what Rimbaud asks of poetry: not to produce beautiful works, or to answer to an aesthetic ideal, but to help man go somewhere, to be more than himself, to see more than he can see, to know what he cannot know—in a word, to make of literature an experience that concerns the whole of life and the whole of being. From this point of view, the abandonment becomes a greater scandal. The poet does not renounce just any activity, or even any privileged activity, but the very possibility that, glimpsed and pursued, cannot be destroyed without a diminution in comparison with which suicide and madness seem nothing. And so great is man's respect for the decision to go to extremes, so great the certainty that one can only betray such an effort by obeying it, that Rimbaud's renunciation, far from being held as an infidelity to the energy that inspired him, has seemed to be its highest moment, one in which he truly touched the summit and which, because of that, remains inexplicable to us. With Rimbaud, not only does poetry surpass the domain of written works and things to become the fundamental experience of existence, but it monopolizes its absence, it establishes itself on its own refusal.

Such a view has become common. Perhaps by being repeated so much it has lost its value. We have forgotten that it would be worth nothing if it were not understood in all its ambiguity, and that, this ambiguity safely aside, it can no longer keep much meaning. To say that the experience lived by Rimbaud at the time of the *Illuminations* and of *A Season in Hell* led him to the silence of Cyprus, to his trafficking in the Harrar, to his communications to the Geographical Society, means that in his decision to break with poetry we recognize only the appearance of sincerity—since, as adventurer, arms dealer, and novice explorer, he would only have been following, in another form and in a baser way, the same designs, the same dissoluteness, the same search for the unknown as he had followed in the time of poetic splendors. On the other hand, if we admit that by leaving poetry, he really and definitively left it, and if we attribute an absolute value to his "I have to bury my imagination and my memories" (as one must for this fact to have the meaning it is accorded), then there is nothing more to say about his second existence. All of its mediocrity is as much a sign of its authenticity as a proof of his failure; all its banality, sordid at times, moves us, and seems extraordinary to us (and also allows Dr. Fretet to think with some plausibility that Rimbaud abdicated only what he had already lost).

We cannot say that Rimbaud's silence adds to his poetry the plan of surpassing it by rejecting it. If we say that, his silence seems a miserable comedy, little by little taken at its word by a miserable reality. And if we avoid saying that, then Rimbaud's story no longer signifies much. After all, if a man who could adventure further than others one day decides to conduct himself like thousands of other men, loving money, limiting his life to the immediate care of life, what can we conclude? That one fine day, he was afraid of the unknown, that he had enough of his "supernatural powers," that he showed himself to be cowardly, weak, terrified before his formidable design, in front of this plan so great that no man could face it? Not even that. Who will ever prove to us that the letter of the Seer was more than an adolescent dream? The *Illuminations*, the *Season in Hell* can indeed let us glimpse that this path was really followed: exactly insofar as, by writing them, Rimbaud touched the extreme, he also surpassed the order of communicable things, and the unknown did not come closer to us. There is actually only one certainty: that these works are literary successes that have shocked men and inspired them in turn; but, concerning the program of the Seer, no one can decide if they represent a trick, a radical failure, a trap full of magnificence, or a truly "legendary" attempt.

This uncertainty makes the power and enigma of Rimbaud. He pushed ambiguity—the essential movement of poetic activity—to the utmost. And this ambiguity is such that the deepest knowledge of his acts, all the new documents that one can imagine discovering one day, no more than "the forty thousand verses from Abyssinia," will ever reduce it. It has become fashionable, after the excessive admiration that we had become accustomed to reserve for his career as adventurer, to portray the silent side of his life in black. We reproach him with his cowardliness because he feared prison, fled military obligations, and, even in the midst of revolt, rather lamentably begged this one and that one to save him from the police. Perhaps, in fact, he was a coward. So? Order, "eternal watchman," was repugnant to him. Disorder did not enchant him. He was not an angel, despite some rather sad whiffs of innocence. He was only a weak lover of adventure and a sometime hoodlum. And, save his literary triumphs, he left us nothing but the testimony of an empty, discontented, mediocre existence that attained nothing and aimed for nothing. And yet no one as much as he ever gave us the feeling of having forced "the impossible," as he calls it in the *Season in Hell.*

Reading the correspondence, facilitated by the Pléiade edition, tends to bring the two Rimbauds closer together, "the angel, the magus" and the "peasant," the Rimbaud who knew hell and the one who turned away from it, still without clarifying the decision that separated the two. But, to speak of only one matter, we are struck by how little change the death of the poet appeared to bring forth in the one who underwent it or provoked it. From without, he remained the same. Two of his characteristics, at least, survived the metamorphosis. All his life, Rimbaud expressed a horror of work, an invincible need for rest and sleep. "The best thing is a really drunken sleep," "sleep in a nest of flames," "the sleep of virginity," "hearse of my sleep." Indeed, one could say that, while he was a writer, he sought, while writing, to bring about an actual breakthrough into the heart of sleep, to flee away into a stupor next to which death would have been nothing, into a nothingness that, even more than death, would have assured the end of life. "What is my nothingness, next to the stupor that awaits you?" And must we recall his "Nothingness Studies," the allusions to the "continuous sleep of the legendary Mohammedans"? Later, condemned by his choice to an "atrocious," "absurd," "mind-destroying" job, he has only one obsession: to rest, "to scrape out, by dint of fatigue, the means to rest." All his letters are torn apart by the expression of this furious need, which assuredly manifests itself without delicacy: it is no longer a question of subtlety or ruse. He comes to wish for rest in marriage, the happiness of one "seated," a position. It is a weakness for which we reproach him. But it only serves to make more important the desperate point to which the need for sleep drives him, the need for any kind of sleep, his "I am extremely tired"; "Don't tire yourself out, that is an unreasonable thing"; "I have to spend the rest of my days wandering in fatigue and privations, with the sole prospect of dying in sorrow."

Dr. Fretet holds against Rimbaud his many complaints, his tears when his leg was amputated, all those frightful cries of misery. Why? Rimbaud made fun of stoicism, and—it must be said here— there was in him (and almost on the same subjects, poverty and money) something howling and ferocious that one finds again exactly in the Marquis de Sade. Rimbaud is one of the men who most strongly asserted their boredom. "I am bored a lot, always; I have actually never met anyone who was bored as much as I." This boredom, as lively in the mature man as in the adolescent, resembles in no way a literary disposition. As far as we can tell, from the time of his first attempts at poetry, this feeling had for him the value of experience; it was a methodical resource, a move similar to sleep that he sought and that, through this sleep, made him dream of attaining a torpor beyond all seeking. When he writes in the *Season in Hell*, "Boredom is no longer my love," he identifies it very clearly with rages, debauches, madness, with all the disturbance that, for some time, was for him synonymous with poetry. Yet, on boredom, in 1881, in the full misery of the Harrar, he writes these strange lines: "Alas! I'm not at all attached to life; and if I live, I am accustomed to living with fatigue, but if I am forced to continue to tire myself out as now, and to feed myself on sorrows as vehement as they are absurd in these atrocious climates, I fear I will cut short my existence. . . . Finally, let us be able to enjoy a few years of real rest in this life; and fortunately this life is the only one, and that is obvious, since one cannot imagine another life with a boredom greater than this!" One should not ask too much of a text, written for "his own," and one that does not claim to say anything singular. Yet singularity is there. Rimbaud builds a strange reasoning: obviously, he says, there cannot be another life, because there cannot be a life with more boredom than this one. As if life for him were action, action were boredom, and as if no more life were always linked to no more boredom, so that when one attains the extremity of boredom, one has always exhausted all possibility of another life, and that one who has known the greatest possible boredom no longer has to fear the boredom of an afterlife. It is the ontological argument come back. Without looking too far, we can see that such thoughts imply a background of singular mental reservations: to know that death is perhaps not death, that to avoid the disgrace of a beyond, one must seek a real death, to know also that boredom has a double aspect, positive and negative, a kind of horror tied to activity and perhaps with the property of coming to the end of activity by means of activity.

Reading this correspondence so full of calls to rest, how can we not notice that in sum he was attached only to himself: with his eight kilos of gold in his belt, which he watches over so grimly, how did he expect to live other than in fatigue? Dr. Fretet speaks of Rimbaud's thirst. Rimbaud, at every age, particularly in his youth, was devoured by thirst: an acrid thirst that dried him out, to which he gave water, alcohol, fire, in vain.

> Et la soif malsaine
> Obscurcit mes veines
>
> And unwholesome thirst
> Darkened my veins

"To say that I never had a concern for drink!" "It is such a crazy thirst . . . ," etc. The need for sleep is not linked in him to some feeble expectation, to a nature already numbed, heavy and malleable, but to a bitterness that rises from fire, that calls the torrid elements and that these elements make crazy. It is a dryness that, to be sated, wants nothing but dryness, the aridity of stone and sand in search of an aridity of flame and poison. Such is Hell. On every page of *A Season*, he "dies of thirst," he is "thirsty, thirsty," thirst of hell, demanding hell, not the coolness of water but a liqueur of gold that makes one sweat. "I demand, I demand! a blow from a pitchfork, a drop of fire."

On one side, this sleep without boundaries, this absolute of laziness and nothingness, that deems suspect all the substitutes for rest—suicide, madness, debauchery. On the other, this unparalleled bitterness without example, this fire of metal that, to refresh itself, runs after the flame, first of drunkenness, of fever, then of work, then the simple sordid fire of money. Thus so many images speak to us, "sleep in a nest of flames . . . really drunken sleep on the shore . . . sea mixed with sun," as well as "I was idle, prey to a heavy fever." Rimbaud was thirsty for pebbles, rock, and charcoal, that is to say, for what is most drying in the world. And starting from this absolute hardness, he wanted the absolute porosity of sleep, innocence of caterpillars, moles, limbs, toad idleness, infinite patience capable of an infinite forgetfulness.

In view of that, what are words worth, even the words of Rimbaud? We would like, to finish, to make this remark again: the silence does not date from 1873. Rimbaud, even when he wanted "to find a language," always spoke as little as possible. In the world, he hardly opened his mouth. He was taciturn, sometimes threw out an insult, offered blows. "I imagine myself meeting him one day in the midst of the Sahara, after many years of separation," writes one of his friends. "We are alone and we are heading in opposite directions. He stops for an instant. 'Hello, how are you?' 'Good, good-bye.' And he continues on his way. Not the least demonstration of emotion. Not a word more." *No more words. I no longer know how to speak.* All his poems, the least of his texts, signify the same superior aridity, the need to say everything in the time of a bolt of lightning, foreign to the faculty of saying that needs duration. *Enough seen. Enough had. Enough known.* Such is the "departure" that by writing he never did anything but begin again, a departure that, one day, takes place and that, in the end, results in these lines: "What do you want one to write you . . . ? That one is bored, one is fed up, one is exhausted; that one has had enough, but cannot finish with it, etc., etc.! That is all one can say; and, since that no longer amuses others, one must be quiet."

The correspondence, beginning from Cyprus, seems in general to lovers of good literature badly written, disappointing, unworthy of such a great writer. Dr. Fretet sees in the "sloppy" and even incorrect style the proof of a ruined intelligence. This proof is strange. First, we find that this style without elegance, miserly and flat, has the same extraordinary dryness as the other, but on a level of such banality that one does not see why he might have distanced himself from it by writing, since that was his way of living from then on. It is in writing "to his own" in the form of the *Illuminations* that he showed himself incoherent, and it is this incoherence that could seem a sign of ruin. And then, why would language not have left Rimbaud, if writing was no longer anything to him? It is not the poor quality of his letters that surprises us but, on the contrary, the forever obstinate, furious tone, without deflection and without return, that, through all the fatigue of work and all the denials, up to his deathbed, continued in him to perpetuate Rimbaud.

§ From Lautréamont
   to Miller

It is a curious coincidence that Henry Miller's first books were able to be read in French at the moment that the work and mystery of Lautréamont were being evoked as an anniversary. (G.L.M. published a document some time ago that fixes the birth of Isidore Ducasse as 4 April 1846.) These blocks of prose that the *Tropic of Cancer* and *Black Spring* are, these fields of words that must be seized in all their breadth and not in parts, give us a way of reading and understanding that, in our mind, is linked to *Maldoror*.

If work in prose could, in our time, either by the novel or by the essay, lay claim to a form reserved generally for the poem, if it succeeded, as well as poetry, in imposing this idea on us that literature is an experience and that reading, writing, reveal an act that not only extracts meanings but also constitutes a movement of discovery, it is to the attempts and to the "madness" of Lautréamont that we owe this. *The Songs of Maldoror* remains one of the strangest works of all literature, because the meaning, always clear, of the details in no way announces the meaning of the whole. There is nothing more intelligible than each sentence; nothing more conforming to our current habits of understanding. There is no language, we know, more classic, in which each proposition links better to that which precedes it, in which the rhetoric carries us more solidly toward a denouement that cannot surprise us. There is neither derangement in the syntax nor rupture in the call of words. The impression that any first reader must have is necessarily that of a text in which the greatest clarity, the most rigorous logic would coincide with a complete confusion and the absolute impossibility of "finding oneself." What he reads is understood, but what is understood is as if subtracted, by this very fact, from the possibility of being taken as a whole, of being welcomed and experienced in the whole meaning that would justify it.

There are, certainly, texts by the insane that, with a logical and syntactical apparatus that is pretty much intact, are able to carry a thought capable at first of deluding. These cases are not as innocent as one would like us to believe, for it remains remarkable that the reader, when he notices that something has been derailed, almost always lags just behind the moment when the anomaly shows itself, and is even uncertain of the point at which it occurs, as if the movement and arrangement of language carried a preliminary meaning solid enough to resist any subsequent breakdown. More so, it is as if the fact of putting words one after the other or of provoking inconsistent series of sounds, as happens with children, were accompanied with a presumption of meaning that the seeming absurdity does not succeed in destroying and that is even the clear background on which this absurdity ends up emerging. That is why the attempts at simulating delirium by Breton and Éluard do not really trouble us, because we feel language can never be completely alienated, because its most complete nullity, its most radical disturbance still carry so much meaning that it will always be possible to bring it close to the richest literary language, a richness that this owes, moreover, to its ability to locate itself very close to its beginning, which is indeed the greatest poverty.

Reading *Maldoror* is remarkable in that it gives the feeling of a text that is not only perfectly clear in its parts but also perfectly composed in its developments, in which the connections, far from being implied, are very carefully prepared, and even, at times, exaggeratedly highlighted, either by a mild mockery of school customs or by a care for coherence that turns into derision, in such a way that the continuity is as great as can be, that there is no hole nor gap, that the tone remains always unified, with a fullness that nothing interrupts, that renews itself from within, without the least alteration, by a veritable crystallization of sound.

One can scarcely imagine another book in which there is so little emptiness. This absence of emptiness, this little rest spared to the eye faced with a compact block in which the succession of lines counts less than their simultaneous presence, can pass as a subterfuge destined to produce a kind of fascination. That is what Lautréamont calls "mechanically constructing the brain with a sleep-inducing tale." Such a procedure explains the change of attention that occurs in the course of certain readings, when, for example, the interest accorded a book separates itself from the attention one brings to it; is no longer tied to the clear or confused meaning that one finds in it, but is oriented on the side of boredom, then embarrassment and annoyance, and finally corresponds to a real floundering to which one abandons oneself without sleep. This phenomenon is not exactly the one encountered in *Maldoror*. The work in itself is fascinating. It does not stop awakening us, and its series of clear acts prepares the mind to understand it wholly. Only this understanding is at once prepared and deferred, hastened and always suspended. Let us examine what happens. In an ordinary text, the general meaning is begun by a series of partial meanings that, as the reading advances, are located in an ensemble sketched more and more clearly; even if the unity of comprehension is failed or hidden or voluntarily broken, it does not exist any the less behind the work, and it is the search for that unity which puts our reading spontaneously in order. In *Maldoror*, there is no unity, no luminous center whence light could shine on each part; there is no actual progression starting from partial unities presenting themselves as momentary sketches of the whole. The reading finds no point of support: no place to stop or rest. Any episode one thinks one can hold onto as the link in a chain is broken inevitably and has no more reality, as a landmark, than "the crystal waves of the old ocean: scarcely has one diminished than another goes to meet it, getting larger."

What is strange in this absence of unity is, on the one hand, that it is realized by a logical discourse—that is to say, by a strongly unified language—and, on the other hand, that it does not tend to produce an unaware, haphazard, and ragged work but, on the contrary, a veritable monolith, a reality that does not divide itself or decompose. *Maldoror* is certainly the most extraordinary effort to make us believe that a book can be an absolute, closed, and finished event. That is what makes reading it so singular and at times so threatening. First, we feel ourselves enclosed in it: in this sphere of language, there is no crack, words have stopped up the exits, the horizon is a horizon of words beyond which there are even more words. At the same time, this language, perfectly significative, coherent, and eloquent, that has thus not abandoned any of its logical traits, begins to exist as a thing: it tries to take us into a kind of presence, to insert us into the body of a monumental object; it even tries to make this global existence serve its ability of expression and comprehension. It is as if we are to understand each sentence, each page, each episode, not starting from the meaning of each sentence or each episode, and even less starting from the general meaning of the book, but by penetrating its reality of thing and the blind, smooth meaning that it takes on.

> Calme bloc ici-bas chu d'un désastre obscur,
> Que ce granit du moins . . .

> Calm block fallen down here from an obscure disaster,
> That this granite at least . . .

We must understand this claim: it is not a question of leading us to read words by assimilating us with the paper on which they are written, or to retain only the physical allure of language and the material emblem of the book. But *Maldoror*, a work that the mind penetrates like a composite of expressions and significative connections, wants also to have a complete existence, without part and without contents, so we know no better than to compare it to a thing, inasmuch as we understand by "thing" a reality that is always exterior to us, that offers to our inspection only an outside deprived of inside, hence always impenetrable because always full.

It would perhaps be easy to show by what ways Lautréamont

inclines us to a feeling of this kind, a feeling that, moreover, is never entirely unaware of the final failure it bears. But we would like to note now that as remote from *Maldoror* as a work like *Tropic of Cancer* can be, it is a similar ambition that it tries to find, thus giving a new chance to an attempt that, for eighty years, has been made many times with an intrepidity never discouraged by failure. Miller claims to write a book apart, not more original than the others, or more true, or more beautiful, but the book, as Mallarmé had said, "a single immense book," "a Bible," that is described to us as a geological ensemble, as a story drowned and lost in the very reality it brings to life. "It will be enormous, this book! there will be vast spaces in it like oceans to move in, to wander in, to sing in, dance in, climb in, swim in, do somersaults in, to moan in, to break the law in, to kill in. . . ." "This must be the Last Book. We will exhaust the century. After us, not one single book." The very word *Cancer* is striking: "I am Cancer, the crab," Henry Miller said from time to time. "My book is a cancer." That is because the work believes it develops with the strength of furious cells, like that proliferation of living substances that, for the very reason of the superabundance of life, is a sign of death. "This world," he said, "is a cancer that devours itself. . . ." The ideal of his book is also to be what is resorbed by being developed, a power than annihilates itself by the very excess of its force.

We know that Lautréamont relished describing violent states, a series of spasmodic, sudden actions, that would give the impression of ferocity, even if they did not explicitly have the force of an attack, of an aggressive spending of energy. "My poetry will consist only in attacking, by all means, man, that wild animal, and the Creator. . . ." Why this choice, why this resort to cruelty? One could argue about it, but the effect is obvious enough: it is precisely that cruelty is a resort, that it is a tension always in reserve and always capable of thundering discharges, that it is the only disposition by which destruction claims to endure, and yet to accomplish acts of instantaneous annihilation. Gaston Bachelard has shown us in the mythology of Ducasse an entire bestiary of aggression, a dream of breaking and crushing actions that claw and tooth come naturally to fit out. Perhaps this is exaggerating the hurried, destructive character of the action in *Maldoror*. If we recall the role that animals with suckers and suction play in it—octopus, louse, spider, leech—we also see clearly that the attack must have something numb, lingering, enveloping, that is perfectly symbolized by the movement of style in which brutality is slowness and the most halting succession, infinite duration, calm, solemnity. What is striking in *Maldoror* is that we are the prey of a devouring power that carries us away into a staggering series of metamorphoses, into a greedy and violent time that drunkenly destroys with a force capable of creating—and, at the same time, we are as if immobilized in the midst of a reality that does not advance, that is there once and for all, pressing us and crushing us under an avalanche, a caving in, that are forever suspended.

One finds in Miller neither such a violence in the pursuit nor such an immobility in the wait. But his work has the same tendency to organize itself like a monolith in front of us, all the while carrying us off in a verbal torrent, following the fastest rhythm he can use. The writer's tenses are extraordinary. A good part of his books is the narration of events that are supposed to have happened to him—his life in Paris, for instance, the life of a foreigner who has no money and who, from one day to the next, stumbles against the usual incidents of an existence that lacks everything. But these narratives do not follow the duration they describe. They occur almost always in the present, and this present is a simultaneous cross section of the most varied moments lived by the writer, not as memory restores them to him but in a strange superimposition. It is as if the proliferation of his language could assure him a true ubiquity in time, a presence in dimensions that are least reconcilable, and, as he says, a crab's existence, "that walks sideways, forward or backward, as it likes." Language creates its duration, and it is this explosive unfolding, this violent, untiring development, this exaltation, that cause to rise from the depths of a text whose details are not exceptional, and whose ideas are not very important, a vexing, overwhelming meaning, an extreme tension that, as in Lautréamont, ends up in a frenzied passivity.

Miller's motivation is neither cruelty nor hatred but insurrection and defiance, a rebellion for ambiguous truth, because it asserts itself against constraints of very different natures, in the name of an instinct for freedom that does not know exactly what it is or what threatens it. When Miller writes, "I am a man of the old world, a seed carried by the wind, a seed that hasn't managed to flower in the moldy oasis of America. I belong to the heavy tree of the past. Body and soul, I am liegeman of the inhabitants of Europe, those who were once Franks, Gauls, Vikings, Huns, Tartars, what else! . . . I am proud of not belonging to this century," we see clearly that his sedition here is mystified by a dream, fixed by who knows what obsession of a lost good that must be found and that the time shows him. If one can say that Lautréamont's vision is made of a fundamental conflict in which violence and slowness associate, acceleration of acts and unified control of rhythm, explosion of metamorphoses and arrest of all duration, then one must notice that, with Miller, on a less profound level, the same disagreement occurs, if the extreme intrepidity of his movement, this rapidity of existence, this multiplicity of presents that the language expresses seem like the returning shock of a consciousness that lacks a future and that seeks only to live again in the past.

This ambiguity is often very dramatic in Miller's work. The pages he devotes to his walks in Paris, pages that in emotion are as great as they are simple, have this ability of freezing us by their heat and making us feel the exhaustion of what is indefatigable. We could compare them to famous pieces by Rilke, on almost the same theme, in which anguish comes from the life that comes undone, and from death that approaches, and from horror that makes itself visible; but here this furious walk-taker, whose heart is on fire, whose walk is endless, is petrified by his very movement, and if he advances, it is in streets where every step is a step backward, where monuments and houses are saturated with dreams already lived out and with sorrows already experienced, where what looks at him is the cold, indifferent certainty that, whatever he does, whatever his rage of running toward the future, it is toward an inaccessible and lost past, toward death already there, that his very desire forces him to turn back. "It is that sort of cruelty which is embedded in the streets; it is *that* which stares out from the walls and terrifies us when suddenly we respond to a nameless fear, when suddenly our souls are invaded by a sickening panic. . . . It is *that* which makes certain houses appear like the guardians of secret crimes and their blind windows like the empty sockets of eyes that have seen too much. It is that sort of thing, written into the human physiognomy of streets . . . that . . . makes me shudder when at the very entrance to the Mosque I observe that it is written: 'Mondays and Thursdays: *tuberculosis*; Wednesdays and Fridays: *syphilis*.' . . . No matter where you go, no matter what you touch, there is cancer and syphilis. It is written in the sky; it flames and dances like an evil portent. It has eaten into our souls and we are nothing but a dead thing like the moon."

Lautréamont speaks of an "invincible and rectilinear pilgrimage." That is what Miller calls his "grandiose obsessional walks" that go from one city to another, from one world to another, and that have no object but an "I go on and on and on," without hope and without fatigue. His very language is this inexhaustible flux, this momentum forward, the most ardent, the most vertiginous, and yet it evokes only an endless return to a life already past, a monotonous standstill, an unrelenting search for the beginning. "I love everything that flows," he repeats with Milton, "rivers, sewers, lava, semen, blood, bile, words, sentences." But he adds: "I love everything that flows, everything that has time in it and becoming, that brings us back to the beginning where there is never end: the violence of the prophets, the obscenity that is ecstasy, the wisdom of the fanatics." The word "ecstasy" plays a large role in the creation, by language, of these new continents, these mountains of cold and solitude that words, in the paroxysm of revolt, try to bring to life in a world of fury, of passion, of action, of drama, of dream, of madness, a world capable of producing "ecstasy." And thus he comes to cast his universe "above human boundaries . . . because to be only human seems to me so poor, so mediocre, such a wretched business, limited by meaning, restrained by moral systems and codes, defined by platitudes and isms." Language seeks thus to separate itself from man and even from language; it penetrates underground, it becomes water, air, night. It enters into the way of metamorphoses.

One chapter of *Black Spring* is titled "Into the Night Life." Verbal virtuosity and delirium of images attain their greatest momentum there. Everything follows everything else in it with an ever-quickening rhythm, with the threat of a final outburst, a definitive catastrophe, lightning that has already left the cloud but remains suspended. But if we pursue our dialogue with Lautréamont, we feel how much here the metamorphosing, dehumanizing power of Miller remains weak. In *Maldoror*, something does not stop slipping below the human horizon, and the most burlesque transformations—the eight-tentacled octopus, seraglio with four hundred suckers that stick one fine day onto the rottenness of the Creator, or the giant crab–turtle resuscitated from the sea and soon mounted on a horse going to meet the All-powerful, himself changed into a rhinoceros, and the louse mine, great blocks like mountains that, when the time comes, dissolve, pierce the walls, invade cities—all these images express an irresistible movement toward a different possibility, a physical adherence to something completely strange. But with Miller, the scenes show themselves in vain in their nightmare strangeness; they do not make obvious to us the closeness of a world where we would not be, and only the annoyance of following them makes us glimpse the effort at rupture of the imagination that supports them.

What is characteristic of Lautréamont is the triumphant thrust, the ferocious running beyond human forms, that still succeeds in attaining this coagulation by the loss of life that metamorphosis signifies. In this sense, Kafka's "Metamorphosis" is the quintessential metamorphosis. As Bachelard has shown well, Gregor Samsa lives more and more slowly; he buries himself in a world of scraps, he is sticky and viscous, he drags along: one could say that, with him, even after the metamorphosis, the metamorphosis continues, that, having become a vermin, every day he falls a little lower, that in the end he is nothing more than a breath taken in by a little decomposing matter; and it is this very progress into the fall that ends up assuring his deliverance. But, with Lautréamont, the strange thing is that everything is ardor, power, exaltation, and that this numbness, this sleep that is metamorphosis, still occurs. "Metamorphosis," he says, "never appeared to my eyes but as the high and magnanimous repercussion of a perfect happiness, that I had been awaiting for a long time." The "failure" is here accomplished as a deranged act; degradation expresses the movement in its paroxysm. If we look closely at the tendency that most of the metamorphoses manifest in *Maldoror*, we see that they result in equivocal beings, half mollusks, half carnivores, at once capable of very fast, dry, heavy movements of a deceitful, dubious life, movements involved in a "flaccid substance" that become unchained in a storm of fury and virulence. It is "the old spider of the great species," whose immense suction has the slowness of an orgy; it is the octopus with four hundred tentacles, which sometimes has wings with which it can glide above the clouds; it is the crab, by his powerful pincers of pure aggression, but, by his marine life, keeping the viscosity of that which slides along, the character of a wet, oozing movement; it is the louse that scratches and sucks; and so on. One could say that each of these new beings, although precipitated into the cycle of metamorphoses by drunkenness and exaltation, experiences the need to be lost in some kind of stagnant substance, and to become something that sticks and adheres, to be unified with a shapeless mass, without which there is no more metamorphosis possible, if, under the pretext of a different form, this is above all making contact with an absence of form, with the density and opacity of pure matter.

That Miller's imagination lacks this sleeping element is what so many pages of his books show, whose coarseness has frightened Anglo-Saxon readers (and, it is said, some French readers); in them, they thought they saw the perfection of impropriety, while they remain almost invariably removed from the category of the obscene, and even of the erotic. Certainly, the words are there and the details are there, too. We know what is happening, and all that one does not say does get said, all that one fears showing is seen in the clearest manner. But the extreme verbal quickness, the writer's time that is a relentless spontaneity, always in advance of the acts it causes to appear, does not allow the metamorphosis there is in eroticism, the slow changing of a mind into a body and from a body into a thing. Everything happens in it as in that story where he describes himself in the act of drawing a horse: the horse does not have time to remain a horse, it becomes a sausage, a kangaroo, a house, a cemetery, it jumps from one form to another, he cannot find the substance that would immobilize it, and, in conclusion, an angel appears, and remains, and cannot be erased, an angel in the middle of a cold blue light. "I wear an angel as a watermark." Yes, he wears an angel as a watermark as much in his apocalypse of unbridled anecdotes as in his whirlwind of improper words, for everything there is blazing, flame, pursuit of stars, and, finally, what surrounds us is still the cold, calm blue light. Yet there are instants that the atmosphere changes: those in which we touch obsessions, precisely those instants in which violence becomes fatigue, in which the thrust forward is nothing more than repetition, mechanical wallowing. So extraordinary scenes result. The most violent humor seizes onto beings who go on advancing without perceiving that they have neither feet nor legs, who couple in emptiness, with the stubborn obstinacy of insects that will never reach each other and, having lost the human signification of their acts, begin to live without suspecting their cancerous existence.

Humor is one of the main enigmas in *Maldoror*. It is difficult, even by obscuring it with the adjective "black," to give any name to this movement of deterioration, of disintegration, by which Lautréamont constantly comes to add a dangerous quality to the ordering of his rhetoric and to the certainty of his excess. It has often been said, for example by Jaloux, that humor was his means to reestablish the equilibrium of his long, emphatic cadences by slipping in a critical element, a kind of denunciatory equilibrium. But it is rather the contrary. Lautréamont does not make fun of what he writes to reassure us of the madness of his imaginings. Sarcasm is not used here as a counterbalance, as a stabilizing medium: if it does add something to the reading, it is a new threat, by taking away from us the possibility of taking what we read seriously. The serious is, in fact, always reassuring, even when it is a question of a dramatic statement; it is the sign that there are stable values, perhaps sadly misled in the situation described to us, but such that they always assure a satisfying dignity and security to our sadness and our tears. Sarcasm in *Maldoror* takes away this support and certainty from us. It substitutes emptiness for them. It opens its language to a disconcerting spectacle that takes our breath away, that perhaps makes us laugh, as, when we stumble in a hole, we are easily seized with a fit of laughter. But Lautréamont took care to underline the equivocal nature of this fit. "Often," he says, "it will occur to me to pronounce with solemnity the most ridiculous propositions; I do not find that that becomes a peremptorily sufficient motive to enlarge the mouth! I cannot prevent myself from laughing, you answer; I accept this absurd explanation, but let it be a melancholy laugh."

One must say, moreover, that "humor" in *Maldoror* is marked with the same ambiguous sign that envelops all its metamorphoses, its paralyzing ardor, and its language, so logical and so obscure, in a contradiction. Of this language, we have seen how slow it was, how patient, solemn (he says), with an obvious search for all that can weigh it down, make it substantial (for example, the constant substitution of the noun for the adjective), and also to give it the solidity of rhetoric at every ordeal (the use of ready-made expressions, expressions made language). Humor, in this implacable, heavy slowness, is the intervention of a different "time": it is the sudden apparition of a menacing rapidity; it comes like lightning, it rises from this dazzling capacity for aggression we see shot through his whole work. At that moment, the sentence is simplified, it reaches us without detour and touches us without warning. It is the sudden, the instantaneous. "The elephant lets itself be caressed. The louse, no." Yet, this work of destruction and negation that humor accomplishes is not only a temporary movement, a kind of alarm bell that, from time to time and suddenly, comes to throw us into emptiness, while after this upset we have the right to regain our feet in the gravity of a faultless rhetoric. It happens, on the contrary, that the slowness, the patience, the solidity of logical language are themselves as if surrounded by the possibility of a rupture: these reasonable qualities endlessly threaten reason, for they conceal, in the depths of their seriousness, a sarcasm that destroys this seriousness and, in the depths of their tranquillity, a shattering irruption that makes tranquillity impossible.

Where does it come from? First, from those propositions that are too long, too sinuous, and as if infinite, that go from one meaning to another, contradict that meaning again, then, insofar as these jumps of meaning are justified by well-reasoned digressions, return to the starting point and finally let themselves glide into emptiness, because of the very solidity of the logical apparatus involved in an absurd order in which this solidity seems a derisory anxiety. Over this stretch of words, sarcasm does not stop watching, it surrounds it, develops with it, making constantly present to us, even if it does not occur, the possibility of a lightning intervention, so that slowness expresses lightning, and the silent functioning of language, the unbearable sound of machinery that derails and destroys itself in the catastrophe. Humor here is the threat of a complete *metamorphosis* of language that would change the meaning not into an absence of meaning but into a thing, a mirage in face of which any correct reading is soon transformed into stupor.

Miller chose the title *Black Spring* to express the element of discord that bursts out in his work. On the level of language, this work also wants to be a cluster of nocturnal lightning bolts, a new ore, a thing, a veritable story without words. And yet metamorphosis does not occur, language is always there, words keep their meaning, images are beautiful images. That is because Miller's world is a world that is too human, in which revolt has its limits. "It is possible," he writes, "that we are condemned, that there is no hope for us, for any of us, but if that is true, let us give voice to a last roar, a roar of horrible suffering, to freeze the blood, a shattering cry of defiance, a war cry!" If he could make us hear this cry, it would still be only a word, like the others: never, in his books, do we approach the last word. Thus we see that a work that is as free as his, aimed as it is against what is "false, derived, that is to say literature," could still not achieve the movement that a work of perfect rhetoric like *Maldoror* does not stop accomplishing. It is a movement that is certainly mysterious and difficult, if it is the passage from metaphor to metamorphosis.

§ Translated From . . .

In *For Whom the Bell Tolls*, Robert Jordan, discovering the importance of the instant he is in the process of living, repeats to himself the word "now" in many languages: *now, maintenant, ahora, now, heute.* But he is a little disappointed by the mediocrity of this vocabulary. "*Now,*" he says, "it has a funny sound to be a whole world and your life." And he seeks other terms: *Esta noche, ce soir, tonight, heute Abend.* He tried to find in these words what they signify for him, his meeting with Maria, one that is also the meeting of his last hour, a meeting with death. He then pronounces the words *dead, mort, muerto,* and *todt,* then the words *war, guerre, guerra,* and *Krieg.* The word *todt* seems to him the deadest of all; the word *Krieg,* what is most similar to war. "Or was it only that he knew German the least well?"

This impression of Robert Jordan is one to reflect on. If it is true that a language seems so much truer and more expressive when we know it less, if words need a certain ignorance to keep their power of revelation, such a paradox is hardly likely to surprise us, since translators never stop experiencing it and since it represents one of the main obstacles and the main resource of all translation. It is a phenomenon to which the author of "The Girl with the Mirrors" came back often and for which he has this definition: "The language to be translated seems at once more *imagistic* and more *concrete* than the language into which we translate it."

This paradox cannot remain without literary consequences. If we admit that one of the objects of literature is to create a language and a work in which the word "dead" is really dead, and the word "war" really war, then it seems that this new language should be, in relation to current language, what a text to be translated is to the language that translates it: an ensemble of words or events that we understand and grasp, no doubt, perfectly but that, in their very familiarity, give us the feeling of our ignorance, as if we were discovering that the simplest words and the most natural things could suddenly become unknown. That literary works want to keep their distances, that they seek to distance themselves from the whole interval that always makes translation the best and a foreign work the best written, that is what explains (in part) the taste of symbolism for rare words, the search for exoticism, the success of "stories of the extraordinary," the vitality of all mannerist literature and a good number of theories aiming to find recipes or formulas to move away from us a language that seems sometimes so close to us that we no longer understand it.

It is well known that classic literature demanded from ancient culture and ancient languages this disorientation intended to raise current language to the dignity of a translated language. To transpose a Greek or Latin work into French was enough to accomplish the essential part of a creative act. Racine, seeking to justify the too-close subject of *Bajazet*, speaks of "the distancing of countries *that* mends, in some way, the too-great closeness of the times." In the preface to *Oedipus*, Corneille regrets having lost the advantage of being only a translator. The moderns assuredly go further. *Translated from Silence*, that work by Joë Bousquet, is like the wish of an entire literature that would like to remain a translation in its pure state, an unburdened translation of something to be translated, an effort to retain of language the only distance that language seeks to keep with regards to itself and that must, if pushed, result in its disappearance.

The influence of foreign works on a literature that the richness of its past, the maturity of its experiences, the certainty of its language make little prone to acts of dependence quickly seems rather dangerous. Many good critics complain of American literature: they judge it not very original, esteem it of a mediocre interest for a culture that for more than half a century has surpassed naturalism; they make fun of young writers who think they are modern by imitating Faulkner, Dos Passos, or Steinbeck while, for Americans themselves, these novelists represent yesterday rather than tomorrow. To these remarks others are added. The technique of the American novel is supposed to be in disagreement with our novelistic tradition; it implies the decline of art; it makes useless the variety of works and diversity of artists that it tumbles together in a lifeless, brutal monotony.

These critics contradict each other curiously. For some, foreign literature would have the fault of being too foreign to us, of distancing us from our art and its means. But, for others, it has the inconvenience of bringing us what we already have: simplicity, objectivity of language, which is the essential part of classic art, concerted, economic art, in which expression attains, by accident and almost while unaware of it, what is to be expressed.

Perhaps such judgments oppose each other because they all demand to be corrected, but perhaps the part of contradictory truth that they enclose is also linked to the paradox of which we have spoken. Simplicity and objective rigidity seem foreign to us, and we seem to have the attraction and danger of foreign qualities, as soon as they appear to us, no longer coming from our language but transported into our language, translated, moved away from us, and as if fixed in the distance by pressure of the translating force. It is from such a change that so many works gain an originality that surprises the literature to which they belong and that does not recognize it in them. Thus are we surprised at the influence exercised by our realist writers (in particular by Maupassant) over foreign writers who to us seem hardly realist. Thus do we learn with wonder that Flaubert was Kafka's master. But, if there is something mysterious there, this mystery will help us perhaps to understand why we do not have to search for the importance of these writers who enjoy such a great renown in France, or for what they bring to original, new American literature. For what counts is the metamorphosis they undergo by entering into a new language, this change of direction of which some become capable; their naturalism can be taken for the strength of an incredible imagination, their chatter for silence, and their most literary researches for a brutal sobriety that distances us dangerously from our own simplicity as too elegant and too careful of its effects.

The influence of what are called the masterpieces of universal literature is part of this character: in no matter what language, the coefficient of deformation or distancing due to translation adjusts itself exactly to the capacity of strangeness that they owe, in the original language, to their creative ability. For some books, the translator's work is added to the initial distancing, doubles it, so that some of them gain provisionally from this supplemental aberration, but little by little the disagreement seems too little grounded in relation to the contents, and in the end disappears like an illusion. On the contrary, for other works, the act of the translator annuls all interval and all distancing: transported into a foreign language, they are less foreign than they were before they were translated; they are, so to speak, translated against the current, against translation proper to the original art, a translation that, we know, must make us discover the word "death" as the one best adapted to death, but equally strange as death, as a term put far before us and that we have to recognize, to relearn, as if it were completely new and first, a word forever unknown, borrowed from an inaccessible possibility of language, although we felt the perfect aptness of it, and because of that it tends endlessly to disappear like a sign without value. Those are works that are called "untranslatable," but only because the translator translates them necessarily too much and reintegrates them into everyday language, from which very little had kept them apart.

Imitation of a work, no matter what the value of the imitations might be, always ends up by seriously wounding it. For a short while and sometimes in a lasting way, the work is as if stricken with death. If in the nineteenth century romanticism underestimated the merits of Racinian tragedy to a point that seems incomprehensible to us, it is because imitations had killed it. Racine, as if he were guilty of all the mediocrities his perfection authorized, was punished by becoming invisible; he was read, his plays were seen, but it was not Racine, it was Voltaire, it was Soumet, who were heard and watched. So the same erosion that one day reduced Racine to the nothingness of an overlong posterity can indeed happen, without dishonor, to the American writers. We note that such an imitation tends to unmake the work of translation, insofar as it acclimates it and thus takes away from it the privilege of the ambiguity, of the instability that make so many great translated works extraordinary, an instability that makes these works, well adapted as they are in their new language, threaten at each instant to return to their language of origin and oscillate mysteriously between many forms whose perfect suitability is not enough to restrain them.

If we reckoned up the elements that the French novel is suspected of having borrowed, with too much complacency, from foreign books, we would find only elementary technical procedures: the technique of the objective narrative, the simultaneity of different actions and stories, discontinuity of narrative movement, application of ellipse and litotes to the narrative, use of as impersonal a language as possible, and of course interior monologue and abundant dialogue. Perhaps their systematic use would make the contemporary novel poorer than traditional rhetoric could. One can always wonder. But no serious reader will presume to be able to form an idea of the richness of Faulkner or Joyce or Virginia Woolf, to cite only the greatest names, merely from the procedures they more or less illustrated, if not invented. In these conditions, even supposing that the fashion for these techniques is due only to their influence, this influence does not measure what they are worth to us, what their original works and their translated works are worth, but measures only the necessity we have to return what we have borrowed from them, those veritable sepulchers.

Obviously, when we call into question the American novel, as if this vague entity designated one particular book, we are thinking about only a certain number of formal qualities, isolated by analysis, not ones we could find only in all important foreign works but also ones we have come to know through French books, not very numerous, that use the same means of expression. This confusion, seemingly inevitable, is favored by the use of key words. The words *objective, impersonal,* are words of this kind that one applies indifferently to the most varied examples of the American novel. It is easy, no doubt, and useful, perhaps, to underline this predominance of objective narrative and to draw general conclusions from it: to know that if the heroes of these books can talk about themselves in an impersonal way, even when the narrative is in the first person, it is because they are deprived of all inner reality, that they are nothing else than the banal opinions, socially interchangeable, that they express, nothing else than the empty actions they accomplish under the pressure of instincts whose violence is without mystery, nothing more than a kind of heavy inconsistency, of powerful absence held in the fabric of a collectivity and of a story that goes where it can. All that has been said, analyzed, and studied in thousands of ways. What we would like to note is that the technique of the objective narrative is in no way linked to such a view of the world. What is it, after all? Simply that of the quintessential novel and, to a certain extent, the fundamental demand of every work of fiction and perhaps even of every literary expression, if the effort to go from *I* to *He* (even naturally when the *I* remains the apparent form), the effort to put distance between language and us, to grasp us again by way of a reality that seems to slip away even less when it finds, to incarnate itself, a collection of events and words more foreign to us—in a word, if this attempt at dispossession both of language and of ourselves is the essential part of literary experience. When we speak of this objective narration as a procedure belonging to our time, it is probably true, but it is also true that its masterpiece was written eighty years ago and is called *War and Peace.* And one can certainly answer that the impersonal form goes much further in the works of today, that it is so rigorous that it excludes all intervention of the author either to illuminate the beings or to tell the story, for in truth, the story is no longer told, it happens, it is realized under our eyes by the acts of the characters, and we know of it only what their actions teach us.

These remarks are correct, but to how many works do they apply? And yet the word "impersonal" continues to serve as a label for all contemporary American literature, as if the impersonal form of *Sanctuary* were the same as *The Big Money* or *The Grapes of Wrath*, as if the language of a Faulkner in which images burst forth and intermingle, in which the words, carried to a dangerous degree of heat, seem to belong to a language in fusion, had nothing in common with the obstinate, furious ingenuity of a Wright or the grave detachment of a Steinbeck.

One significant example of the use of key words seems to us the following: after having spoken about the impersonal form of Dos Passos in his trilogy, excellent critics speak in the same tone about the impersonal form of Hemingway in *For Whom the Bell Tolls*. Hemingway seems to the French public to be the representative of all American literature. If one speaks of the novel from across the Atlantic, it is of Hemingway that one thinks. If one wants to show that Camus's *The Stranger* uses American technique, one asserts, following Sartre's remark: "It is Kafka written by Hemingway." Yet, it is somewhat remarkable that the most accomplished works of this novelist, those in which he truly showed what he was capable of, escape the genre of which he is usually taken as the master. That is because exactly this impersonal form (the category in which one tries to grasp it for convenience) resembles much more that of Tolstoy than that of *The Stranger*. *A Farewell to Arms* is a narrative in the first person. This narrative is certainly remarkable for the sobriety of expression, the discretion of feelings, the care of the hero to stay at a distance from the action in which he participates, but this erasing of the character behind what he says and behind what happens is not more complete or more systematic than in *War and Peace*, and it succeeds wonderfully in making us aware not of the crushing of an individual in the impersonal debacle that is war, but of the legitimacy of his refusal, his inclination to withdraw from an absurd story, his decision to give to his own fate a conclusion that does not concern him. And no doubt this decision itself has a certain fatal nature: it is born from the incoherence of war in which the act of desertion seems to be imposed by those who make a crime of it and, moreover, it results in a failure, for into the most accomplished individual fate the most impersonal of all forms insinuates itself, that of death. But such a theme, it goes without saying, does not belong to the philosophy of American technique.

So we, too, can share in the pleasure of comparisons, let us cite two texts. The hero of *A Farewell to Arms* has just been wounded, and is led to a field hospital: "They picked me up and took me into the dressing room. Inside they were operating on all the tables. . . . The major was unhooking the forceps now, dropping them in a basin. I followed his hands with my eyes. Now he was bandaging. Then the stretcher-bearers took the man off the table. 'I'll take the American Tenente,' one of the captains said. They lifted me onto the table. It was hard and slippery. There were many strong smells, chemical smells and the sweet smell of blood." And here is a well-known passage from *War and Peace*, when Prince Andrei has just been wounded: "One of the medical officers went out of the tent. Between his thumb and little finger he delicately held a cigar that he feared dirtying, for his little hands were, like his apron, covered with blood. He raised his head and let his gaze wander above the wounded. He obviously wanted to take a little air. After turning to right and left, he sighed and brought his gaze back to the ground. 'Yes, right away,' he answered the nurse who was pointing out Prince Andrei to him, and he gave the order to bring him into the tent. A murmur rose among the wounded who were waiting. 'Seems that in the other world too, there's room only for sirs!' said one. They placed the prince on a table that was free and that a nurse had just rinsed. Andrei could not make out in detail what there was in the tent. The plaintive cries that rose from everywhere, the sharp pain he felt in his side, abdomen, and back absorbed him completely. The spectacle that was in front of his eyes was confused in a single impression of human flesh, naked and bleeding, that seemed to fill this low tent."

The narrative of *For Whom the Bell Tolls* is in the third person. But the most casual reading shows how much it remains foreign to the rules of so-called objective narration. The narrative is not made from above, following the easy methods of what we can call a false, bad objectivity; it unfolds almost exclusively from the point of view of Robert Jordan, reproducing, with few exceptions, what he knows of the story, what he learns about it, what he does in it, and what he sees done. But this gaze by which things are illuminated is not a simple light that would give them the emptiness of its transparency. Robert Jordan is united in the strongest way to the action that carries him along, he chose to participate in it and, in his eyes, it is not distinguished from this free, personal choice. It would be easy to show that the progress from *A Farewell to Arms* to *For Whom the Bell Tolls* is at the expense of the impersonal form. Having joined the 1914 war, as Robert Jordan had joined the Spanish Civil War, the American lieutenant of the first book remains, however, on the surface of the conflict, of which he experiences neither the force nor the profundity, so that his individualist refusal of the end also has the nature of a game, of a light touch, of fleeing from the surface of things, and seems to us exterior to itself, lightly impersonal, so that its description of war is affected with this same disinterestedness. On the contrary, the volunteer in the Spanish Civil War forms one body with the story, he has neither the will to take himself away from it nor the hope to get out of it; this little collective episode, this light burst in the Spanish conflict, itself like waves in the midst of a vaster conflict, in four days expresses and absorbs his entire life. But to the very extent that his life has become that of the little group of partisans, with whom he must, behind the fascist lines, on the night before an offensive, blow up a bridge that commands the transport of enemy reinforcements, to the extent that this life can no longer separate itself from the common lot or evade the mortal outcome that will also be common, he keeps his personal feeling, and the freedom of his gaze, and his search for a fate that will be unique to him, in the most startling way. From many sides, this witness is not an extraordinary type of man. Little developed politically, as he knows, professor on vacation, whose vacation deliberately took the form of a serious adventure that he decided to follow not out of dilettantism, or out of a taste for violent actions, or even out of simple sympathy of Spain, but out of a deep instinct of which his liberal

ideas, his faith "in Freedom, in Life" are only rather weak indica-
tions, he remains essentially a man like others, who knows fear,
believes in his work, and continues to the end of his job, without
drunkenness and perhaps with a certain heaviness, but this tranquillity is not the ignorance of what threatens him, it is indifference
to grandiloquence, to theatrical gesticulation, outside of tragedy,
not inside.

It is generally accepted that the characters of the American novel
have the air of robots, led by what they do rather than masters of
their acts. Robert Jordan is a man who, at the grave moments of his
life, struggles for lucidity and self-protection. "It was the greatest
gift that he had, the talent that fitted him for war; that ability not to
ignore but to despise whatever bad ending there could be." Neither
is this lucidity an incomparable quality: it is hardly like the extreme vivacity of reflection of a Julien Sorel that neither passion nor
madness lessens; it is even more the expression of an inner solemnity, the result of a patience that waits for the right moment to
direct an exact gaze on men and events. His gaze needs to be
correct, out of a need for justice, and since this need is also the
profound reason for his participation in the conflict and for the
conflict itself, we comprehend how, all the while playing his role in
it, by approaching step by step the death that will be the dawn of
the fourth day, he can remain a witness capable of reflecting, according to their correct meaning, on the events and beings of a
great tragedy.

That under this gaze the other figures of the drama keep an
extraordinary power of expression and life is what all readers have
seen and admired. It is enough to recall the image of Pilar, that
woman about whom there is something barbarous, as her companions say, but whose barbarism is a wonder of civilization. That is
because her fury, her ardor, and her coarse strength, though in
contact with an existence always open to the worst, do not stop
finding the greatest freedom and a rigor of appreciation, a demand
for true things and feelings that do not put up with, on her part or
anyone else's, the least averted gaze. One will notice that almost all
the members of this little band of *guerrilleros* are capable, with

regard to themselves and others, of lucidity and sangfroid. And that is why the drama of the head of the partisans, this Pablo who was a very good agitator, but who now thwarts Jordan's work out of fear and fatigue, and who does not stop, during the entire story, being on the edge of betrayal, is the drama of clairvoyance that sees the fatal outcome and, fascinated by it, transforms through a crafty change into this bizarre sadness that is the sign of decline.

Because each one has formed a pact with the pride of an impartial judgment, each one can also participate in the story he lives, not as an amorphous spectator but as a witness who will be the very impetus and the hard, dispassionate necessity of this story, if it could stop for an instant and turn back to see itself and speak itself. Thus the narratives of Pilar enlarge the episode to the level of the whole civil war, just as the narratives that Jordan makes for himself put the events of these days on the level of all that he lived in the distant past and in the near past, as if through the swiftest action these could open, for each of them, the perspective of another duration, of an already historical existence, able to be told and to be judged as definitive. Hemingway's novel unites the structure of the tragic narrative to that of the epic narrative. He reconciles, in a very simple composition, the violence of an action, as narrow as possible, and the scope of a story that is not hurried by its denouement. For Jordan, it is a question in these four days not only of preparing and carrying out the operation assigned to him, of surmounting unforeseen obstacles, of conquering Pablo's resistance, of triumphing over snow, and conquering the presentiment that this operation will be of no use, the Republicans' offensive being almost surely doomed to failure, but also of accomplishing his own personal destiny by living with the young Spanish woman, the young woman with the short hair, whom he meets at the very moment when everything is ending for him. And of course the more the action builds toward a climax and speeds up, the more the tragedy profits from this tightening of duration to raise feelings and acts to a tension such that we are rooted to the spot, and at the same time hurled forward toward a conclusion that is so inevitable that it is already lived through for everyone. There is no possibility of resting in this drama whose law is to know respite no more. Yet it is also at this moment that the tranquil present of the story is introduced into the breathless present of tragedy, and in the midst of an end that already consumes us the patience and the truth of the past take their place, the truth of just those days to which the narrative returns to fix them, without complacency or denigration, as the unmoving foundation of a fatality even stronger than the lightning approach of the last instant, which is coming.

For Whom the Bell Tolls is scarcely different from classical compositions. It is not innovative, and if it does use techniques like interior monologue, such procedures are themselves classic. These monologues are often very fortunate, because they keep the silent nature of words that, although accomplished from the formal point of view, do not seem to be entirely said; they give the impression of a used language, still to be made or to be remade because it has been stretched too thin. In French novels (except in Sartre), it seems that this impression is not often met with: it must be said that monologue turns sour in them, and seems either an exercise of loud rhetoric or a commodity that lets itself be too much on display; interior speech in them seems always more exterior than interior, and its stammering, instead of lessening it, gives it a paradoxical character. Why are translated monologues more likely to seem to us silent and turned within? For many reasons, but first, because they are translated. Translation, if it is good, brings with it, without recourse to an artificial incoherence, the feeling of a light space between the words and what they aim at, of a possibility for them to slip outside of this form they have been given to return to the starting point, that is here the original language but that also symbolizes the original background on which words are imposed to be born from a language that scarcely separates itself from emptiness. Monologue in French novels is generally not translated enough. It does not send us back to another language and, too sure of its stutterings, it succeeds only in drawing attention to the words it finds, not to the words it replaces, and for which its only role should be to make their silent, ungraspable presence felt.

We could ponder dialogue in modern novels from a similar

point of view. We know how it always takes up a larger space in them, but that at the same time it keeps even more to the level of narrative and action, either so that it allows the characters to assert themselves without explaining themselves, or so that the quality of banality (with which they are reproached) serves to embody the events and to coat them, to make of them no longer pure events, direct object of a narrative, but the events of the characters themselves, as they experience them and live them. The result is that dialogue is quite important, but also that it must remain not very visible, that it can make itself understood only as the beginning of acts that it announces or as the means of a presence with which it is confused and from which it borrows its taciturn nature. So dialogue counts very much and is very silent. That is almost exactly the nature it has in *Sanctuary* or in Steinbeck. In other books and, to stay with Hemingway, in *A Farewell to Arms*, dialogue does not seek to attain silence by terseness but by an excess of chatter, by a come-and-go of easy conversations beneath which the seriousness of what must be understood is revealed. Thus, in *She Came to Stay*, the interminable dialogues in which some have seen, wrongly, a badly calculated move, are there to distract us from themselves and to make us aware, behind the brilliant ease of the words, of the obstinately silent voice of one who, even when she speaks, does not speak, a presence that is eager, free, and also absent, because foreign to words.

Let us admit it, these successes are rare. It is dangerous to appeal to the futility of rigor as image and to what is said too easily as a sign of what cannot be said. The greatest danger is not that the words are poor or null, but that this nullity, far from making them invisible, fixates us on them. In translated novels, dialogue, often long and dragged out, serves usually as filler, but less actually to mask holes in the continuity than to make us see the emptiness that it cannot fill. It is not the natural that helps them, or a special aptitude to preserve, in the midst of verbiage, a minuscule zone of silence, but even more (it seems to us) this impression that the language that is spoken in dialogue is a borrowed language, to which the characters remain foreign, in which consequently there always remains more for them to say than they say, and in which their words are not actually words but a *translation*, a text for which they are not responsible, and that is only halfway their own. Because of that, they seem more distant to us because they adhere less to their words, they overflow them, they wait behind, and the feeling of imperfect communication that every skillful translator knows how to handle involves us in restoring to them in silence all that the passage from one language to another has made them lose, and all that no language would ever have allowed them to express.

Hemingway, writing a novel on Spain, throws Spanish words from time to time into the dialogue. Rather a naive convention, for it has the air of wanting to remind us that the Spanish sometimes know how to speak in Spanish. However, the effects are not so simple. Tolstoy himself posed the question to himself: "Why is it that in my work not only Russians but also the French speak sometimes in Russian, sometimes in French?" And Tolstoy justifies himself in a curious way, by acknowledging the right to make dark areas—shadows—and light alternate at his will. Well, it happens that in Hemingway's work Spanish words play the role of shadow, of a glittering, provoking shadow, and that they thus hollow out the surface of language, introducing into it all kinds of differences of level and rather neatly disorienting languages to make them all foreign (which is again the case in *War and Peace*, in which French phrases placed in the mouths of characters seem to us from a language that is as different from our own as Russian can be, glimpsed behind the French of the translation). But nothing else happens in no matter what well-translated novel capable of welcoming the translator's work: there is no need of any *Qué va, guapa*, or *nada*, or of any term in italics, for the distancing of the text to work. The slight gap indicates that what we are reading is not exactly what we should be reading, and also the metamorphosis by which we feel, all through our usual language, interstices and emptinesses open up, when we are at liberty to watch the extremely mysterious approach of another language, completely unknown to us.

It is perhaps unsuitable to recognize in translated works, from the fact of their translation, merits that might be lacking in similar works written in an original language. But first, we do not see why the act of the translator should not be appreciated as the quintessential literary act, one which proposes that the reader remain ignorant of the text it reveals to him, and from which his ignorance will not distance him. Instead, it will bring him closer by becoming active, by representing to him the great interval that separates him from it. It is true that these merits are perhaps only apparent; they have the value of a mirage; they vanish if we are too attentive to them. Even more, one can evaluate such dangerous qualities. Too good a bargain, a translated text mimics the effort of creation that, starting from everyday language in which we live and are immersed, seeks to make another language be born, same in appearance and yet, with regard to this language, like its absence, its difference perpetually acquired and constantly hidden. If foreign works encourage and stimulate imitation more than our own works, it is because imitation, in this case, seems to reserve for us a greater personal role, especially because the imitator, fascinated, in the translated text, by the strangeness that the passage from one language to another provokes, thinks that it can take the place of the originality he seeks. Unfortunately, even if he borrows from his model only what he has the right to borrow, he will forget to be in his turn a translator and he will renounce making his language undergo the transmutation that from one single language must draw out two, one that is read and understood without deviation, while the other remains ignored, silent, and inaccessible. Its absence (the shadow of which Tolstoy speaks) is all that we grasp of it.

§ The Novels of Sartre

People wonder why the novel of ideas has a bad reputation. The complaints are many. The "idea" itself complains of the excess of truth that it is supposed to acquire from the adventure. Alive in the theoretical milieu where it took shape, its transplantation among the reflections of real things makes them into dead thoughts. In novels of this kind, the characters are reproached for being lifeless, but it is the idea that is lifeless: it no longer resembles anything but itself, it has only its own meaning; the artificial world hides it too poorly, it is more visible there than in its original bareness, so visible that it scarcely has any secrets to offer us. Of La Rochefoucauld and other moralists, we are told: these are the novelists. So be it. But, if their maxims are living (sometimes), it is because they make us think about novels that would not make us think about their maxims.

On the side of the work, the objections are no less categorical. Still, they are strong only from the point of view of a certain conception of the work of art, one from the end of the nineteenth century, according to which art, being an absolute, does not have to have its goal outside of itself. But the novel has never wanted to accommodate itself entirely to this ambition. Willing to represent imaginary lives, a story or a society that it proposes to us as real, it depends on this reality of which it is the reproduction or equivalent. If it is a copy, it is a prisoner of the things it describes; it does

not want, certainly, to prove anything, yet it is in collusion with the
world, with the idea that we form of it, with literary verisimilitude,
with our own condition, etc. Even the novel that is only a narrative
made to please carries in it all kinds of ideas, extremely consequen-
tial ideas, since it is the whole horizon of ideas and prejudices the
reader requires if he is to be capable of being amused. And what
about this purest art, which does not know today that it is the most
impure, made guilty by its innocence, art of propaganda because
disinterested, an art in which the society, in the perfect world of
culture, finds a warrant for its abuses?

So there is no literary art that, directly or indirectly, does not
want to assert or prove a truth. Then why do we tend to discredit
the literature of ideas? Doesn't such a condemnation amount to
rejecting the writer who knows what he wants to say in favor of the
writer who knows nothing of it and pushes the unconsciousness to
the point of thinking he has no ideas, while he is the servant of
everyone's ideas—is that what is called impartial, objective, true?
Must a work necessarily mean something? Why should it signify it
only by chance or by luck? And since, as readers, we are destined to
be associated with some particular view of the world, shouldn't
honesty be there to present it to us clearly, without playing an
underhand trick on us? Shouldn't it play candidly with us (the
characteristic or defect of ideological works)?

Unfortunately, fictional work has nothing to do with honesty: it
cheats, and exists only by cheating. It is hand in glove, in every
reader, with the lie, with the equivocal, an endless movement of
trickery and hide-and-seek. Its reality is to glide between that
which is and that which is not, its truth is a pact with illusion. It
shows and it takes away; it goes somewhere and pretends not to
know it. It is in the mode of the imaginary that it meets the real, it
is by fiction that it approaches the truth. Absence and constant
disguise, it progresses by oblique ways, and the obviousness that is
its own has the duplicity of light. The novel is a work of bad faith,
bad faith on the part of the novelist who believes in his characters
and yet sees himself behind them, who does not know them,
realizes them as unknowns, and finds in the language of which he is

a master the means of manipulating them without ceasing to believe that they are escaping him. Bad faith of the reader who plays with the imaginary, who plays at being this hero that he is not, at taking for real what is fiction and finally lets itself be taken for that, and, in this enchantment that keeps existence at a distance, finds again a possibility of living the meaning of this existence. There is no doubt that literature despises the philosophical novel because of the good faith of this kind of novel, because it makes obvious what it means, and because it puts itself honestly, entirely, in the service of truth: it is not divided against itself, or it would perish. (Gide's sentence "With beautiful emotions one makes bad literature" has perhaps no other meaning: good feelings weigh heavily on this wickedness that art has in it. If La Fontaine's *Fables* often seem immoral, it is not because of bad morals but because of the indifference of the narrative to the moral that concludes it: too visibly, the work makes fun of the meaning it gives itself. On the contrary, the most immoral novel, if it is a philosophical novel, ends by giving an impression of crushing morality, as with the first *Justine* by Sade.)

Yet honesty is not the only fault of the philosophical novelist. Suspect because of his good faith, he is also suspect on account of the good faith that he cannot get rid of. He remains, in fact, a novelist: he also makes use of fiction, he seeks out characters, he wants to represent reality—it is a way open to abuses. In vain does he people his books with uncomplicated heroes, in vain does he rigorously submit his story to the test it proposes; nothing comes of it; or, rather, everything works, but against him. Now his propagandist honesty seems dishonest to us; his characters without dissimulation smell of hypocrisy. What has happened? This: for good or for evil, he has embarked into fiction, that is to say, in the most banal meaning of the word, into lie. His truth is now a lie. He has entered into the bad, and can save himself only by the worst.

Literary art is ambiguous. That means that none of its demands can exclude the opposing demand; on the contrary, the more they oppose each other, the more they evoke each other. That is also why no literary situation is definitively settled. Literature is made of words, and these words work a continuous transmutation from the real to the unreal and from the unreal to the real: they breathe in events, real details, tangible things, and project them into an imaginary construct and, at the same time, make this imaginary real and offer it as actual. This activity that makes us live what we know as if it were unknown, and regard as true what we could never live at all, must sometimes necessarily give the one who practices it the feeling of a remarkable power, such that he can, thanks to it, make discoveries and learn more than he knows. When he writes, he comes to feel that he is either the agent of higher powers or—more modestly—to recognize the original experience in his activity as a kind of way of knowledge and means of research.

No need to point out how current this idea is today. The possibility of fiction becoming a revelatory experience haunts all our modern literature. But recognized as means of knowledge, art and even the novel are inevitably called to meet with other intellectual disciplines. This meeting has nothing extraordinary about it; it was almost constant in the entire history of thought. From the pre-Socratics to Dante, from Leonardo da Vinci to Goethe, from Cervantes to Kafka, history is marked by works of art that not only expound ideas but also discover them, that are not content with illustrating a certain image of our condition but deepen it and make it change. Let us go further. Philosophy, giving up hope of getting it all sorted out by means of systems, abandoning preconceived ideas and implicit constructions, turns back to things, to the world and men, and seeks to grasp them in their unobscured significance. This philosophy describes what appears, that is to say, what really shows itself gradually in what appears, it is interested in real situations, it immerses itself in them to find itself on the level of profundity in which the drama of existence is played.

We might think that if Jean-Paul Sartre, at the same time as important philosophical works, wrote novels, plays, and critical essays that are no less important, this capacity for such different works is peculiar to him and expresses only the diversity of his gifts. It is a fact, however, that union in one man of philosopher and writer of equal excellence also comes from the possibility that philosophy and literature offered to combine in him. It is clear that he is only a striking example of an almost general situation: if we think of Simone de Beauvoir, Georges Bataille, Albert Camus, Jean Grenier, Gabriel Marcel, Brice Parain, Jean Wahl, we feel how distant the time is when Bergson had recourse to Proust to compose novels, when Taine abandoned philosophy without doing better than *Thomas Graindorge*, when Voltaire could not manage to be either a novelist or a philosopher. That is because in truth, works of fiction are more and more besieged by theoretical aims, and because theoretical works are more and more addressing problems that demand concrete expression. Existentialists or not, poets, novelists, and philosophers pursue similar experiences and researches, they are involved in a similar way in the same drama to which they have to give an image or whose meaning they have to seek. If they work out their salvation, it is by ways so little different that one is tempted to take them all together.

Naturally, these general remarks explain nothing. Even purely literary questions that are posed starting from such a phenomenon are just as difficult as problems we call "fundamental," since from then on, literature and, consequently, technique have a meaning and value that are extraliterary. For example, one could try to see why Sartre's novels are viable, but that would lead us to pose questions of this kind: Why does Sartre need to seize certain philosophical problems by way of novelistic fiction? To what extent is novelistic work for him not a mode of exposition, or a means of persuasion, but a field of experience, a possibility of discovery, etc.? All these questions still evade us for now. If we leave the books themselves, it is only to arrive at rather banal reflections. This first: that Sartre, in his literary works, is in the grip of questions that are central for him—in *Nausea*, it is the problem of existence, in *Roads to Freedom*, the problem of freedom. Each time, he puts into question his vision of the world, he seems to take it up again from nothing, he exposes himself to its risks and dangers, and the way out he heads toward (admitting there is a way out) remains as unknown to him as it is to us.

That, at least, is the most remarkable trait of *Nausea*. That novel

is an experience and the narrative of an experience. Antoine Roquentin confronts an impulse which escapes him and from which,
he feels, everything is going to slip. The approach of this impulse is
as important as the revelation by which he grasps the meaning of it,
or rather, it is part of this revelation, it is this revelation: trial and
error, blind progress, methodical obsession, presence of a radical
change that is already there and that yet conceals itself, meeting
with what one has found and that one is unaware of, that one
touches and that flees, in which one is constantly embedded and
drowned, and that one loses and lacks constantly. When Roquentin is finally face to face with existence, when he sees it, understands it, and describes it, he actually has nothing more and
nothing changes, the revelation does not enlighten him, for it has
not ceased being given to him, and it puts an end to nothing; it is in
his fingers that feel and in his eyes that see, that is to say, it is
continuously absorbed by his being that lives it. If the critical
moment of every novel of ideas is the conclusion, when the thesis is
unveiled and suppresses ambiguity, *Nausea*, which is a quintessential novel of revelation, emerges intact from this trial, insofar as the
idea that shows itself cannot be distanced from the character who
sees it, that enters into him, takes him, and, as Sartre likes to say,
sticks to his consciousness, as it tends to stick in the reader's. Thus
we always lack the word of the story, if this word, as soon as we hear
it, fills our ears; as soon as we read it, becomes the murkiness and
density of our gaze.

In *Nausea* we do not know where the experience is going, and
the experience does not know where it is going, and when we see
where it arrives, on the one hand, the anticipated presence of this
denouement that was always there causes there not to be any
denouement, and on the other hand, the meaning of this denouement necessarily becomes what we are, throwing us back into the
experience and involving us in it more and more. Two of the
essential conditions of literature are safeguarded: the tendency
belonging to fiction and language to offer themselves as a means of
discovery and not as a means of expressing what has already been
discovered; and the ambiguity of the message, an ambiguity that is

here at its height, since it confuses itself with the existences of the author, the character, and the reader.

In *Roads to Freedom*, it is certainly not so easy to see where they lead, since we do not know the destination. Enough to say that, despite the two large volumes that have already appeared, the novel does not exist, it is entirely yet to come. Naturally, we know that it is a question of a novel on freedom, but when that is understood, we understand that we do not know anything. What will this freedom mean? How will it reveal itself to itself? What ways will it take as goal without being exhausted in contradictions? Finally, how will it involve itself in the world, since it will probably be real only by becoming the freedom of the world? To all these questions, we have a premonition of an answer, but this premonition is theoretical and it is more of a threat (for this book that also has the right to be free) than an aid to understand what we know of it. In *The Age of Reason* and *The Reprieve*, freedom is certainly always present. One of the main characters, Mathieu, professor of philosophy, is openly in battle with it; with him it is at once an obsession and a choice, a "vice" and a "bet." As an adolescent, he had one day the full, abrupt, inexplicable sensation of his existence. On this impression the entire plan of his future has played: to be free, to draw his entire life into the ease of this exceptional moment.

This plan, when the book begins, is at a standstill. It is July or August of 1938. Mathieu is struggling with various personal troubles: his girlfriend tells him that she is pregnant, he has no money, the only doctor he can find is too expensive. One day, he becomes aware that his girlfriend would like to keep the child. What can he do? He is ready to marry her, without enthusiasm he offers to do so, she refuses, marries a friend, etc. One cannot say that this little story of his during one fine summer is extraordinary; it is no more so than his conduct, which seems to us that of just about everyone. It is true that at a certain moment he steals (he takes some money that he needs from a woman's house), and in this form it is an unusual action. (There is a lot of stealing in these novels: one of his former students steals from shop windows out of methodical pleasure, out of a taste for a well-devised act. In Simone de Beauvoir's

The Blood of Others, a young woman steals a bicycle she wants. It is an innocent survival of the gratuitous act.) But, aside from this prank, Mathieu is rather scrupulous, excessively involved in moral and, on the whole, good concerns. What happens to him is that, in the smallest deeds of his current life, he clashes with his freedom and feels only emptiness. He wants to "keep his freedom," as they say, he reserves himself, he conceals himself; and this is not out of egotism, it is not even to obey his "plan," for this plan has nothing deliberate or theoretical about it: he chose that his life be this way, and he lives his choice poorly. "If I didn't try to assume responsibility for my existence," he says, "it would seem absurd to me to exist." So instinctively and desperately he tries to take control of himself by refusing to be just anything. At each instant this obsessive fear appears: Is the die cast? Am I not a once-and-for-all settled being, a "lost" man? He needs to be unattached, and is, to no purpose. He is free, single, nothing ties him down, but his life is dead, he is fixed in place, everything is empty. That is how we arrive at the "age of reason," this serious age that takes the side of failure and knows how to build a comfortable life on it.

The difference between Antoine Roquentin's adventure and that of Mathieu is obvious. The former is involved, from the beginning, in an experience from which he will not emerge, whatever happens: he is taken, he has felt existence, existence will not let him go. And no doubt Mathieu has also felt freedom, and freedom will not let him go either: he is not free to stop being free; his freedom is in him, his freedom is him, it shows itself in each one of his actions, it holds him. Still, both situations cannot but evolve in different ways. For Roquentin, it is such that revelation will not change him, that it can in no way become new: when he comes to understand that his unease, this sly, deceitful, and capricious nausea, is only the unveiling of things that exist, he will have reached the bottom of his story, yet, in a certain way, he will not know anything more about it; in any case, there is nothing more he can do. Mathieu's freedom, on the other hand, is not just a situation that is experienced and elucidated. Mathieu certainly has his revelation, too, his "discoveries." The most important is described to us in *The Re-*

prieve, in the course of that evening before Munich in which war seems inevitable and in which the mobilization and fear disturb everything. Mathieu is on the Pont-Neuf: suddenly he discovers it, this freedom he has sought in vain, that he wanted to meet in some special act or in an exceptional moment. "I have been looking very far for this freedom; it was so close that I couldn't see it, I couldn't touch it, it was only me. I am my freedom." It is the imperceptible distance that separates him from all things, the inappreciable margin starting from which they show themselves and that can never be filled in. "Freedom is exile, and I am condemned to be free."

But this revelation must be a new starting point: it is a question of knowing if Mathieu is going to take responsibility for it, if, now that he knows the meaning of his freedom, inalienable, always present, he is going to claim it, to take charge of it completely and assert it in the world, by acting in such a way that it can choose itself and locate the situations thus produced as situations of freedom. In other words, Mathieu first of all experienced freedom as an original deed, in the same way that Roquentin experienced existence. What separates them from each other is, first, that Roquentin battles with an unknown phenomenon, about which, if he is wrong, he still is not mistaken, while Mathieu seeks freedom more or less deliberately, is mistaken about it, confuses it sometimes with an empty gratuitousness, sometimes with personal independence, and, in a general way, with the need to be without chains, to be finally led, late, before the authentic awareness of that which is. What also, and more profoundly, separates them is that this revelation is not a new beginning for Roquentin, but that it must be one for Mathieu. The latter, on his Pont-Neuf, makes one think very much of Orestes in *The Flies* at the moment when, before the useless miracle of the gods, Orestes, suddenly feeling the void, cold night, becomes aware of his lightness and prepares to make himself heavy by means of an appalling act. We have the foreboding that Mathieu is also on the threshold of a new day, and perhaps on the threshold of a moral. But that is the end of the book, and we know nothing more.

It must be acknowledged that the shadow of a moral always

weighs dangerously over a work of fiction. There is much to be said about that also. If we take Simone de Beauvoir's two novels, we see a much clearer difference between them than between *Nausea* and *Roads to Freedom* (at least as we know them). *She Came to Stay* is also the story of an experience: Françoise, one of the characters, goes to meet the other; that is to say that little by little she discovers in herself the fact that someone exists in her presence, someone who, like her, is awareness, pure presence, indestructible reality, someone who sees her from without, who judges her, against whom she is powerless and without recourse. The heroine pulls herself out of this experience as well as she can. It is a drama with multiple facets, or more precisely a drama in which each movement goes in opposite directions. For example, Françoise, in front of her girl-friend, has the impression of being nothing more than a "white mask," she floats, naked and empty, on the surface of the world. But at the same time it is with this meeting that she begins to exist: the appearance of Xavière is the test that makes her become aware of her freedom in the loss of which she sees herself threatened; it is by the other that she is returned to herself, and her unease is the anguish of an awareness that discovers it is absolute, at the moment when it is alienated and enslaved. Thus the novel does not con-clude, it finishes neither by the crime that is only a meaningless measure nor by a development that goes somewhere: the ambiguity remains complete.

Is the same the case in *The Blood of Others*? That is less certain. In the latter book, we are present at an evolution—more than that, at a veritable overturning, a conversion. And everything makes us be-lieve that this conversion will be definitive, it has "value," it desig-nates itself to us as a solution and an end, announcing the deplor-able appearance of the *Sollen*, of that *Sollen* for which Hegel condemned Fichte to philosophic calamity.

From certain sides, Blomart in *The Blood of Others* has the opposite experience of Françoise in *She Came to Stay*. Françoise learned to know the threat that other people always are to the self. Blomart has changed into this very threat, he is other to everyone, his fault is being an other. Such is his "plan," his choice: he has determined to feel himself responsible. "How can you not find that agonizing? . . . To think that it is you who shape the life of another, despite him." The object of the book, however, is not to describe this experience to us; rather, it shows us how one can surmount it, how, starting from it, by following a road that leads somewhere, we can, to a certain extent, sort things out. That, in fact, is very striking. Blomart's experience is, in appearance, without an outcome like that of *She Came to Stay*. Once involved in this story of responsibility, he is caught. Whatever he does, he sinks. If he acts, he is responsible for the results of his actions that, directly or indirectly, are inevitably defeating; if he does not act, he is responsible both for the meaning that others attribute to his refusal and for the refusal that makes him complicit in the faults that he does not prevent. His abstention is never an absence, it is a gap that for others is always full. "Yes, it's very nice to leave people free . . . it's all in vain: one is always responsible."

But then arise war and defeat and the necessity to choose anew: to accept by doing nothing or not to accept by acting. Blomart, this time, chooses action, and he chooses it, in full lucidity, in a wholehearted way: "Real acts, very visible acts," that is what he prepares to carry out in the clandestine campaign, and he utters the keynote of the book: "I learned from this war that the blood one spares is as inexpiable as the blood one causes to be shed." Undoubtedly, this decision does not settle anything. The death of hostages, the death of his fighting companions, the death of those who consented to die and of those who were not consulted, this entire tragic flow of blood gives the path the feel of a quagmire. So this is not an easy way, but it is the way. From then on, Blomart forges ahead, making himself responsible since he cannot renounce being so, and finding his justification in this responsibility, once accepted and assumed, in the face of the transgression it brings out.

Neither in *The Age of Reason* nor in *The Reprieve* do we find any sign of a comparable clarity in the resolution. That is perhaps the property of the third book, the one we do not know. It is possible: as *Work in Progress*, the novel actually has the advantage of seeming to escape us forever. Still, one of its most remarkable traits is that even when it gives the hint of a movement toward something, it remains undecided, it has no slope, or one that is so slight, so uncertain of itself, that it inclines us without having us believe too much that an author is there who is leading us. Let us admit that this is an effect of art, but art also has its reasons, which have content as well as form. On this subject, it will be necessary to develop the resources that this famous fashionable notion of a *project*—"an existential project"—offers to the novel, to release it from the danger of "ideas." It is obvious that a philosophy professor, with his theories—to be free, to seek conscientiously to be free—undergoes a terrible risk to play his drama out on the level of clear ideas, lucid arguments, and meditated results. Yet he has none of that. Naturally, he speaks, he philosophizes, he has a vocabulary of technical words. But this is not the main thing. If he heads toward his story of freedom, it is not as a man who goes toward a goal already determined that he sees or glimpses. Here, the goal is linked not to a preexistent representation but to the orientation of all of life: it is Mathieu's life that, in its profundity, is polarized toward the need for freedom; it is this life that, to the extent it is directed toward it, causes this goal to exist; at each instant this goal is there and at each instant it conceals itself, it is constantly real and absent.

Even though this project is his own, and he has the ability to revoke it when he likes, it weighs terribly on him, that is why he is enclosed in it as in a cage, "a cage without bars." We are told what a spineless person, how spiritless he is, etc. That may be so, but his spinelessness is probably part of his project, it feeds him and perhaps gives him a reality, a density thanks to which his project will take on a new meaning and will transform even his cowardice. Mathieu is the first to feel that the freedom he gives himself does not work: he would like to be no longer in suspense, to have a destiny, to accomplish an irremediable act. "Everything that I do, I do for *nothing*; you could say the results of my acts are stolen from me; everything happens as if I could always take back my actions." Yet each time he has the chance, he does not succeed at seriously involving himself: to his Communist comrade who asks him to enter the party, he answers no, and this no is despairing. Is it cowardice, uncertainty of mind, skepticism of the heart? It is all that, no doubt, because all of that accompanies his profound decision and forms it and joins with it, this decision that perhaps will be nothing at all except the lamentable dream of a reasonable man, but that perhaps also is reserving him for the moment in which the decision will become all that he is, and will give his involvement the very weight of existence.

The drama does not take place in interior debates. Neither is it expressed in a story that, as we have seen, is nonexistent. But it comes to rest on things, it streams through the world, it mixes itself with outer reality the way water and sand form cement. That is Sartre's great gift, the one that best shows in him the perfect correspondence of the theoretician and the novelist. Mathieu's unease and what can seem to be his (momentary) failure are legible, perceptible in the very objects he touches, in the people he approaches, in the voices he hears. They say of a candidate who is embarrassed by his shyness and unable to handle a question, "He is floundering." That has to be understood in the right sense. Mathieu flounders, he wades through a waterlogged matter. Even his gaze becomes thick, his thoughts are blurry. Everywhere mud, turbid secretions: a universal stickiness, a vile mixture of matter and awareness, a hell in which one does not see, as in Dante, men changed into trees or, as in "The Metamorphosis," a salesman transformed into a cockroach, but thought itself turned into thickness, viscosity, quicksand.

In a certain way, Mathieu's world is almost identical to that of Roquentin. Roquentin sank even more completely into the pitch, into a shapeless reality that "rose to the sky," "went everywhere," "filled everything with its gelatinous collapse"; and certainly it cannot be otherwise, since that is the general condition for man, whose existence is just this being stuck to the world. Yet more must be said: if Mathieu's "plan" is his own, it is also his special nature, his failure that throw him back into a situation similar to that in *Nausea.* With what characteristics did Mathieu appear to us? As a man for whom freedom is confused with empty possibilities, the need to hold back, to conceal himself. His Communist friend describes him very well: "You have put thirty-five years into cleaning yourself and the result is emptiness. You are a funny body . . . you live in the air, you have cut your bourgeois attachments, you have no tie with the proletariat, you float, you are an abstract, an absentee." This exactly defines the condition of the bourgeois intellectual who, to be free, withdraws into an inner refuge, the refuge of his culture, his intellectual, aesthetic, or moral comfort.

At first sight, what is there more distant from the drowning of Roquentin than this high reserve, this retrenchment away from everything? But we are quite deluded. Mathieu thinks he denies and guards himself while he accepts no matter what. He thinks that he breaks his chains, that, having taken refuge in his freedom, he is disengaged from everything, and he is already deeply engaged, lost in the universal swamp that, as much as he climbs, climbs even faster and reaches over his head. For example, he escapes marriage, but only by sinking more deeply into "the misfortune of being single" of which Kafka speaks. And even more so, his availability puts him at the mercy of things: he is free and captured by each of his glances, ready to do everything and immobilized by an inert wadding that absorbs his gestures, dissolves them in an invisible bath of lime. "No one hindered my freedom," he says on the last page of *The Age of Reason*, "it is my life that drank it." His freedom now wanders everywhere, it is left on the edge of café tables, coagulated with the light, caught in the mood of a look—a passive, opaque, dead thing. Hence the murky impression the world gives, his world, this feeling of a spongy, soft reality, of a reality that "drinks" you, that dissolves into you and dilutes you in it. Hence this obsession with cowardice that separates itself from all contacts, that makes the paper thick, the light "yellow, sad, and creamy," the air sticky and muggy. Hence also the role that so many homosexuals play, avowed or ashamed, men who please themselves with men, women who attract women: it is a "mixed" world—half feminine, half masculine, in which softness is gluttonous, inertia is voracious, in which activity is not that of an active decision but of a passive invasion, a deceitful and gelatinous appropriation. One does not live there, one does not act: one flows and sticks. Such is the other side of this illusory absence by which one would like to express one's freedom.

Nausea was written in the first person. *The Age of Reason* is an almost impersonal narrative, with some shreds of interior monologue, of sudden passages from *he* to *I*, but on the whole, whatever margin is left to other characters is composed from Mathieu's point of view. It is in relation to his hidden *I*, diluted everywhere in things and beings, that he unfolds his perspectives and reveals his illuminations. He is objective, in the sense that he sometimes skims over the point of view of a single individual, but it is only to mesh provisionally with another point of view, or to show the vague reality behind which the same awareness stays lying in wait. *The Reprieve* marks an important change in this mode of expression: that is even the principal meaning of the book. There is no more intrigue. People continue, undoubtedly, to have their ways of doing things and their individual situations, but their acts do not set time in motion for them. What happens to them in particular is the inner disintegration of a Something Is Happening, vague, giant, of an Event that no one can embrace any longer because everyone is caught up in it. It is already this feeling of extraindividual duration, of variation in time, a change of scale, of measure, that Malraux's *Man's Hope* gave, in a very powerful way.

In *The Reprieve*, the narrative becomes a whirlwind, it is an aberrant cyclone, in this species of Pascalian universe, that has its center everywhere and its circumference nowhere. Where it reigns, it reflects and radiates events and things from the center of awareness that it has momentarily chosen, but this stability is fugitive; as sentences turn, it carries itself elsewhere and begins again to turn vertiginously around a new center that it obeys until it abandons it because of a veritable sudden shift of wind for a new fixed point and until some new abandonment. Thus, during these days in Munich, we are carried along to the four corners of Europe, into the thousands of little individual cyclones that represent the slow and fatal progression of an immense common cataclysm. We go without rest from Berck to Paris, to Munich, to Prague, to Morocco. An action, begun in Marseilles, merges with another completely different one a hundred leagues from there, where it is completed. A riposte, snatched from its speaker, continues in another mouth that receives it as if it belonged to it and that speaks, thus, in the language of another. All images, all scenes follow each other, change, take each other's place in an infinite diversity, and yet what takes shape is an identical fate: this will be, tomorrow, our destiny.

Besides the mastery that such a mode of composition implies, many difficulties make its use dangerous. This narrative that is not that of any single one risks resuscitating the point of view of the absolute spectator, of seeming to represent the imperious, authoritarian, and lifeless gaze that is always that of the author. Or, on the contrary, it will be everyone's narrative only in appearance, since each time it poses itself, it is on an individual awareness, it is the solitude of this awareness that it unites with: it will never be able to escape the fatality of a point of view.

The composition of *The Reprieve* is art's recompense. Certainly, what happens in it at no time seems contemplated from a falsely impersonal observation post of the hidden author, and on the contrary this will-o'-the-wisp narrative is illumined each time by a little real light, that of a wavering awareness that, as much as it may project itself on greater spaces, always sees only itself. We have, however, the impression that the narrative, during the very time that it arranges itself exclusively around such or such a character, is vaguely aware of arraying itself also around an immense collectivity. Each individual in whom the narration incarnates feels it oscillate in him, feels it is almost somewhere else already, already someone else's narration, and this oscillation, this movement of seasickness, is like the lost and uncertain call of a sick atom that wishes and fears to go out of itself to be no more than its environment. In a word, it is a question of a kind of narrative metempsychosis, of a series of avatars into which narration plunges, dies, and comes back to life in an endless transmigration, like a half-divine consciousness that can be true and real only in the totality of its incarnations, and yet never presents itself except in a ridiculously fragmentary form.

In *Nausea,* Sartre asks little of technique, yet succeeds in pushing all threat of abstract aims away from his work. In *The Age of Reason* and in *The Reprieve,* he pushes the concerns of art even further but also dangerously further away from theoretical preoccupations, to the extent that the experience he describes is probably linked to a moral, and the roads he has us follow head toward an end that he may recommend to us or a certain goal that he is pointing out, and risk not being able to be retraced from their end to their beginning (but that is the secret of the third book).

In sum, we see it better now: the novel has nothing to fear from an idea, providing that the idea is willing to be nothing without the novel. For the novel has its own moral, which is ambiguity and equivocation. It has its own reality, which is the ability to discover the world in the unreal and the imaginary. And, finally, it has its truth, which forces it to assert nothing without seeking to counter it, and to make nothing succeed without preparing its failure, so that every argument that triumphs in a novel immediately stops being true.

§ A Note on Malraux

Malraux's work has certainly lost nothing in the silence to which the critics have abandoned it for five years. And it is to be feared that it meets today with more admiration and commentaries than it would like. So it is fortunate that the first comprehensive study devoted to it is worthy of this silence, and has all the seriousness and the spirit of rigor and decision required for it. Gaëtan Picon's little book, *André Malraux*, while it is an effort to approach a very complex work, is also an absorbing account of the meaning that the generation to which he belongs finds in him.

Perhaps he hesitates to see it such as it was for the one who wrote it: not only a means of personal assertion or an instrument of metaphysical awareness, but also an irreducible experience whose results, as important as they are, are only forever imperfect products. The only reservation Picon expresses about a work that he understands and loves, and that is even his favorite, touches on the art of the novel. Malraux's novels are not novels: they are at once too close to their author and too close to the events, too focused on one single being and too much dispersed throughout the current events of the world. How strange this reservation is. For what makes Malraux's case unusual, perhaps, is that he does nothing but look for himself, but meets himself in the most immediate and general historic reality; he sees and describes only it, and he describes the most important events, those that reveal his own time and decide the future. Perhaps he creates nothing else but his universe, but the movement of this inner universe coincides with that of history, and, in that way, he also creates history, that is to say, the meaning of history.

Gundolf distinguishes, among creative minds, those who, bringing the world to them, give it the solidity and shining of their own mind, like Dante, and those who express themselves by finding the world, by re-creating it in its infinite richness and value, like Shakespeare. He notes, moreover, that, in order for there to be a Dante and a Shakespeare, there must be a stable world, a strong unity, or a sufficient historic profundity, or else the mind that brings the world to it finds no more than itself and loses itself in fantasies, like Byron, and the one who seeks himself outside finds no more than social etiquettes, facts and not poetic values, like Balzac and, to a certain extent, Goethe. Such distinctions leave us rather mistrustful. But they at least make us aware of the originality of those who, like Malraux or Kafka, indeed create, outside of them, a world to meet themselves, but an entirely imaginary world that has nothing in common with the real world except the profound meaning that they lend to it. The originality of a Malraux, if he seems to take everything from current happenings and events and still expresses himself in them, continues through them as profoundly as if he invented them to his own measure, to find in them the substance of a unique experience.

It could well have been that *The Conquerors, Man's Fate,* and *Man's Hope* were a fascinating expression of our epoch, but a personal one of inner adventure, irreducible as any image is. Why do these books that investigate and trace an individual passion nevertheless answer to collective reality? Why do they assert an extreme bias, all the while representing the course of things not subject to bias? Why, faithful to the vigor of a solitary "I," are they also faithful to the objectivity of a historic awareness that dominates all choices and, finally, to the choice peculiar to this story? That stems from the very strength of experience, capable of re-creating, from within and in a perpetual reference to itself, the meaning and value of events from without, that we observe, that we undergo and do not create. In Malraux's case, novelistic experience, in battle with facts that it does not invent, finds in them the chance to experience its truth. These great facts, this imposed reality constitute the role of the irremediable, what the novelist would not know how to change, and whose mastery he does not accept except by an art that makes him feel its domination more strongly. By going to meet history, Malraux's novel goes before what denies it and perhaps what crushes it, but it also welcomes this test as the supreme chance that is given to it to accomplish itself faced with what threatens it.

Picon insists on the dialogue, the constant tension we find in such a work. That is the character of all art born from an experience and tied to it: it is endless, without rest, it draws to a close only by questioning itself. To say of Malraux's work that it chooses despair or death or solitude has, obviously, very little sense. To say that it uses powerful political struggles to find in them the drunkenness of strong actions does not have much more sense. To say, finally, as Picon does, that it tends to surpass the fascination of death by hope, to reconcile the powers of day with those of night, is perhaps truer only in appearance. What is at the heart of these books, in the most varied forms, is an absolute demand, always ready to sacrifice all the rest, but one that at the same time is not enough for itself and wants to preserve the values it sacrifices. Whoever recognizes the necessity of the revolution, for example, cannot just do a small share of it; he must follow it to the end, accepting all its disciplines, loving all its constraints. But the more this demand seems like the order that frees man, the more mindfulness and the sense of values whose sacrifice this freedom demands momentarily awaken. Man must be free, but he must be oppressed to become free, he must consent to this oppression and refuse it, he must become aware of this insurmountable debate and surmount it, for he has to act, he must act without ever losing sight of what he is acting for, and he must act without taking that into account, for one must not act but succeed. Then where is hope? Perhaps in history that saves us. And despair? Perhaps in the man who is lost. But just as well, hope is in the lucid awareness that exalts itself by sacrificing itself, and despair in the definitive arrival of a freedom with which everything will come to an end.

Picon emphasizes that Malraux's last book, *The Walnut Trees of Altenburg*, makes one hear a hymn to life, and marks a stubborn assertion in favor of the victorious role of man. It is true. We can even find a striking symbol of it. In *Man's Fate*, Chen, after his first murder, suddenly sees the world change, decompose beneath his eyes. "The killed individual," he says, "has no importance. But afterward something unexpected occurs, everything is changed, even the simplest things, the streets, for instance, dogs." In *The Walnut Trees*, there is indeed change, even metamorphosis; but it is not from having caused death, but having escaped it, that Berger is present at the transformation of all that he sees, and meets purity, innocence, joy of living. Chen and Berger thus face each other, both carriers of a secret, both before a universe that they no longer recognize; and for one, this secret is joy, while for the other it is the impossibility of living. "This morning, I am nothing but birth." And the other: "Bloodshed is strong enough to decompose the state of distraction that allows us to live."

Is that the sign of an evolution, of a definitive preference? But what would such a choice signify? Malraux has always chosen hope, but he has also always chosen to go all the way to the end of hope. That is why the terrorist who is obsessed with the idea of death signifies the impossibility of living and signifies hope, since his death will be the sign that he has fulfilled himself. And the wonder before the refound world signifies grace and happiness, but also anguish and distress, for this happiness is already lost.

§ Gide and the Literature
of Experience

Anyone who tries to look fairly at the work and person of André Gide must be struck by this trait first off: one can hardly speak of the work except in an unfair way. If one sees one aspect of it strongly, one neglects the important characteristic of that aspect: not to be alone, and to admit the truth of its opposing aspect. If one stresses this assertion of contraries, one forgets the tendency to equilibrium, to harmony and order that has not stopped animating the work. Work of excess, work of extreme measure, completely given over to art and yet given a design to influence that is not aesthetic but moral, a work that counts more than the man and that for the man who shaped it was only a means of shaping himself, seeking himself, finally an immense work of an extraordinary variety, but also scattered and narrow and monotonous, open to the richest culture, turned toward the least bookish spontaneity, naive in its taste for effort, free through care for constraint, discreet in its frankness, sincere to the point of affectation and as if pushed by anxiety toward the repose and serenity of a form in which nothing could be changed.

We recognize that the work that best represents him is in the *Journals*. But why? For we also recognize that his most successful works are *The Immoralist*, *Strait Is the Gate*, and *Pastoral Symphony*, novellas wonderfully composed and completely foreign to the unlimited movement that carries the *Journals* to a fortunately unforeseeable end. These stories are faultless. *Lafcadio's Adventures* and *The Counterfeiters* are books considered failures, but the influence of these imperfect works has been considerable, even too important, to the point that their ability to shine has been momentarily exhausted—they seem old today because of all the new things they authorized and made possible. On the contrary, the treatises that success has never entirely recognized—with the exception of *Fruits of the Earth*—and that perhaps desired only this semi-celebrity, continue to exercise a profound influence and, in the same way as the strongest works of Rimbaud, Lautréamont, and the surrealists, are responsible for the need contemporary literature feels to be more than literature: a vital experience, an instrument of discovery, a means for man to test himself, to try himself, and, in this attempt, to seek to surpass his boundaries.

Gide, by his work and the way in which he linked it to his life, gave a new meaning to the word essay. One can find his precursors through our entire literature. What does that matter, if it is precisely he who illuminates this kinship by giving the writers with whom he is likened the new meaning that justifies such a filiation? One can say that he created those from whom he came, and that they owe to him all that he himself owes them. Such is the value of what we call culture. In 1893, about *The Amorous Endeavor*, he wrote in the *Journals*: "I wanted to point out, in *The Amorous Endeavor*, the influence of the book on the one who writes it, and during the writing itself. For going out of us, it changes us, it modifies the current of our life. . . . So it is a method of action on itself, indirect, that I have given there; and it is also, quite simply, a story." Is this the preoccupation of extreme youth? But thirty years later, looking at the totality of his work, Gide writes again: "It seems to me that each of my books has not so much been the product of a new inner disposition as its completely opposing cause, and the first provocation of this disposition of soul and mind in which I had to maintain myself in order to lead its successful elaboration. I would like to express in the simplest way that the book, as soon as it is conceived, completely has me at its disposal, and that, for it, everything in me, down to the deepest part of me, is orchestrated. I have no other personality than that which is appro-priate to this—objective? subjective?—work. Those words lose all their meaning here; for if it happens that I portray things drawing from my experience (and sometimes it seems to me that there can be no other exact portrayal), it is because I began first by becoming the very person I wanted to portray" (*Journals*, 1922).

This last remark aims at the art of the novel. It is often asserted that the novelist wants to be a writer capable of making distinct beings come to life, whose freedom would claim him. But when one attributes to literature the ability to create a life different from the one who creates it, it is to admire the power of fiction's freedom and not to recognize in this freedom the means, searched out by the author, to put into play the meaning of his own freedom. We have been shown the author in battle with his heroes, given over to them and possessed by them: Jarry becoming Ubu. These "dramatic" cases remain of little interest because of the simplistic notion of a character, understood as a quality, a temperament that is petrified and assimilated with a thing. Completely different is the ability to challenge oneself, to risk oneself in this vitally dangerous experi-ence that art must be for the artist, the novel for the novelist, and, in a more general way, the fact of writing for one who writes.

When Gide notes in his *Journals*, "For a long time, too long a time (yes, until these past years), I strove to believe that I was mistaken, I was wrong; to accuse myself, to contradict myself; to bend my way of seeing, feeling, and thinking to that of others, etc. One could have said that my own thinking made me afraid, hence the need that I had to bestow it on the heroes of my books, in order to distance it more from me. Certain people, who refuse to see me as a novelist, are perhaps right, since that is what inspires me to the novel, rather than the wish to tell stories," we recognize in these remarks the care to make literature serve an actual experience: experience of oneself, experience of one's thoughts, not to keep them and confirm them, even less to persuade others of them, but to distance them, to hold them at a distance, to "try" them by trusting them to another existence, that is to say, to alter them, make them wrong. Undoubtedly, Gide's experience was too often the experience of his thoughts and not that of his existence itself, and that is why he comes to be unfaithful to the movement that inspires him, for experience occurs only starting from the moment that, as he says more or less, everything and everything of oneself is put in doubt. But insofar as he followed this impulse, and despite his very scruples that make him accept the objections according to which the only real novelist is a storyteller and a creator of characters, he was not only a great writer of novels but he contributed to giving the contemporary literature of the novel its essential nature, that which allows one to say that *Maldoror* is a novel, *Nadja* an admirable novel, on the same level as the works of Malraux, who was also a great creator of novels of "experience."

It is easy to assert that literature is an activity in which whoever exerts himself tends not only to produce beautiful, interesting, instructive works but also to experience himself completely, not to tell about himself, express himself, or even discover himself, but to pursue an experience in which the meaning of the human condition in its entirety will be uncovered, in connection with him and with the world that is his. It is simple to repeat: writing has a fundamental value of experience for the one who writes; we say it, we repeat it; but we wind up repeating only a formula without content, illusory, one that resists examination only by escaping the criticism whose integral value it nevertheless asserts. One of the characteristics of Gide's work is that it helps us understand these difficulties, since it was itself made starting from these difficulties, in the debate they provoked in him, and without surpassing them, but by welcoming them, by experiencing them with an indulgence at once uneasy and jealous, in the very real suffering of not being able to surmount them and the satisfaction, finding them insurmountable, of drawing from them the chance to delight an infinite curiosity and spirit of seeking.

From the instant the writer writes with the ulterior motive that what he writes "takes over" him "entirely," the terrible question of art's proper demands begins to be posed. Gide's situation enlightens this debate. Coming from symbolism, he does not renounce his faith in the idea of perfection, in the virtues of a perfected form and a fine style. His writer's existence is dominated by the desire to be in conformity with the ideal of a harmonious, true art. To be faithful to the act of writing well is for him to be unfaithful to nothing, to betray nothing; it is to follow the road that leads the farthest, that allows the most important and daring adventure. Why? It is an act of faith, based on the cult of centuries and the example of masterpieces. The mature Gide, instructed by experience, can still write, "It is quite difficult to me to believe that the healthiest, wisest, and most sensible thinking is not just the one that, projected into writing, gives the most harmonious and beautiful lines" (*Journals*, 1928). The elegance and harmony of a beautiful form are not, then, simple aesthetic satisfactions that the writer grants himself out of indulgence for his gifts. The hope is deeper. It is the certainty that, when everything has been questioned, at least the form of the sentence subsists as a measure and safeguard of its value. "I wanted to make an instrument of my sentence so sensitive that the simple misplacing of a comma suffices to ruin its harmony" (*Journals*, 1923). Wanting to be sincere, questioning himself on the meaning of artistic sincerity, the very young Gide defined it in these terms: "I find this, provisionally: that the word never precedes the idea. Or even: that the word is always necessitated by it; it must be irresistible, unsuppressable; the same is true for the sentence, for the entire work." Between these two assertions, that of the sincerity of youth, that of the "write well" of mature age, there is no disagreement, but profound harmony. *To be perfectly sincere*, asks the Gide of 1892, and the other Gides answer with faith: so, write in conformity with the harmony of the language and so that once the sentence is traced, once the work completed, the resources of language do not allow anything in them to be changed.

Often bolder but, in all, less skeptical than Valéry, Gide is infinitely less so on the point of the truth of art and rhetoric. Valéry sees only arbitrariness and conventions in the means and effects of art, and that is because he denies the real value of the form that he asserts and whose demands he observes: he is a perfect writer only because perfection has no truth for him. But Gide is not so impious. Art, in his eyes, means something. To write a work is not a simple exercise; to write well is also to give the greatest chances to truth, to the effort to remain true without ceasing to be utterly daring. If one comes from that to question the power of language and the value of rules and form—whether they are traditional or not does not matter—if one writes: "I believe that everything must be called into question" (*Journals*, 1931) and if one does not keep an inmost confidence in the words that introduce this complete calling into question, one has only the choice between becoming the author of masterpieces in which one claims not to believe, and losing oneself in the repetition of a silent chatter. Valéry took the side of masterpieces, and in the end masterpieces triumphed over his skepticism, reducing it to a state of mind, light, brilliant, and rather vain.

Gide's possibility of negation, less radical and because of that more profound, less easy to appease, had extraordinary faith in the resources of culture and literary art. Too much, perhaps. For we do not see that the desire to write in order to head toward the unknown or to fight against oneself, as he says in a letter to Francis Jammes in May 1902 ("Don't you understand, then, that I hate *my thinking*? I use myself to fight against it; but I can deny it only through it, the way one chases a demon through Beelzebub, the prince of demons. What else did I try to show in *Marshlands*?"), ever led him to abandon the ideal of writing well, or even clashed in him with the demands of the work to make, to compose, to create something worthy of the test of time. While it is quite possible that writing well is, for the one who writes, the best means to venture and question oneself, the opposite is also possible. When Valéry reproaches Pascal for his too beautiful sentences on man's misery, he claims that Pascal's misery, if it had been more real, could not have been experienced in such beautiful language. Why? That is not clear, for where Valéry recognizes a beautiful style, too sure of its effects, anxious to attain them, Pascal perhaps saw only the expression of the decay that he had to find in himself with such anxiety. Yet the doubt remains. We have seen, in fact, great writers stop writing, we have seen others discover their poverty thanks to the richest language, or torment themselves by the consolations of superb images, but we have never seen any, in the movement of a real experience, continue to write and strive to write mediocrely, to ask of their gifts the means of ruining their gifts. And yet, who knows? By becoming François Coppée rather than a merchant in the Harrar, would Rimbaud not have become a visionary, would he not have spent his real season in hell? And if "with beautiful emotions one makes bad literature," by condescending to bad literature, the one who is capable of the best literature would perhaps rise more truly above himself, would better surpass his boundaries than by following his bent, which is to produce great works that will endure through the centuries.

Good literature often worried Gide; we cannot forget that. It seemed suspicious to him, and he, who served it with so much faith, also regarded it with mistrust. The sincerity about which, from youth, he questions himself, enters into disagreement with the necessities of writing. "The desire to write these journal pages well takes away from them all merit, even of sincerity. They no longer mean anything, never being well enough written to have a literary merit; finally, they all rely on a fame, a future celebrity that will give them some interest. That is profoundly contemptible" (*Journals*, 1893). And twenty years later: "Perhaps, after all, this belief in the work of art and this cult that I dedicate to it prevent this perfect sincerity that I would like from now on to obtain from myself. What do I have to do with a lucidity that is only a quality of style?" Sincerity is an excellent siege engine against the rights of fine language and even of all language. Sometimes it suspects it of saying too much, of saying more than there is ("This amplification of emotion, of thought, of which *writing well*, in French literature, sometimes consists" *Journals*, 1931). Sometimes sincerity finds language lacking: to say is always to say too little ("If I have, for a long time now, stopped writing [the *Journals*], it is because my emotions were becoming too complicated; it would have taken me too much time to write them; the work of a necessary simplification made them less sincere then; it was already a literary fine-tuning" (*Journals*, 1893). Or again, as we have just seen, it reproaches him for his *lucidity*, blaming him for being too pure, with a transparency that is too perfect—a very grave objection and, for classic art, completely ruinous, since it implies that blurred feelings allow as correct expressions only those that betray them, that express them without clarity, without decency, without that minimum of order that there is in something real. Then the temptation to write against style appears, or to write against oneself, to ask from spontaneity the hope of a more sincere expression, as if swiftness, the absence of reflection, the natural could here offer greater guarantees than patience, study, and the naiveté that is the result of effort.

Sincerity is an admirable principle of questioning. Nothing contents it, neither the natural, which is the lie of the first impulse, nor artifice, which is a satisfied awareness of the lie, nor banality, which is a consent to common bad faith, nor the cult of differences, which wants to save the imposture by considering it—untruthfully—unique. Silence itself is false, for it is only a language that does not know itself and that, moreover, by its renunciation of language makes itself very well understood. "I am stirred by this dilemma," wrote the young Gide, "to be moral; to be sincere. Morality consists of supplanting the natural being (the old man) with a preferred factitious being. But then one is no longer sincere. The old man is the sincere man. I find this: the old man is the poet. The new man, that we prefer, is the artist. The artist must supplant the poet. From the struggle between the two is born the work of art" (*Journals*, 1892). But why would the new *preference* be less sincere than the former state? It has the truth of desire, the richness of that which comes; it is promise, it is life; factitious perhaps, since it concerns the being who makes himself, but because of that it is less falsified by usage. Later, however, Gide, reversing these assertions, will find the naive beneath the natural, like the reward for the effort, sincerity obtained, conquered, and no longer inherited.

Art is a trap, Mallarmé has said, and that is why sincerity is such a precious enemy to him; nothing is lacking for it to be the supreme rule, if sincerity itself were not imposture. Hence the uneasiness that accompanies all his judgments; hence, too, the fact that he must succumb to the condemnation that it utters. "The word *sincerity* is one of those that is becoming the most uneasy for me to understand. . . . In general every young man of conviction and incapable of criticism believes himself sincere" (*Journals*, 1909). Gide, before Freud, considered the defects and vices—in the non-moral sense of this word—of sincerity—and, before making his way to Marx, he held as insufficient its cunning authority, completely altered by the blinding of an inner gaze that lays claim to purity by ignoring both history and the world. It is, however, at the moment when social problems present themselves to his mind that he most categorically dismisses art, and seems to advocate its disappearance. "That art and literature have only to deal with social questions, yet, if they venture into it, cannot help but lose their way, I remain pretty much convinced. And that indeed is also why I am silent since these questions have occupied the foreground of my mind. . . . I would rather write nothing more, than bend my art to utilitarian ends. To persuade me that these must today take the foreground, is at the same stroke to condemn me to silence" (*Journals*, 1932). And this in July 1934: "For a long time, it can no longer be a question of a work of art."

This questioning of art in view of objective freedom is one of the most important that can be imposed on an artist. Gide's debate with communism is the pathetic moment of this existence, his supreme moment and one that must be regarded with the most seriousness. Such a meeting put him in the presence of a wall that he could neither climb nor stop seeing, in front of which he contented himself with stepping back, while feeling that this shrinking away did not satisfy him. Let us note that political men can be Communist and then stop being it; for them, this stage does not always have much importance. It is not the same for the writer. From such a confrontation, if he withdraws, albeit for the strongest reasons, he does not withdraw intact. In his vocation something was touched by death. What once questioned him, even if later on he comes to regard it as questionable, continues to make him suspicious of an activity when he sees all that it costs him by the satisfactions it brings him.

But in Gide, we cannot help noticing with what precautions, or rather with what reticences, the "It can no longer be a question of a work of art" is accompanied, from the moment it is uttered. Art renounces itself because it does not want "to bend itself to utilitarian ends"; it sacrifices itself, but it also keeps itself pure. There may be in the world a task for the writer that is more important than that of writing, and Gide recognizes it with a gravity from which he is ready to draw all the consequences; he hears "moans" that are too pressing for him to have any desire to make himself heard. So he is going to condemn himself to silence. Extreme sacrifice, not only the sacrifice of literature to the world's distress but just as much the sacrifice of art to itself, of art that, in the order it has given itself, does not tolerate purposes that dominate it or foreign laws that can corrupt it. Art's failure is also a victory of art; it closes up again in silence and rests for the future.

The questioning was not then complete: not to write anymore, yes, if the best interests of humanity require that; but so long as you do write, write well, write in accord with the obligations of writing well, considered apart, in themselves, as you can recognize them in the closed sphere of literature, because they are the least deceiving, the most fitting to help whoever expresses himself to express more than himself, more than he knows, to help him, in a word, to create. The *Journals* are from one end to the other shot through with the torments of style: "I no longer like things that are slowly written. The purpose of this notebook, like that of all the other 'journals' I have kept, is to teach me to write quickly. . . . These pages have seemed to me overwritten and lacking spontaneity. . . . I have just reread the last written chapter of my Memoirs, that I promised myself I would write without lifting the pen, and over which I have already labored so much. Nothing of what I would have liked to put there is there; everything seems to me devised, subtle, dry, elegant, faded." Just as "vice" was virtue for Gide, to the extent that virtue was natural to him and getting away from it entailed the difficult conquest of effort, even so, too naturally tempted by elegance and the precautions of language, giving way too willingly to the research of *number*, to the point of asking the truth and meaning of the measure of sentences, he would like to refrain from this inclination, to let impropriety rule the choice of words, incorrectness the syntax (*Journals*, 1914), and especially to write quickly, to write ahead of himself, preceding himself, by a veritable movement of anticipation and discovery. In this, his scruples are not only those of a writer whose taste would become ever more classic and who would learn to prefer cleanness, exactitude, dryness over the music of the sentence. Anxiety with regard to form is an anxiety touching the value of the writing experience. If Gide so often repeats to himself the sentence from *Armance*: "I have spoken much better since I began my sentences without knowing how I would finish them," it is because it represents to him this mysterious, dangerous movement of the act of writing by which the one who writes, beginning a sentence without knowing where it is leading him, undertaking a work in the ignorance of its end, feels himself tied to the unknown, involved in the mystery of a progress that surpasses him and by means of which he surpasses himself, a progress in which he risks losing himself, losing everything, and also finding more than he seeks.

But at the same time such a preoccupation, far from weakening the rights of style, reinforces them and takes place in the midst of fine language. "I have spoken much better. . . ." It is always speaking well that is the question, writing well thought of as the law; and finally Gide admires in Stendhal "this quality of alertness and impulsiveness, of impropriety, of suddenness and bareness that ravishes us always anew in his style." He admires that style. But, for as long as it is a matter of style and not of a way of seeking or a means of discovery, he does not stop preferring his own. This slow, insinuating form that he chose, with its seemingly interior movement, its indecisive and firm progress, reticent and enveloping, his sympathy for the sensuous qualities of words and their cadence that is corrected by the exceedingly supervised and thought-out elegance of syntax, this mixture of study and abandon, exactitude and call to indecision, of natural rigor and contrived tremblings, of heat and ice—he knows well how it corresponds to the being that he is and that he never wanted to reject entirely, he knows how much this way that is so common and so rare of writing well is like him, to the extent that distancing himself from himself—but only up to a certain point—dissembling himself, is part of his resemblance, it is the movement by which he asserts himself and assures himself. "You will not easily find the trajectory of my mind; its curve will reveal itself only in my style and will escape more than one."

This "only up to a certain point" is the secret characteristic of André Gide. Whether it is a question in him of the artist, of the creator of forms or the creator of his own life, of the one who, living, lives in desire, entirely at the disposition of the experience to which he gives himself, yet never pushing it far enough to make any other impossible, he always ends up by meeting, at the moment of forgetting himself, the moment that recalls him to himself, at the extreme point of innovation, the guarantees of a traditional rule, in the greatest daring a regret, a yen for measure and harmony. The times are such that, during one part of his life, Gide saw himself rejected because of his audacity and, during another part, because of his lack of audacity. That is because the times welcomed this intrepid curiosity of extremes from him, but did not accept either his patience, or his honesty, or his faith in works, or his spirit of prudence and, as he calls it, of parsimony. And in that, his example remains ambiguous and mysterious. Some disapprovingly see him as a writer who is too much master of himself, who, all the while writing because he "calls everything into question," writes also to "shelter something from death" (*Journals*, 1922), who wants very much to be unbelieving but without consenting to impiety, and, as soon as he touches the extremity of experience, is afraid of losing himself completely and hurries to get hold of himself again, to take himself in hand ("Necessity of connecting the frontier to the center. It is time to return"). We can answer that he is daring in proportion to his caution, that his restlessness has all the more meaning because he wishes for repose, and his struggle for emancipation all the more value because it is the deed of a mind incapable of the disrespectful and the irreligious. But, at the same time, if Gide's characteristic is patience in impatience, reserve in excess, honesty in error (the move that breaks the rules), one can tell oneself that true reserve would have been to abandon himself completely, and the absolute honesty to be completely disordered without hope, and the most fertile patience to live without waiting, far from the spirit of fame and the subtle design of influence that he loved and served with a great disinterdness, and that today recompenses him by the most widespread and honorable renown.

When we see Theseus come out of the labyrinth, glorious conqueror in a battle at which no one was present, we rightly suspect him of trickery or illusion. For there is no labyrinth except for the one who tests it, and the test is real only for the one who really gets lost in it, and the one who gets lost in it is no longer there to bear witness to his loss—and to tell us, "Entering the labyrinth is easy. There is nothing more difficult than to get out of it. No one finds his way there who has not first gotten lost there." Gide's Theseus, because he knows how to retrace his steps, wonderfully quick at transforming Ariadne's burning feelings into an attachment of which he remains the master, will always expose himself to these suspicions: that he never entered the labyrinth, since he came out of it, and never met the Minotaur, since it did not devour him. That is an insolvable dilemma. Theseus finds his way because he stays attached to something certain, but, not having broken the thread, he remains one who has never really known the labyrinth. To which he can answer that whoever does not return was even farther away, and that getting lost is possible only for one who preserves the meaning, knowledge, and love of the right way.

Literature is a dishonest and confused experience in which one succeeds only by failing, in which failing means nothing, in which the greatest scruples are suspect, in which sincerity becomes comedy. It is an experience that is essentially deceiving, and that is what creates all its value, for anyone who writes enters into the illusion, but this illusion, deceiving him, carries him away and, carrying him away by the most ambiguous movement, gives him, as he chooses, a chance either to lose what he had already thought he found, or to discover what he can no longer lose. Gide is the meeting place of two conceptions of literature, that of traditional art which places the good fortune of producing masterpieces above everything, and literature as experience, which makes fun of works of art and is ready to ruin itself to attain the inaccessible. Hence his double destiny. As a model of literary honesty, he passes for a long time as the prince of the equivocal and as the demon itself. Then classic immortality discovers him. He becomes the greatest living French writer. And fame lowers him to being no more than a wise man.

§ *Adolphe*, or the Misfortune of True Feelings

Benjamin Constant's *Adolphe* counts for much in the conception we have of the French novel. To what extent does this notion of a novelistic tradition influence even the writers who most distance themselves from it? And what does this tradition represent? A small number of judgments that epitomize it, rules that we elicit from it? Would it not first be the feeling of a mysterious reality, represented by the ability to endure that some works have shown, to remain stubbornly in the background of our literary experience and of our language? When a literature becomes classic, it is this temptation to conquer time that its influence brings to all those who feel themselves charged with continuing it. The temptation may be a worthwhile one, but it is also full of dangers. It is the temptation of the timeless. It is the hope of existing beyond history, and of acting and being admired independently of historic conditions of success. It is the thought that literature offers us the chance of climbing back up into the Platonic sky and imposes on us the duty of finding again the purity of its essences, which are eternal. From this come all kinds of constraints, claims, calculations. Whatever we may think of the idea of *involvement*, it at least has the merit of being only an involvement with a time limit, limited to our own brief lifetime, and not this hypocritical, vague, but endless involvement, for all times and even for beyond time, that the little hell of artistic immortality signifies.

As soon as we wonder by what traits the works that last succeed in lasting, we enter the classic influence game. Yet, the answer changes with the times themselves. Sometimes *Adolphe* triumphs by its purity and simplicity: it is a book "without a date," says one, a book "without a country," says another. Sometimes we love it because it represents the passions of its time, thanks to an art that remains foreign to it, a nineteenth-century hero who uses the language of the eighteenth century, a modern hero in a form that eludes fashion. Or we may even admire the spirit of analysis of this little novel, the violent, dry, and impersonal lucidity that seems one of the constant qualities of our tradition and makes all that is connected with it lasting. But later we begin to love *Adolphe* because it has something unique and even suspect about it, because, far from being the result of a pure art, it expresses the singular experience and the seeming madness of a man who is difficult to understand, in many ways one of the strangest that we know. And at this instant it suddenly seems to us that this novelistic tradition whose main characteristic seemed to be the search for universal values is manifested essentially by works in which the author looks only to himself, expresses only his secret, encloses the most surprising and scandalous things: *The Princess of Cleves, Manon Lescaut, The New Heloise, Les Liaisons dangereuses, Justine, René, Adolphe, The Charterhouse of Parma, Aurélia, Maldoror,* unique works, for what is expressed in them indeed adds to the heritage, but like something that is not inherited and so, remaining whole, is transmitted without being lost.

From this double appearance of being a work that is suitable for all times and for everyone, yet that is suitable only for one alone and closes back on itself, *Adolphe*, like all classic art, has kept its right to survive. But the contradiction here is particularly strong, and all the simplicity, the rigor, the purity that we see in the book make the singularity of the movement that emerges in it all the more unusual. Undoubtedly, Adolphe's mood can be reduced to simple feelings: Adolphe or the helplessness of loving, says Jean Mistler; Adolphe or the greatness of severity toward oneself, says Charles du Bos, while many others say indecision, weakness, the mania of remorse, Adolphe's cruelty. You will note that these epithets contradict each other. According to Delecluze and according to Martineau, who cites him, Stendhal complained by turns of the affectation of the book and loved its extreme truth of feelings; he thought it well expressed what it expressed, but that it featured a kind of tragic banter [*marivaudage*]: affectation in truth, tragedy and game, a just language, but nothing but a language, Beyle's uncertainty about *Adolphe* is not less than that of Adolphe himself. It is too true that the stylization of this character, the extreme paring-down of anecdote, the ordinary nature of the passion that it illustrates are paired with some indescribable quality that we cannot come to understand and that lends the work its secret. It is the same mystery, the same strange necessity that Constant discovers in himself, that he sees and penetrates lucidly without ever being able to accept or reject it.

Charles du Bos, in lectures that have been published (*Grandeur and Misery of Benjamin Constant*), has tried to be no less fair to Benjamin Constant than Constant wanted to be to everyone, Constant to whom his friends were so unfair. His extreme intelligence has been acknowledged, but in order to make him responsible for the mediocre use that he managed to make of it. He is accused of being weak because, beginning many affairs, he shows himself incapable of ending them, cruel because he destroys himself in the ties he cannot break, insensitive if he confesses to being cold and scarcely more interested in himself than in others, inconstant finally (*sola inconstantia constans*, he says), for he becomes attached only to detach himself. And, moreover, cowardly enough to condemn Napoleon when the Empire collapses and to rally to his cause at the moment of the Hundred Days, servile enough to ask of power the material advantages that he pays for by the loss of his independence. These judgments are nearly those of Sainte-Beuve, who felt too close to him to understand him, and too far beneath him not to envy or condemn him. It is against these injustices that du Bos, by an analysis in which his delicacy of mind patiently examines the texts, has undertaken a work of restoration from which Benjamin Constant emerges as a hero of lucid mind and a martyr to pity.

These conclusions of du Bos are rarely arguable. Constant's lucidity is extreme. Working through him, it is incomparable: lively, strong, without hesitation as without vanity, great enough to understand while conserving the mysterious points it meets. Adolphe and his creator have traditionally been made into the victims of excessive analysis. Constant accused himself of this: "I hate this fatuity of a mind that thinks it excuses what it explains; I hate this vanity that occupies itself in telling of the evil it has done, that intends to get itself pitied by describing itself, and that, gliding indestructible in the midst of ruins, analyzes itself instead of repenting." But this mind, so guilty in appearing to abuse its intimacy with itself, by leaving us a personal diary, leaves us the surest document, the least complacent, one perfectly foreign to the spirit of analysis. They are almost always short notes, in which he does not seek to relive what he has lived, or to take his revenge on what he was not able to live, or to say "I alone," or to "lay his heart bare," or to give himself the temptation or the excuse of an impossible sincerity. He succeeds at that rare effect of being more natural than Stendhal, because he is more indifferent to not seeming natural, and even simpler, for he does not always try to be simple: "To occupy my evening I reread my Diary; it amused me passably well. . . . When I began I promised myself to speak only for myself, and yet such is the influence of the habit of speaking to the gallery that sometimes I forgot myself."

This demon of analysis who writes a diary in which analysis is almost absent is also a mind that is most closed on itself, and yet most capable of justly appreciating others. Twenty-four hours after having met Mme. de Staël, he judges her with this spirit of truth: "I think her activity is a need, as much as, or more than, it is a merit; but she uses it to do good. . . . What you say of her jibes is true: she cites the great like an arriviste from yesterday. . . . But I do not think that she prides herself on her wit; she just feels that she has a lot of it, she has a great need to speak, to give herself over, to know neither limits nor caution. . . . She praises people too much because she wants to please them in order to give herself over to them without reserve. When they are no longer there, she naturally retraces her steps: one cannot call that positively bad faith." Later, he will speak of her less honestly: she will be a "torrent," "the disturbance of the universe and the movement of chaos," the blazing of a volcano, "the most egotistical, the most frenzied, the most ungrateful, the vainest, and the most vindictive of all women," but that is what she will be then with him, what her own madness will force her to become, when he will write in the height of the storm: "Dreadful scene, horrible, demented; atrocious expressions. She is mad or I am mad."

We see now that Constant's lucidity is not that of indifference. It is a neutrality that passion overexcites. At the moment when his feelings for Mme. Récamier reach paroxysm and ought to have made him blind, he writes of her: "She loses herself in the little flirtations she makes her trade of, and pleases or pains herself by turns by the pain she causes to her three or four wooers, of whom I am one; then she does a little good, when that does not disturb her, and puts the Mass above everything else, and sighs that she thinks come from her soul and that come only from her boredom." Which does not prevent him from writing, on the same date, "Juliette must love me . . . or kill me. Vowed to give twelve thousand francs to the poor if she loves me. The death I have chosen is not painful; despondency deadens the physical and mental pain; let us not shrink back." These texts would be enough to dissipate the myth of an insensitive Constant. That he was sensitive only prompted by a certain impulse, we will see. But Constant himself, all the while noting his reserve, his coldness, his weak curiosity, did not stop pushing back this suspicion of insensitivity. "I prefer the madness of enthusiasm . . . ," he writes to his aunt. And in his *Diary*: "They quarrel with me over my scant sensitivity. No, I do not have scant sensitivity; but it is susceptible and that of others is never perfectly suitable for it. . . . I see in it only a means of getting rid of the pain that seems ignoble to me. In a word, my sensitivity is always wounded by the demonstrations of that of others." And even more than these abstract judgments, the remarks of his *Diary* on the events that touch him show the violence, pushed to madness, of what he feels and what he suffers. On Mme. Récamier: "Agitated and frightful day . . . horrible awakening—

Night and morning delirious. I cry continuously, etc., etc." On the
death of his father: "My father is dead! my head is clouded and my
blood frozen." On his own life: "No one suspects the kind of
madness that inundates and devastates it," and again (this in a
letter): "I am a stricken creature."

Constant's drama is quite banal in appearance, and what is more,
in reality it is banal. But what makes it unique is that at the same
time that he underwent it, he gave us the means of understanding
it, revealed to us its true meaning and real breadth. His passions
were among the strongest. Mme. de Staël made a fuss about loving
him, he took poison, and there he was, dying. Mme. de Staël gave
in finally, she stopped "being a goal and became a bond": then
more love, even more attachment, no doubt, but especially out of
the boredom of feeling himself attached; the pleasure of what he
obtained made him regret the freedom he no longer had, and since
Mme. de Staël was obsessed with involvement, because she did
not suffer anyone to escape her and demanded a constant, assidu-
ous presence, and one not exclusive of many others, she quickly
enough transformed this connection into a crushing burden that
cut her off from life and made her crazy. Well, why didn't he break
this tie? But that is the other movement of the drama, he could not
break it, and he could not break it not out of weakness or irresolu-
tion, but because he could not bear the suffering it caused. Both the
spectacle and feeling of suffering represented a torment and an
enigma that overwhelmed him. He knew how to perceive the
subject clearly; he made of it a fatality of the human condition:
"The great question of life is the pain we cause. . . . All that I respect
on the earth is pain and I want to die without having to reproach
myself for having held out against it." He sees in it a trait of his
nature: "I know only that I am one who is always carried away to
feel for others more than for myself, because pity pursues me." It is
such a carrying away that filled his existence with dismay. When he
no longer had passion, he had the passion of breaking off. But if he
wanted to break off, he destroyed the one from whom he was
separating, and this pain made him beside himself. ("She uttered
frightful cries of pain and desolation. A heart of iron would not

have been able to resist it." And about his wife, whom he does not love, whom he deceives and ridicules: "The idea of what she is suffering and will suffer . . . poisons the feeling of my freedom.") If he resigns himself not to breaking off, he must feign feelings that he no longer has, for a lack of feelings would be as painful to the other as a breaking off would be. And if he dissimulates, this dissimulation ends by stifling him until he explodes and puts all his strength into breaking off, which provokes a thousand sorrows, provokes so many that he cannot go on with it; then he becomes resigned, then dissimulates again, until the next vain attempt to free himself, tear himself to pieces, and fall back into his bonds.

Constant is a gripping example of the paradox there is at the bottom of all human relationships, when they give themselves as their purpose the lack that makes them up. He often calls out to solitude, but as we shall see, and shall see why, solitude reserves as much torment for him as communal existence. He cannot do without another; his entire conduct proves it: he marries twice, has weightier affairs than twenty marriages, lives in the world and of the world, a world in which his wit is brilliant. But he can no longer suffer another as soon as he no longer conceives of existence as what he lacks, but as something he holds. The principle of all these movements is the feeling of distance that separates him from the others. He knows and he feels that this distance is at once the condition and the object of his relationships with the world. He must be distanced from the world if he wants to get closer to it, and he can communicate with it only if he becomes master of this emptiness. So it is not Mme. de Staël whom he wants to attain, but the very distance that will push him away from her, the absence that, in the truest sense, is the only way for men to make themselves present. Ten texts would furnish the demonstration of this. This emptiness is often perceptible to him only in boredom, he is satisfied with it, he lives in apathy and laziness, lives confronting his own emptiness. But let someone transform this interval, let him hollow it out even more, make a burning, brilliant, unscalable emptiness of it, let obstacles be multiplied, let the chasm seem always vaster and deeper: then Constant's desire blazes up, spreads out, becomes irritated, madness, desire for death, and does not rest until it attains the other whose possession suspends his desire, without even giving him what provoked him: the irreducible distance of beings that makes others, as he writes, never be oneself. So it is not because he is fulfilled that he stops desiring. He is not fulfilled; what he wants, what such or such beautiful appearance reveals to him, is not only the absence of her to him but also the absence that is the ground of all his relationships with others, and that he tries in vain to live and to appropriate. Loving Mme. Récamier, and loving her even more madly when he cannot obtain her, he begins to suffer from all that he is missing and even from the coldness of his wife, who is so unimportant. ("Without this wretched need for loving that Juliette has given me, I could console myself.")

"Vexation makes me crazy." "My heart wears itself out with all it has and regrets all it does not have. . . . If Juliette loved me, I would tire of her. . . . I love only in absence, with gratefulness and pity." The moment does not come when, less out of weariness than to restore the possibility of human relationships, he is going to try to break off, to substitute an absence for the presence that offends him. Then the ambiguity of tearings-apart and the contradiction that, each time he wants to distance himself, arises with the pain he causes to make the distancing impossible. We cannot say that this suffering is a pleasure to him; it is a suffering, but he experiences it only through others and in others, in the loss that it brings them and thereby, because of this mutilation, makes them present in a murkier way. He has told us his personal pains are almost nothing to him, while the pains of others weigh infinitely on him. He tells us again: "My affection has increased with the pain that I have caused her." Someone who suffers puts him in an inexpressibly feverish state. When Mme. de Staël loses her father whom she loved so much, the thought that he is going to see her in this extremity inspires feelings in him of an extraordinary violence: "There is in my situation something like waiting for an execution whose time is fixed." Even the pain of unimportant people exercises a fascinating power on his imagination. He speaks of a twenty-three-year-old woman who was hanged in England for counterfeiting. Caught in the act, dragged before the tribunal, this young woman does nothing to defend herself, she goes from swoon to swoon. Condemned and brought into prison, she remains in the same place, immobile, without taking any food. On the day of execution, she lets herself be carried without resisting and without seeming to see what is happening around her. At the last moment, when she feels the board giving way beneath her feet, at this final instant, uttering a great cry, she finally gives a sign of existence, the first and the last. Before this solitary suffering, despised by all who go by without seeing it, Constant is "gripped and frozen." And it is not only the profundity of this misery that touches him, the scene itself moves him; this young woman whose suffering is muteness, whose life is nothing but fainting, is for him the incarnation of this absence in which he finds the existence of the other, and of which he makes the place of his desires and the object of his impossible dream.

"For more than a year, I sighed after complete independence; it has come and I tremble. I am as if appalled with the solitude that surrounds me. I am frightened at not holding onto anything, I who have moaned so much to hold onto something." There he is alone: he no longer has anything; he no longer holds onto anything; under the form of his freedom, he enjoys the emptiness that he has sought and that he meets in himself. And yet this solitude frightens him, he "trembles" from it. What is he lacking, then? When, separated from others, he meets love that illuminates this separation, he can dream of reconquering it by conquering the one whom he loves. When, bound to another, he suffers from no longer communicating with another because he is no longer separated from her, he can again live this absence in the presence that is its obstacle, struggling to distance it. But if he wins that very absence, if it stops being a lack and becomes what he has, he has more than he can live, he falls into a state of satiety, he is more dead than alive; his illness can be expressed in this form: when he has nothing, he has too much.

Much more could be said. The main part of Constant's drama is that he lives, in its pure state, in the vivacity of a singular sensitivity, this paradox: we have relationships with another only if we are not confused with another. We communicate fully with someone only by possessing not what he is but what separates us from him, his absence rather than his presence, and, even better, the infinite movement to surpass and cause this absence to be reborn. It is clear that Constant associates with this emptiness that obsesses him all the states that can become its symbol. We know that the idea of death hardly left him. "I am all dust. Since we must end there, it is just as well to begin there." "I am not, will not be, cannot be happy. . . . At the end of it, nothingness." But even more remarkable is the strange need to begin his passions by making himself die, either seriously or through an uncertain comedy in which he honestly divides his chances. One could say that by seeking the real emptiness of death, he looks for a magic way to trap this emptiness, more difficult to grasp, that is the condition of all attachment and the object of all desire. Even faced with Mlle. Pourras, who is only a passing fancy while he plays out alone a romance in which he scarcely believes, he has to drink his little vial of opium. With Mme. de Staël, he sets himself to death, and we learn that Constant always had with him what he needed to kill himself, and to prevent himself from dying. Finally, when he meets Mme. Récamier, death is at each step.

We have noted that Constant's lucidity went hand in hand with his sensitivity, and that, far from harming them, his reflection gave strength to his passions. "His sensitivity increased by the reflection that diminishes it in others," said his cousin Rosalie. But that is because his lucidity expresses the same impulse as his desire. He judges and looks deeply because he remains at a distance from what he sees; he knows himself better than anyone else because what he feels is felt as the absence of what he would like to feel, thus this pure margin endlessly authorizes the neutrality of his gaze. So the extreme vivacity of his consciousness finds more resources than obstacles in his desire, if consciousness is so much more lively when it tends less to confuse itself with its object but separates itself from it, that is, if it seeks to know by the absence of what it knows, as desire wants to realize itself by the lack of what it desires.

It is an extraordinary adventure, because it is complete and because it illustrates the motives of human actions when they devote themselves to achieving their own possibility. We can discern their originality by comparing it with Proust's. Proust, too, comes near only to what he distances himself from. What he possesses is too much to him, what he knows is nothing to him. The reply to "My heart wears itself out with all it has and regrets all it does not have" is the remark in *The Captive*: "Every being who is loved, even a little, every being is for us like Janus, presenting a pleasing face to us if this being is leaving us, a sad face if we know he is at our constant disposition." If Proust loves Albertine only when she begins to go away, if, when she is there, he loves only the being in her who escapes him because she contains "so many days slipped away," a time forever unknown and forever lost, if he attaches himself so desperately to her each time he feels that she is living elsewhere, that she belongs to another life and other beings, it is indeed undoubtedly, under the most diverse forms, an absence that he seeks and that is the object of his love. A necessary absence, since he can enjoy reality only in imagination. ("My imagination, which was my only organ to enjoy beauty, could not apply itself to it [reality] by virtue of the inevitable law that wants us to be able to imagine only what is absent." Even more strongly, Constant says of Mme. Récamier: "In her absence, one remakes her for oneself to one's liking, and the obstacle, along with the material difficulty of seeing her, get one excited.") It is an absence that, representing as it does time that is irremediably lost, the time of a being whose past is doubly inaccessible, gives the most burning desire to find it again, finally an absence, always threatened, that measures the impossibility of making itself master of another and preventing it from belonging to another.

We are thus very close to Benjamin's sentiments. Proust, like Adolphe, experiences the paradox of all communication (a paradox that is also one of language), according to which what establishes relationships is their impossibility, while what unites beings is what separates them, and what makes them foreign to each other is what brings them closer together. Both men become weary of presence because it is only a contact, not an authentic relationship. Only (it seems), Proust does not desire this absence as the motive of all communication, in the way that Constant does: he does not desire it at all, but it is absence that makes someone desirable to him, while making him suffer from not being able to attain the person. Suffering and desire come in Proust from the part that is inaccessible to him, inalienable to everyone, that he finds in the one he loves; in Constant, suffering comes from finding too great access to the person, an access that makes everyone else inaccessible to him, comes, too, from the necessity to lose in one single person alone the possibility of communicating with everyone, and thus of communicating with even that one person. Proust desires in the Captive what he cannot capture, his freedom. Constant desires in a being the freedom of desiring in general. That is why in Proust love is suffering, he loves only in jealousy, and he suffers not because he has lost his freedom to love others besides Albertine, but because Albertine still remains free for others besides him. Constant, on the contrary, is hardly jealous. Adolphe is satisfied enough to see the friends with whom Ellénore surrounds herself and who threaten to detach her from him. If he suffers, it is because of what he has, rather than because of what is taken from him; and if he suffers, it is to give birth, at the moment of separation, by means of the suffering that breakup causes, to the reasons for not breaking up.

These differences are delicate. They are not essential. Proust loves because he suffers, and he suffers from feeling all the absence there is in a forever fleeing presence; but it is also because of this absence that this presence can found real relationships. Constant begins to love when a particular being appears, magnetizing the whole void that separates him from others, and whose possession is far from restoring to him the embodiment of the unknown. As soon as this too-demanding involvement exhausts the possibility of his relationships with all, which he wanted to experience with one single person, he is stifled, he succumbs. He needs to be free, but he is always tied down. This is so because his freedom is not for himself, it is the freedom of belonging to others. Without succeeding in breaking off with Mme. de Staël, he secretly marries Charlotte, with whom he is no doubt in love, whom he found again with surprise, with delight, twelve years after a first affair, but of whom he writes on the day after their delicious reunion: "Evening with Charlotte. Will the fever pass, and will boredom begin again? I am hellishly afraid of it." The secret marriage with Charlotte represents an attempt at restoring, by means of the ambiguity of a double presence, the absence that alone makes him master of his affairs with everyone. Finally, if he considers grave and culpable the suffering of which he is the cause, it is because this suffering marks in another person the same mutilation that the loss of his freedom represents for him. A being whom he causes to suffer is one with whom he unites himself by destroying. Hence the tangled and equivocal nature of his feelings after each appalling scene: when he sees Mme. de Staël at his feet, twisting and screaming with pain, he feels strongly how much he has acquired rights over her, and this excess of power is the sign of the excessive connections that unite them, of the distance that has been erased between them, of their double lost freedom, and he develops as much shame as disgust at it. At the same time, this suffering he inflicts is a way of diminishing the other, of destroying him, of sending him back beyond himself. And he feels a lightening of spirits from it, and perhaps a renewal of desire, so much so that after each mention of "frightful scene, convulsive night," he must also write, "Everything is reversed, a magical power dominates me, attachment takes hold again," for the tearings-apart that are the sign of their mutual destroyed freedom are also like the cloudy dawn of a newly glimpsed freedom.

Two characteristics are striking in this Proust-Constant community. With both, lucidity accompanies the violence of feelings: their way of coming near others to love them is their very way of coming near them to know them well. Moreover, it is remarkable that the symbolic images Proust uses to describe Albertine's love are just as sketched out in Constant. It is when Albertine is asleep that Proust's strange love for her arises: her absence is as if present, sleep realizes the unknown that is in her without dissipating it, it hands over this stranger who cannot be surprised, this freedom that cannot be confined; the young woman is finally completely herself, and all that she is, is revealed, avowed, and given. "Her self did not keep escaping all the time, as when we chatted, through the exits of unavowed thought, or through her gaze. She had called back to her all that used to be outside of her; she had taken refuge, enclosed, resumed in her body. Holding her in my gaze, in my hands, I had this impression of possessing her entirely that I did not have when she was awake. . . . My jealousy calmed, for I felt Albertine had become a being who breathes, who is not something else, as this regular breath signified by which this pure physiological function expresses itself, that, completely fluid, has neither thickness nor speech nor silence; and in her ignorance of all evil her breath, drawn rather from a hollowed-out reed than from a human being, was truly paradisiacal, was the pure song of angels for me who, in those moments, felt Albertine removed from everything, not only materially but morally."

Proust indicates in a famous passage that the true meaning of a novel is found in images and sentence types that reveal its haunting secret. Albertine's sleeping is one of these images. And one of these same images, the young Englishwoman of whom Constant spoke to us with so much agitation, this living-dead woman who progresses by swoon to swoon from mistake to death. And another of these images, the sleep to which he compares the attachment of certain women in his *Diary*, a comparison that, by a strange coincidence, Julie Talma takes up to define "the eternal loves" of Constant that he enters the way some men enter sleep. This metaphor cannot be without importance. If sleep shows us Albertine's life removed from everything and made perceptible in this universal distancing, it is because it represents to us not so much beings as their place between parentheses, their suspended relationships, incarnated in their pure state, the profound drowsiness that only awakening makes known to desire.

Adolphe is a calm, discreet novel, says Albert Thibaudet. Discreet, yes, calm, perhaps, if calmness is what hides violence and conceals beneath its surface the most considerable tragedy. We see clearly, now, that the work's interest is not found in the single naturalness of the passions, nor in the subtlety and strength of analysis. Feelings and analysis are here nothing but a way of lighting up a fatal path, one of the thousands of detours that must make us perceive the circle of human relationships whose outcome, whatever the route followed, is universal misfortune. There is no mistaking it, and Constant writes: "Some people have asked me what Adolphe should have done to experience less pain and cause less pain. His position and Ellénore's were without resources, and that is precisely what I wanted. I showed him tormented because he loved Ellénore only weakly; but he would not have been less tormented if he had loved her more. He suffered because of her, because of a lack of feeling: with a more passionate feeling, he would have suffered for her. . . . When one has entered on this path, one has only a choice of evils." Could this warning be clearer? So let us stop seeing in *Adolphe* the tragedy of a particular feeling, of a particular nature, since it is a drama inherent in our condition, wherein all feeling and all personalities whatsoever are doomed to the same fate.

This drama comes from the madness in the sphere of human relationships when those who live them choose to live them by testing their potential, that is to say, their truth. One who chooses to seize again in the other the impulse that carries him toward the other will only be able to repeat with melancholy Benjamin's own conclusion: "With true feelings, I made nothing but misfortune for myself and others"; for it is truth that makes this misfortune, just as it is lucidity that precipitates it. Once the point of departure is established, once the need has been accepted as necessary to get in touch with the impulse in the other by which one contacts the other and to live that impulse, and, living it, preserve, save the possibility of this impulse, then neither the strength of feelings, nor the nobility of one's character, nor the strangeness of circumstances will change anything in it. If Adolphe had loved Ellénore more, he would have experienced even more acutely the need to break off with her, for her passion would have contradicted even more the truth of his passion; but he would also have been all the more strongly prevented from breaking off, and more incapable of bearing the suffering that this rupture could not help but entrain. As for

Ellénore, less attached to Adolphe, she would have consented to set him free only to the extent that he would have refused this freedom, would have suffered from it, and, through his suffering, would have obliged him to take her back. What is more, this very movement is that of the book, since this peripeteia marks its last episode. When Ellénore is dead, by an ironic revelation the letter is divulged in which she finally consents to separation: "Through what bizarre pity do you not dare break a tie that burdens you, and destroy the unfortunate being at whose side your pity keeps you? Why do you deny yourself the gloomy pleasure of at least believing yourself generous? Why do you show yourself furious and weak? The idea of my pain follows you, and the spectacle of this pain cannot stop you. What is it that you want?" Thus at the death that has untied the ties and has just given him the freedom of feelings that he is no longer capable of experiencing, Adolphe receives, from the same woman who always held him back, and as a last reproach, the permission to make himself free. The permission comes too late, but it could only come too late, and seems now to be given only to corrupt the enjoyment of a freedom that now burdens him more than all his connections.

On almost every page in *Adolphe* we find the description of feelings whose causes keep vainly switching back and forth; everything sends them back to themselves, everything confirms their inescapability. That is because the point is reached in which the diversity of events and the whole infiniteness of the world tirelessly repeat the circular movement in which the heart that is greedy for the truth is enclosed. When Adolphe writes, "When she appeared, I was grieved by doubting a love that was so necessary to her; I did not grieve any less when she seemed to believe in it," or again, "When Ellénore found me somber or depressed, she grieved first, wounded herself afterward, and tore from me by her reproaches the avowal of the fatigue that I would have preferred to conceal; on my side, when Ellénore seemed content, I was irritated at seeing her enjoy a situation that cost me my happiness, and I vexed her in her short enjoyment by insinuations that enlightened her about what I was feeling inside," we feel that the balance of clauses, their symmetrical opposition, only translate into form the demand of a situation in which one goes from one extreme to its opposite without change and without rest. All the book's rigor comes from the inescapability of this movement. All its tragic power comes from this repetition, which does not stop making the feelings it exasperates ever more violent, or, owing to this violence, making the return of these feelings ever more inescapable. The repetition thus makes monotony the principle of an extraordinary march toward catastrophe.

Constant, in his *Dairy*, on the subject of suffering, observed how passions become destiny. If one betakes oneself to pain, one must suffer it in order to distract oneself from it. If you flee it, you suffer even more (for it always reaches you) from the weakness of having fled it. "Pain is a snake that glides through all barriers and always finds you. The very action of fleeing gives you a feeling of weakness that makes you more incapable of mastering it when it reaches you." It has often been thought of as an irony due to chance that the two symmetrical adventures of his life should have shown him, in the first one, incapable of loving and, in the second, powerless to make himself loved. But the symmetry is even more profound, and it is not the work of capricious fortune. He did not love Mme. de Staël less than he had Mme. Récamier: letters, his conduct, his madness, everything demonstrates it. But once he had chosen true feelings, he could only choose the inextricable, and his two great passions exposed him to the same disaster, by putting him in the presence of the two opposite sides of his sentimental destiny. He loves and we love him strongly; that is the first good luck. But the one whom he chose to love, who is neither intolerant nor exclusive ("Many people must love me," she said; "as soon as there are two of us, there must be many more"), and who consequently offers him the rare chance of freedom, has as her main trait a "quasi sacred" (Charles du Bos) horror of separation—she cannot bear the idea, she needs pacts and engagements, the very things most likely to exhaust the feelings that she wants to bind. And Benjamin gets caught up with exhilaration, because he himself always hopes to find in marriage or an enactment of marriage the means of holding back a passion that presence causes to flee. But as soon as he is involved, passion becomes impossible, and what remains of it in him pushes him to break off precisely with the single person for whom breaking off is worse than death. What more can he attempt? To love in freedom, to love without the servitude of a shared love? So he meets Mme. Récamier, he meets the person who has the greatest impuissance of feeling, the most extreme naiveté of indifference and coldness toward him and toward everyone, the one who, according to Sainte-Beuve, would like everything to stop in April. Truly she is the one who is best made to goad passion to dementia, to make him madly desire all the satisfactions of summer, and to drag him along to lose himself in pacts and slavery.

Such is the rigor of the code. Assuredly, situations sometimes get untangled, but this resolution is only appearance. Although Constant can indeed leave Mme. de Staël and can resign himself to the shallowness of Mme. Récamier, whatever truth there is in his feelings returns endlessly to the first one ("Mme. de Staël is quite lost to me. I will not recover from her") and burns forever in the coldness of the second. Thus, this indifferent man, model of the ennui'd heart, finds, to express the meaning of his life, the very words that Nietzsche's burning solitude will meet half a century later:

> Ungesättigt gleich der Flamme
> Glühe und verzehr' ich mich.
> Licht wird alles, was ich fasse,
> Kohle alles, was ich lasse,
> Flamme bin ich sicherlich!

> Unsated as the flame
> I burn in order to be consumed.
> Light is what I touch,
> Ash all that I leave:
> Assuredly, I am flame.

And Constant to Juliette Récamier: "I am destined to illuminate you by burning myself up."

§ Gazes from Beyond
the Grave

Michel Leiris prefaces the new edition of *The Age of Man* with an essay that makes the most accurate commentary on it and makes all the others useless. In this essay, entitled "On Literature as Bull-fighting," he clarifies completely the intentions to which we owe this book, one of the central works of so-called "modern" literature. What did he want in wanting to write it? First, to escape the gratuitousness of literary works and to accomplish a real deed, threatening for its author and capable of implying the same danger for him that "the bull's sharp horn" represents in other sports. Further, to achieve a work that could enlighten him about himself and enlighten others about him, and at the same time deliver him from certain obsessions and allow him to attain a veritable "vital fullness." Finally, to write a book that would be dangerous both for his other books and for literature in general, by revealing "inside information," by making us see "in all their unexciting nakedness the realities that formed the framework more or less disguised in brilliant exteriors" of his other written works.

All these intentions answer to problems from which literature is not remote. Writing is nothing if it does not involve the writer in a movement full of risks that will change him in one way or another. Writing is only a worthless game if this game does not become an adventurous experience, in which the one who pursues it, involving himself in a path whose outcome escapes him, can learn what he does not know and lose what prevents him from knowing. Then write by all means, but only if writing always makes the act of writing more effortful, if it tends to take away from him the facility that words do not stop receiving from the most skillful hands.

The Age of Man is not an autobiography or simple confessions; it is even less a matter of memoirs. Autobiography is the work of a living, vital memory that wants to, and can, grasp time again in its very movement. Autobiography, outside of its content, depends on its rhythm, its pouring forth, which is not here synonymous with confidence but evokes the power of the stream, the truth of something that flows, stretches out, and assumes form only in the flux. *Henri Brulard, Memoirs of an Egotist*, sometimes De Quincey and the second part of *If It Die* are examples of this history that is discovered, not a history that is already made and congealed, but an existence turned toward the future and that, at the moment it is told, seems always in the process of happening, unknown to the very one who is telling it in the past. As for memoirs, we know what they are: deliberate, methodical reconstitutions, works of reflection, sometimes of art and science. Existence here (even if it is a question of a private existence) is history because it is historic. It is presented as having always been, with that dignity and solemnity that it owes to the monumental presence of a past over which the author himself no longer has any right. The *Memoirs from Beyond the Grave* have this exemplary virtue: they rise up from the grave, says Maurice Levaillant, and Chateaubriand, with this incomparable sense of the past, confirms it in words at which we dare not smile: "I have been urged to let some excerpts of these *Memoirs* appear during my lifetime; I prefer to speak from the bottom of my coffin; my narration will always then be accompanied by those voices that have something sacred about them, since they come out of the sepulcher." But, to tell the truth, in these *Memoirs*, it is not death that speaks, but existence as if dead, as if an existence that has always been, always past, immobilized in a life that is dauntingly alien to any future, even to the future of death.

The Age of Man comes close to confessions. As in confessions, its author wants to "expose himself . . . publicly confess certain deficiencies or weaknesses that make him the most ashamed." The purpose of confessions is to make public what is only private, and to do so with a moral, or at least practical, intention. One confesses, first of all, to place what is hidden into the light of day, then to make the day judge these hidden depths, and finally to disburden oneself of this secret life onto the day. Michel Leiris told us in his preface: "By means of an autobiography having to do with a domain for which, ordinarily, reserve is required . . . I thought to rid myself of certain tiresome representations at the same time as setting free my characteristics with a maximum of purity, as much for my own use as to dissipate any erroneous view of me that might take hold of another." And he then speaks of *catharsis*, deliverance, of a discipline coming to complete the first results of a psychoanalytic cure. Perhaps this is a somewhat obscure intention of the book. One might say that this intention contradicts all the others, that if the author writes to free himself of dangerous obsessions, this "good" that he expects from his book greatly diminishes its menacing nature. That by dint of sincerity he thinks he can be cured of "certain deficiencies and weaknesses," yet could even, at the same time, experience all the dangers this sincerity holds for him, by making the relationships with some of those close to him more problematic for him, but that finally will be only a wrong for the sake of a right, a momentary inconvenience that he accepts to get rid of much more serious disadvantages, an effort risked to live ever after sheltered from the risks that obsessions and deficiencies represent.

We could note again that confession implies a strange entanglement of motives and results. It is certainly not easy to confess one is cowardly. Yet precisely that cannot happen without courage, and the witness to the confession risks perceiving behind the defect the courageous firmness that confesses it, and he will see it even better when the avowal is frank, harsh, accurate. And if the one who confesses his defects counts on this avowal to deliver himself from them, if, confessing himself deficient, he finds, after this confession, that he is the most courageous of men, we see how the procedure is revealed as a winning strategy, one suitable for rewarding the one who attempted it for its risks.

The author of *The Age of Man* not only does not ignore these difficulties but he denounces them, or at least he denounces others that are their equivalents. First of all, that the danger to which one exposes oneself by writing is rarely mortal. The bull's horn that threatens the writer is only a shadow of a horn. The scandal can be great, but literature is that sword that cures the one it wounds: the aesthetic value of scandal, its beauty, soon transform it, and the book for which one has risked scorn brings in the end admiration and fame. So trickery is the point of departure of any literary undertaking like tragedy. But there is something more serious: "What I misunderstood is that at the bottom of any introspection is the taste for contemplating oneself, and that at the root of any confession is the desire to be absolved." In truth, this taste and this pleasure are the only immediate "benefits" that confession has in store for whoever abandons himself to it; the other advantages that we have pointed out remain very ambiguous: to portray oneself as one is, that is, as more mediocre than one would like to appear and than as others see you; this avowal promises us in vain important consolations later on, at the moment it is made, only the annoyance and difficulty of making it count; whoever confesses his defect perceives the defect he confesses and not the courage of his confession, and the book in which this confession is written is still only a stuttering outline that is completely unaware of its coming destiny as a successful, praised, and admired book. So the confession is indeed a risk; a remedy, too, but perhaps an illusory one that, far from making obscure things disappear, will make them more obscure, more haunting, and will precipitate the failure that it was supposed to prevent.

"To look at myself with complacency was still to look at myself, to keep my eyes fixed on myself instead of directing them beyond, to pass over me toward something more broadly human." On this level, confession is in fact secretly undermined by the satisfactions it brings. Some people draw pride from their humiliations and pleasure from their humiliating confessions—that is sometimes the case with Rousseau. But the pleasure can be of a more subtle and formidable kind. Thus we take satisfaction in looking at ourselves without satisfaction, we find a confused sensual delight in putting everything out into the open, and rigor becomes weakness. The more sincere we are, the more sincerity satisfies the duplicity at the heart's core. The more exacting we are with ourselves, the more this exactness will be a source of dangerous divergences. There is a sin in confession that no confession can atone for, since it is committed by being avowed and is aggravated as soon as it is absolved: the offense here is linked to justification, innocence. Yet wanting this innocence is necessary, we cannot do without it, so that everything is an offense, both the avowal and refusal of the avowal. Such is pretty much the category of the demonic of which Kierkegaard spoke.

Leiris chose the sin of confession, and this sin is probably a *felix culpa* since to it we owe a book that is a classic from now on. But it must again be noted that satisfaction is here the opposite of satisfaction, that it not only signifies an excessive inclination to speak but has its origin in the refusal to speak, in an "I cannot speak" that by its excesses ends up opening the mouth. "All my friends know it: I am a specialist, a maniac for confession; yet what pushes me—especially with women—to confide is timidity. When I am alone with a being whom sex suffices to make so different from me, my feelings of isolation and misery become such that, despairing of finding anything to say to my interlocutor that could be the basis for a conversation, incapable, too, of courting her if I happen to desire her, I begin, for lack of another subject, to talk about myself; as my sentences flow on, the tension mounts, and eventually I begin to institute a surprising current of drama between my interlocutor and me, for, the more my present situation distresses me, the more I speak of myself in an anguished way, relying for a long time on this sensation of solitude, of separation from the outer world, and ending by not knowing if this tragedy described by me corresponds to the permanent reality of what I am, or is only an imagistic expression of this momentary anguish that I undergo as soon as I enter into contact with a human being and am placed, in some way, in the position of speaking."

We see how the most profound speech is born from the vertigo that rises from the impossibility of speaking, and we also see that the motive and single theme of this speech is its own impossibility: it is spoken as if it were not speaking, and, because of that, it is limitless, nothing can interrupt it since it has no contents to exhaust—nothing, if it is only at a certain moment that it discovers itself speaking, speaking endlessly and thus, aware of its trickery, sends itself back to silence, in shame and hatred of this vain speech. From oral secrets to the book, the distance is great. To speak, the author here deliberately, and with a concern for mastery, willed a severity of examination that does not authorize the excess of an unreined language. In speaking, however, its aim is still to give speech to what does not speak in him, to violate the silence of that which wants to be quiet. *The Age of Man* is exactly this moment of maturity in which the reign of silent intimacy, of muteness in oneself and about oneself that belongs to childhood and adolescence, is brutally brought to an end by a demanding, analytic, and denunciatory speech. For the complacency of silence that is the offense of the first three months, an offense of innocence that wants to say nothing and has nothing to say, manhood substitutes the complacency of language, the offense that wants to be recognized as an offense and thus find innocence again, the innocence of the offense.

Michel Leiris's book is no sort of vertigo, it refuses the spontaneity of open-mouthed secrets whose depth is revealed with the incoercible strength of moods clearing a path to the outside. To write this life "seen from the angle of eroticism," he tells us, he imposed rules on himself. He did not trust himself to the surge of memories or to simple chronological order. Like any author of an autobiography, he wants to take hold of life again, "to gather it into one single solid block," but he does it by means of an ordering vision, a preliminary clairvoyance that arranges this existence according to the profound themes that it has perceived within it. These strict rules, this discipline that he observes both in self-expression and in self-interpretation, are what seem to assure the greatest chance of truth in his undertaking, and also to make it most like bullfights, where the combat compels a danger risen from instinct to take the form of a ceremony in which nothing can be changed. The paradox of these confessions, if it is one, comes then from this: the author feels them dangerous to him, not because of their liberties and their turbulent movements but because of the severity of the rules that he imposes on himself in order to write them, and because of the lucid objectivity that he wants to attain by writing them. And this other paradox follows: that the tone of these confidences is almost always reserved, reticent, and yet this reserve and this reticence, far from diminishing the frankness that seems as great as possible, on the contrary guarantee it and give it the nature of necessity. Frankness that says everything says only itself, and it says it perhaps by accident. But frankness that holds itself in reserve to say everything also says the reserve from which it speaks, that forces it to speak, makes a duty of it by forbidding it all denial, all retraction, and all excuse. The "objective" tone of *The Age of Man*, the vigilant, sometimes almost formal coldness that emerges in it are promoted by the underground "I do not want to speak," and are like the echo of timidity that he told of, of this fundamental reticence that first prevents, then deranges, all communication. But here the dizziness has become lucidity, and the anguish is cold-bloodedness.

The Age of Man is an attempt at interpreting oneself, in which all the detail of tastes, the chance of one's actions, all the anecdotal dust of life, generally thought to be insignificant, are related to themes around which the profound meaning of existence is organized. It is quite a different attempt from that of an ordinary autobiography, and all the more meaningful in that it escapes the trap of causal explanations and systematic views, such as that of psychoanalysis or even of interpretation, of understanding at any price. In it are rare measure and mastery: a concern to see oneself in a way that does not change what is seen, an ability to understand oneself that makes order out of impulses not easily understood, a tragic feeling of the human condition glimpsed through its own difficulties, without being either exalted or lowered by it. In his little book entitled *The Confession*, Arthur Adamov also attempted a confession whose pathos and sincerity do not conflict with each other, and he tried as well to link obsessions that are his to the situation of the world in general, as it is today. But he could not fully pursue either of his aims that endlessly interrupt and are confused with each other. The very pathos of his story obliges him to keep to the single pathos which he cannot master and of which he gives us only brief images; and the feeling that his pain is also the world's pain places in his hand the oversimplified possibilities of explanation and justification that turn him away from himself and from the rigorous, demanding scrutiny without which "confession" perhaps remains a temptation.

The very "form" of *The Age of Man*, the stiffness of expression, the ordered constraint that allows unleashing, the reticence that is frankness, all these characteristics are not simple writing procedures but are part of the existence that they help to bring into the open. Leiris explains to us that, starting when he was fifteen, he sought in his dress as well as in his manners "the English look . . . the sober, correct style—or rather a little stiff and funereal." And he adds, "That corresponded to a symbolic attempt at *mineralization*, a defensive reaction against my internal weakness and the disintegration I felt threatened with; I would have liked to make myself a kind of breastplate, producing the same ideal of *stiffness* in my exterior that I pursued poetically." However, this "icy coldness," this affectation of impassiveness, this plaster-cast mask were themselves chosen only through the most profound care and urgency. The "coldness" and the face of stone are used as a means of defense, but that is because "coldness" is also desired for itself, and moves of the liveliest sensitivity are associated with dreams of marble. In *Aurora*, a literary work seemingly entirely gratuitous, with no other purpose than the work of words, but in which one finds, embedded among the images and symbols, all the themes whose vital significance *The Age of Man* shows us, one of the characters declares, "I must say that from time immemorial life has been confused for me with that which is soft, warm and measureless. Loving only the intangible, that which is outside of life, I identified arbitrarily all that is hard, cold, or even geometric with this invariant." And this Damoclès Siriel says later, "Night and day death hung over me like a dismal threat. Perhaps I forced myself to think that I could elude it by this minerality that would constitute an armor for me, and also a hiding place (like the kind insects make of their own body when they feign death to resist danger) against its moving but unerring attacks. Fearing death, I hated life (since death is the surest crowning of it)."

We do not want to go into the movement of themes, into this intermingling that joins what is torn apart and what is loved, what wounds and what reassures, what one loves as an image of death and what one loves as a chance of not dying. All that is part of the book. But we would like to show how far the ambiguity of the motives deepens their meaning. Damoclès Siriel talks to us of the threat of death that hangs over him night and day. This threat hangs constantly over *The Age of Man*, too. But it is not some vague threat, ignorant of what it represents and foreign to that nature. One of the most important passages of the book seems to us to be this one: "I cannot rightly say that *I die*, since—dying a violent death or not—I am only partly present at the event. And a great part of the dread I feel at the idea of death is due perhaps to this: bewilderment of remaining suspended right in the midst of a crisis whose outcome my disappearance will prevent me, for the great forever, from knowing. This kind of irreality, of *absurdity* of death is . . . its radically terrible element." We see by these utterly clear words that the fear of death is also the fear of not being able to die. The fact that we cannot experience the reality of death to the end makes death unreal, and this irreality condemns us to fear dying only unreally, not really to die, to remain as if we are held, forever, between life and death, in a state of non-existence and non-death, from which our whole life perhaps takes its meaning and its reality. We do not know that we die. We do not know either that others die, for the death of another remains foreign to us and always incomplete, since we who know it, we are alive. We certainly do not think of ourselves as immortal, but we see ourselves, rather, as condemned, in death itself, to the impossibility of dying, to the impossibility of accomplishing, grasping the fact of our death by abandoning ourselves to it in a determined and decisive way.

Such a vertigo between living and dying explains, according to Michel Leiris, that in life, a loss of self, which is an enactment of death, can sometimes reassure us against death and help us face it. "If we think of love as a means of escaping death—of denying it or, practically, forgetting it—it is perhaps because obscurely we feel that it is the only way that we have to make so much or so little of our experience, for, in mating, we know at least what happens *after*, and can be the witness—and a bitter one—to the ensuing disaster." But what is at stake is not "the need to know," and as to what happens *after*, we only indirectly have the desire to know: we want to be certain of death as completed, as a real and true totality, and that is why *after* interests us, because "after death" would be the proof that death is, if not gone beyond, at least really and truly past, finished. We do not want something beyond death for its own sake, but craftily, we desire to be able to see ourselves dead, to assure ourselves of our death by directing a veritable gaze from beyond the grave toward our nothingness, from a point situated beyond death. According to Michel Leiris and traditional myths, love is death lived in advance and known to the end, so love is always afraid of the next day, its future, because it fears becoming its own awakening, the profoundly miserable moment in which it finds itself not ended but, in this very ending, finds it is unfinished, having never been, only the vain and interminable duration of what, after all, it never was. And that is why love sometimes calls on death to complete it, as if death, itself unfinished and always incomplete when it is the death of a man alone, could truly be completed by becoming the single death of two beings already dead to themselves, so that "love stronger than death" would have this mythic meaning: love triumphs over death by putting an end to death, by making a real end of it.

"For a long time, I have conferred upon whatever is *ancient* a frankly voluptuous nature. Structures draw me by their icy temperature and their rigidity. I sometimes imagine myself stretched out on flagstones (whose coldness I feel on my skin) or standing against a column to which my torso is stuck." And in *Aurora*, where Damoclès Siriel makes love with alabaster figures with bare skulls like stones, we read: "Love for me was always linked to this idea of hardness; my teeth, cold loose stones in my mouth, seeming to me from that time on the organ that, more than all the others, was destined to love." Thus we understand that "coldness" is not a simple defense mechanism to preserve a threatened intimacy from another person and from death, but that it is also what opens this intimacy to another, because the coldness of marble and the intangibility of stone are privileged images by which death and the other are confused, and by which, too, death is anticipated in order to impose itself from this world onto the monumental plenitude withdrawn from the disintegration of time. The subterfuges of sensibility, we see, are infinite. What is shown to us as an attempt to outwit death is already the presence of death, and introduces it into the heart of the being, causes it to love and desire, and entertains fear of it only to make it better recognized as a full, substantial form that makes it remote from the incompleteness of life and the irreality of "I am dying."

In *Aurora*, we read these sentences: "It is always more difficult for me than for someone else to express myself in any way other than with the pronoun *I*; this is not some particular sign of my pride, but because the word *I* sums up for me the structure of the world." But a little further on, we read: "Here I am at the Death Cathedral, at this third-person singular that just now I crossed out with a stroke of the pen, death, grammatical pitchfork that subjugates the world and myself to its ineluctable syntax, rule that makes all discourse only a paltry mirage covering the nothingness of objects, no matter what words I utter and no matter what *I* I put forward." *Aurora* is the tale of metamorphoses by which the *I* is changed into *He* and the *He* tries in vain, by transformations that are more and more extenuating, to fall below *That* to attain a true nothing. But *The Age of Man* has already shown us how at the bottom of the *I* and joining endlessly with it, in the very fear that it inspires and the anguish it causes to be born, the *He* of death offers itself with its eternity of marble and its cold impassivity. In the collection of dreams entitled *Nights Without Nights*, the following dream is told, under the date 12–14 July 1940: "Awoke (with a cry that Z . . . prevents me from uttering), having dreamed this: I place my head, as if to look around, into an orifice somewhat like a bulls-eye window giving onto a closed, somber place that resembles a cylindrical clay-plastered garret. . . . My anguish is due to the fact that, bending over the cramped space that I surprise in its inner darkness, it is myself that I am looking into." *The Age of Man* is this lucid gaze by which the *I*, penetrating this "inner darkness," discovers that what is looking in it is no longer the *I*, "structure of the world," but already the monumental, gazeless, faceless, nameless statue: the *He* of Sovereign Death.

§ Pascal's Hand

In his beautiful essay on Pascal, Marcel Arland wonders what gives the *Apology* such a powerful, heartrending resonance. It is because "the man of the *Pensées* is always present to our eyes." "Pascal, uneasy, burning, greedy for the absolute. . . ." "We are in the cell where Pascal is looking at the crucifix, prays, suffers, draws a line, throws an accusation at human nature, with the same passion with which he drives the nails of a belt into his back. Is it night? The sound of drops of blood that fall from the cross prevent him from sleeping. Jesus is in agony until the end of the world. We can see nothing but this cross, we hear nothing but this blood and these sighs." Pathetic expression of the pathos characteristic of Pascal, that of a man who impassions us, since he himself is passion.

Albert Béguin, however, in a study entitled *Pascal's Quietude*, shows that the *Pensées* are indeed supposed to move us, but that this disturbance is prepared, methodically provoked by a mind that is master of itself, a thoroughly assured soul, firm and commanding. Joubart had already written, as Béguin quotes: "Behind Pascal's thought, we see the attitude of a firm mind, free from passion. It is that more than anything that makes him very important."

This is not a paradox. Need we recall that the *Pensées* are the debris of a methodical discourse and the moments of a demonstration, that Pascal's aim is to lead an indifferent reader away from indifference toward a concern for religious things, to take repose away from him so that, out of anxiety, he can be led from the false assurance of knowledge and the vain tranquillity of mind to the real certainty of faith? The *Pensées* are only groanings, calls, threats, prayers, Arland tells us. But the man to whom they are addressed does not know torments, for he is satisfied with his reason if he is an intellectual, and satisfied with worldly life if he is a libertine. And the man who writes does not know them either, for if he has been "dulled," he is now awake, and to feel anxiety, fear before the empty universe would represent in him only a lingering impiety and a forgetfulness of God's presence.

"The *Pensées*," says Béguin, "are by no means composed to answer a fear, as we too often imagine, but rather to disturb a peace that is dangerous to the soul. . . . Above all, Pascal will devote himself to reviving new fears in his interlocutor by showing him that, if one holds on to the claims of intelligence, everything is absurd, incomprehensible, grotesque, or rather that everything is terrifying, heavy with menace. 'I will not suffer him to rest.' It is at this precise moment that he composes, with all the care of a writer weighing his words and calculating the effect of his rhythms, the famous *Pensées* through which the shiver of anguish passes: eternal silence, realms that are unaware of us, the last bleeding act, we run into a chasm. . . . These are in no way, as it seems so often to be acknowledged, notes made in a personal diary, still palpitating with the memory of frightened instants. They are for the use of other people, they are calls to order that are to be meticulously placed in conversation at the precise second most favorable to disturb false certainties. A fine fight is begun, in which Pascal, who has exercised his weapons in the fencing of the *Provincial Letters*, handles his feints and his points."

So it follows that the anguish and trembling that make of the *Pensées* a book that is almost not a book, these cries, these terrors, these terrible images are the work of a writer who is neither frightened nor lost nor stammering but, on the contrary, admirably reflective and capable of language, perfectly aware of the words that are best suited to produce feelings that he wants to provoke, a man

who has meditated on these words, on their order, who chose them
deliberately for their effects and knows how to overwhelm others
because he is supremely master of himself. Pascal's anguish is the
result of a calculation. The calculation was accurate: his anguish
has tormented centuries.

That is not a paradox. Yet this view that is so probable, so
reasonable, so in tune with the spirit of the time and the spirit of
Pascal, whose imperious nature is the most visible of all, collides in
us with a reticence that does not give way. Is it the persistence of the
romantic image, the authority of a tradition? Surely it comes from
something quite different: it seems that we feel we are deceived if a
book moves us that wants to move us; our feelings seem to us to
lose all truth if the words that arouse them were chosen with these
feelings in mind and not under their constraint, to make them be
felt, not starting from feeling them. For the language of the *Pensées*
to be read as the language of uneasiness and anxiety, the *Pensées*
must be born from an anxious heart that anxiety alone has caused
to speak.

That is, to a certain extent, a surprising demand, yet an all-
powerful one even in those who challenge it. We have recalled
many times the judgments of Valéry on Pascal, whom he reproaches for being too perfectly despairing and for expressing this
despair too perfectly. Strange reproaches, and incomprehensible,
coming from Valéry; moreover, they are contradictory. For if Pascal
is indeed that writer who makes use of "his great resources," his
"powers of logic," the "admirable virtues of his language" to give
men the feeling of an absolute distress, to frighten them with a
nothingness in which neither logic, nor language, nor resources of
any kind support them, if only Pascal's art is responsible for such an
effect, the greatest, the most constant that our literature has produced, it is almost inconceivable that Valéry did not make a hero of
him to set beside Poe, Mallarmé, and Leonardo. He reproaches him
for the freedom of his mind, his art, his industry, the sureness of his
hand—that is to say, everything that makes the author of *The
Raven*, the author of *A Throw of Dice*, and perhaps the author of

The Young Fate* seem admirable to him. Pascal is the writer who from lucidity drew bewilderment, who made use of a language perfectly governed and controlled to make men feel their condition as random and aimless beings, who knew how to make them despair as he wished, knew how to frighten them, abase them, then raise them above themselves, who opened an abyss beneath their feet and made from this abyss a throne for their glory—and all using only the resources of an art we all know is capable of everything, and first of all of making itself absent, so that everyone forgets it and yields to the movement that impels it, without ever recognizing its nature.

Pascal is the model that Valéry should have held as exemplary. And yet he holds against him the hand that guides him, that he sees, that he is alone in seeing, as if for this Pascal, Valéry would have preferred unawareness and blindness. And, after having begrudged him his mastery, he shames him for his servility of a hunted man—and, thus, reproaching sometimes his shipwreck, sometimes his inability to founder, sometimes the baseness of his cries, sometimes their too-pure harmony, he himself is carried along in all the contradictions into which his author knew how to divide men so as to make them regret more acutely their lost unity.

Valéry's attitude is instructive. It teaches us that in art, effects seek to return to their causes, and demand to form only totality with them, a single world with two poles. Valéry, opening the book of the *Pensées*, is not unaware of their demonstrative purposes. He knows that they must disturb, cause despair, in order to give souls the feeling of their emptiness, and through that lack teach them to know fullness. This aim, which also shocks him, assures him thus that Pascal does not write to express himself or to confess, but to convince, that this groaning, shivering book is thus one whose groans are planned and whose emotion is calculated. Yet Valéry, who claims to reduce all art to a calculation and all poetry to a long reflection on its means, here sees only lies and impropriety in this thought-out use of art to persuade. And even more: he cannot

* Valéry himself.—TRANS.

believe that the writer can be safe from the anguish he deliberately intends to arouse. Pascal must have trembled before the emptiness of the sky, because he wanted to make us tremble before the empty sky, even if for Pascal the heavens are full of God and do not stop speaking of his glory.

Does the form of the *Pensées* lend itself to such a confusion? Does an author who writes, "The eternal silence of these infinite spaces terrifies me," place himself side by side with those to whom he communicates this fear? Perhaps. But, without even seeing in this form a fiction of art meant to please, everything suggests that this *I* is the impersonal *I*, the same one that discusses itself in the most abstract way—"Why is my knowledge limited? my size? my life span one hundred years instead of a thousand?"—and whose fear and surprise immediately enter into the most general reasoning, in a discourse whose pathos relies visibly on eloquence: "When I consider the short length of my life, absorbed into the preceding and following eternity, the little space that I fill, or even that I see, sunk in the infinite immensity of spaces that I am unaware of and that are unaware of me, I am frightened and surprised at seeing myself here rather than there, for there is no reason whatsoever why." Who does not feel all the authority of this fear and the powerful voice of this surprise, whose entire reason for being is to assert itself in conjunction with its consequences, and to aspire to some conclusion? We can certainly be moved by the austerity summoned by a thought of this order: "It is unjust that people become attached to me, even though they do it voluntarily and with pleasure. I would be deceiving those in whom I might cause desire to be born." But let us read further. This pathetic refusal of a soul that does not accept feelings, neither those that come to it nor those that come from it, is only the beginning of a formal argument that ends with "Thus" and in which confession is changed into an abstract instance of a completely general proof.

There is in the *Pensées* all that is necessary to dismiss the image of a Pascal who found in his human condition the means to lose his footing and lose heart. We are in the presence of reasons, images, words, impulses, whose effects on us depend only on these reasons and these words and not on the particular state of the one who writes them. The book exists, and it is intended to produce a feeling and to establish a situation, not on the basis of authority but solely on the basis of our consenting to ourselves. Let us go further. It may be that Pascal was foreign both in mind and in faith to the work he proposes to us. It may be that this was the pure master-piece of a man who writes on command, as Valéry said, and who no more believes in what he asks us to believe than he is afraid because of the reasons for fear with which he misleads us. How should this work touch us less, convince us less, if this were so? It is the same work, not a line is changed, just as unfinished as the other—for writers of pure rhetoric die, too. It is the same, yet, quite obviously, it is its opposite.

Why would the "I enter into fear" and the fear into which he leads us both stop being true if, beyond the motives and the language of this fear, both more than sufficient to impress us, we were to discover an impassive mind, a soul that has freed itself from fear? It is because in truth, in a work made of words, language, to fulfill itself even imperfectly, needs existence to lend it support, to come raise it up from a kind of downfall, and to try to warrant its invincible bad faith. In one of his essays, Brice Parain recalls that the truth of art is lie, and he tells us, too, that art seems like death itself, whose image it places among us.* These are assertions about whose meaning it would be hard to reflect too much, even if we agree with them only out of misunderstanding. Language at one and the same time entertains the most extreme dreams of the absolute and constantly rejects its claims. More exactly: it exists only by the very abrogation of the conditions that make it possible. Poetry is this double impulse. We have seen, for instance, in poets like Mallarmé and Hölderlin, how language is not the simple ability to utter words in someone gifted with this ability, but asserts itself previous both to the one who names and to what he names,

---

* *Critique of Dialectic*, and likewise *Language and Existence* and the older essay "Everything Works Out," in *The Confusion of Choice.*

claiming moreover that the one who speaks, the one who listens, and that which is spoken all take meaning and existence only from the original deed of language. Language, in its poetic claim, asserts itself as an absolute: it speaks itself without someone who speaks it, or at least without depending on the one who speaks. On the contrary, the speaker, the listener, the thing spoken—all three have reality and value only because of the language that contains them.

It is under these conditions that language exists. But this language as such is impossible. It realizes itself only by renouncing itself. In this renunciation, we see the three manifestations of language regain their independence and exist for themselves, manifestations that really have meaning and reality only together: we see a man who writes, a man who reads, we see what is written and what is signified by the writing. The primordial book that was everything is reduced to a few loose leaves, things among things, whose apparent independence is only an illusory reminder of the original independence of language that depended on nothing because it embraced everything. That is why the attitude according to which the work should be sufficient unto itself (a view that Valéry shares) has the truth of an idolatry: it applies to a derisory object what can have meaning only for absolute language. The work remembers this absolute, and the memory deceives it. Sometimes torments it.

The more language renounces its claims, the more easily is it realized. But having become completely real, this very facility, this daily chatter by which we are scandalized as easily as we participate in it, speech has also lost the whole quality of language, for it no longer speaks, it no longer listens to itself, it no longer names, it is only an emptiness and a profound silence that across a deafening and yet scarcely heard rumbling cannot make itself heard. From this everyday language—an extraordinary work of art thanks to its double perfection of nullity and efficacy—from this language that is entirely possible and no longer real, literature in all its forms tries to get back to the language of origin, which is all impossibility and all reality. It returns there by the most varied ways, by the most unexpected subterfuges: that is the secret of genres and of creators.

But whatever the resources might be and whatever the artifices, the language of art cannot be realized, and can have a share in the claim to complete reality only if it has a share in the impossibility. That is why there is no true language without a rejection of language by itself, without a torment of non-language, an obsession with the absence of a language in which every man who speaks knows that he holds the meaning of what he says. Language as totality is language replacing everything, posing the absence of everything, and at the same time the absence of language. It is in this first sense that language is dead, presence in us of a death that no individual death satisfies.

One of the gravest problems that this return to the possibility of speaking through the search for impossibility poses is the problem of the relationships of the author to his work, the relationships of the reader to the author. The more that what he writes matters to the writer, helps him to fulfill and test himself, in a word, the closer his language is to his existence, the more he also feels how much, on the single level of language, his existence is a lie and how much, on the level of existence, language is always possibility and capability. What happens to the one who trusts himself to the spirit of absolute death that lives at the depths of speech? Immortality. And what happens to the one who devotes his existence to language so as to give the truth of existence to his language? The lie of a paper existence, the bad faith of a life that just represents life, that is experienced in tests of words and avoids existing by dint of miming what it is not. The purer the success, the greater the failure. Poetry in this sense is the realm of disaster. At the instant in which language is most intent on wanting everything for itself, and closest to shrouding everything in its unreality, we see poets throw themselves body, life, and soul into the words that they bring to life, at once to win from these words their existence as a poet and to precipitate, by this veritable death, the annihilation of which art is the supreme horizon in the world. But we also see other poets exclude themselves as much as possible from the poem of which they are the origin, not only to keep from mixing their life with their song but, in face of this song, be to nothing but a perpetual absence, a forgotten nonexistence such that it pretends never to have existed, so that the work can believe itself alone. Rimbaud (to a certain extent) is such a poet, and (to a certain extent) so is Mallarmé.

Like no other work, a poem needs the presence of a poet, and, like no other work, it does without it. All the different manifestations of language demand, according to infinitely variable relationships, the participation of existence in language. These relationships, it goes without saying, are not fixed according to a preestablished schedule, and it is just such a particular work (or, in other words, the degree of language that it fulfills) that, in every genre, changes the demands of the genre. At the other extreme, daily language is in the same situation—but in an opposite direction—as poetic language; for, to be spoken, it is so close to the void that the intervention of an individual voice is indispensable to it, but it needs this voice so little that any voice at all contents it: it really wants the voice of no one.

The language of the *Pensées*, to be true, must be a language overwhelmed by existence. Brice Parain often uses this striking expression: "It is always the individual who stops up the gaping hole around words, between each word and the others and between them and the object: he closes it up by stuffing his body into it." We have seen that in this gaping hole the poet would stuff his body, not to stop it up but to become a gap himself, sometimes to the point of actually disappearing, like Empedocles, in order to make this hole real, to realize this void. Existence can do no more, when it has to do with a region where language is too close to its original contradictions. And that is also the case in the *Pensées*, since they call into question not the ordinary regions of faith but the very possibility of religious experience. It must be understood that, on the level at which language disturbs everything (even if it be only for a short moment), the level of "I enter into fear," Pascal's sincerity is not enough for us and even does not matter to us. No more would his good faith be enough for us: that, for example, of a Christian who, sure of the truth that he wants to prove or have recognized, uses ways that he himself has not experienced and that he knows only through his language. The *Apology* does not ask

Pascal to assure his words by a conviction or his demonstrations by his faith. Or if it does ask him that, it asks something else first.

Whether to every instant of this immense discourse the moments of experience unique to Pascal correspond or not, whether here he speaks only as a man who speaks, there like someone who has lived what he says, there like a sufferer who suffers to say it, there again like a believer who prays by saying it, these differences are answerable only to an analysis that distinguishes in the whole that which is foreign to analysis. In reality, what the *Pensées* postulate or demand are not the details of his life or the details of his sincerity, but existence in its entirety, which naturally does not signify his whole existence, the entire history of this existence, but existence as such. There is no need to resort to technical exegesis to understand what such a word implies. Everyday meaning recognizes very well that we can begin to speak of existence only with certain critical moments, states of excess in which the violence of the fact of living submerges life and seems no longer to depend on it, but on the contrary threatens it and is ready to sacrifice it. Existence begins thus to reveal itself when it calls itself into question. In one form or another, this revelation of existence is existence itself when it tends to experience itself as impossible, either because it comes to exist outside of its conditions or because in this trial it discovers its truth, which is impossibility. In one form or another, this revelation is in proportion to this impossibility.

Béguin recalls justly that "Pascal's joy, which is hardly ever spoken of, illuminates his austere apology." That cannot be forgotten, if the only written piece that gives testimony about Pascal also bears witness to that joy, to a joy pushed to tears, pushed to a point where feelings lose their meaning and their own expression and, thereby, lose themselves, and the being himself is lost and undone. This joy can indeed be called joy and certainty and peace. But it is also *Fire*, limited, moreover, to two hours of life, "from about ten-thirty in the evening to about twelve-thirty," and only reflection could seek to contrast it with completely opposite states that are called "I enter into fear."

If Pascal had become aware of humanity's distress only through his two hours of joy, no one would have had more authority than he to frighten us about it—and that not as a man whose only knowledge of the abyss is the joy of not having fallen into it, but as one who in this very joy has known and lived this fall into the abyss, has gotten lost there, and has not found his way out. We can call the *Apology* the effort of Pascal's all-powerful reason to get hold of itself, to give itself the reason for an experience that goes completely beyond it and that it can account for only by a more intense feeling of man's tribulations and a more distinct vision of the incessantly traversed movement between nothingness and infinity, nothing and everything. That Pascal's joy made him experience his existence as infinitely close to nothing and infinitely close to everything, infinitely above and infinitely below existence, that it was infinite distress and measureless exaltation, feeling of the void in its fullness, firm assurance in its instability, and in the very moment it touched these extremes, that it was the feeling of agreement between these extremes and their "peace" in the midst of destruction—there is really nothing here that goes beyond ordinary descriptions of analogous states, nothing, moreover, that is not written all through the entire movement of the *Pensées*. The *Apology* consisted of unfolding in the abstract time of discourse and articulating in a dialectical way, confronting with the themes of faith that experience of an instant by which Pascal's existence became fire.

"I do not at all admire the excess of a virtue, like merit, if I do not see at the same time the excess of the opposite virtue. . . . For, otherwise, this is not a rising, it is a falling. One does not show one's greatness by being at one extreme, but rather by touching both at once, by filling up the entire space between. But perhaps this is only a sudden movement of the soul from one extreme to the other, and it is never in effect except in a point, like the flame of a torch? Perhaps; but at least that marks the agility of the soul, if it does not mark its breadth."

It is because of Pascal's agility of soul that, behind the opposing feelings where his language leads us, we find his own as guarantors and models for ours; in this agility we do not find the vivacity of a mind simply intent on living everything "aesthetically," but the authority of an experience that is perhaps unique, in which extremes have been known together and in which anguish was peace and peace was rapture. After that, it does not matter much that the language of the *Pensées* is a planned discourse in which a too-beautiful form commands the reader. First, because this language, too, wants to be everything and nothing. Everything—for it has the pride and the imperious power of the first word that in itself alone takes the place of everything: without any other reference except to words, it convinces, it surprises, it lowers, and it raises up, it has the reader at its disposal as if the reader were part of itself. And it wants to be nothing—and already it rejects itself, it finds itself in the midst of the misery that it shows: "Those who write against want the glory of having written well, and I who write this. . . ." Undoubtedly he draws language and argument from it, but this new speech also signifies its lie, and if this lie is in turn the beginning of a proof, the proof will serve only to make vain the language that poses it. It must also come to humiliate itself before the reader, of whom it first wanted to be master: "By no means let hearing a thing said be the rule of your credence." And finally he no longer has any other hope but silence, yet silence is still too talkative, too much language, too distanced from this nothing that could perhaps be everything: "It is better not to say anything; and then he judges according to what he is, that is, according to what he is then, and according to what has been placed there by other circumstances, of which the author is not one. But at least he will not have put anything there; if it is only this silence that is active there. He judges according to the turn and interpretation that he will be in the mood to give it, or according to what he will conjecture from the movements and look of a face, or from the tone of a voice."

In this everything and this nothing, despite the seriousness of questionings and the force of contradictions, language, if it is reduced to its bare resources, risks at every instant either asserting itself too much or asserting itself too little and, in both cases, showing the reader what the reader must not see in it: a simple

language, instead of the everything and nothing that is its truth. It
is then that existence comes to fill in the voids, existence that is
nothing else than everything and nothing. And it fills by deepening
them. It does not stop giving value to the fictive deficiency of words
by the reality of its deficiencies. And now this deficiency seems
better to us, having to do not only with man's anguish before the
misery of his condition, but also with this movement in which
existence discovers itself by putting itself in play, in which it feels
itself justified only as far as it feels itself impossible, impossibility of
which its self-sacrifice, its death, are feeble images.

In his *Overview of French Philosophy*, a little book of few words
and many ideas, Jean Wahl recalls the Pascalian litany: Jesus Christ
is dead and hidden in the sepulcher. He has not performed any
miracles in the sepulcher. That is where he takes a new life, not on
the cross. He has had no place to rest on earth except in the
sepulcher. His enemies have not stopped afflicting him except in
the sepulcher. And Wahl remarks, "We understand how Pascal's
apologetic supposes Pascal existing, Pascal believing." If the truth
of Christ supposes him dead and hidden, if he takes form and life
only in the darkness, abandon, and peace of the sepulcher, all the
more reason for it to be likewise for the one who "holds out his
arms" to him. His peace is peace only in the tomb, his reconciliation can happen only in the abandonment of the tomb, and his
march toward the light brings him closer only to the darkness of
the tomb. Assuredly, it would be absurd to give this tomb that is the
truth of the language in the *Pensées* a tempestuous appearance, to
make a theatrical mausoleum of it near which would be shown "a
kind of French Jansenist Hamlet feeling the weight of his own
skull, the skull of a great geometer." For this tomb is itself hidden,
and as Hegel says in another sense of the Holy Sepulcher, of that
tomb we see only the emptiness, and this absence of the tomb that
is the tomb proves the resurrection as well as death, shows the
anguish in the solitude of death and the joy of union in death, so
that someone who perceives only the tomb commits the same
mistake as the one who does not see it at all. So Béguin is justified
in remarking, "It is wrong—as the interpretation of a musical work

can be wrong—to utter in a pathetic tone the Pascalian passages that express despair or anxiety."

We might add that the *Pensées*, this language leaning against a tomb, were not written by Pascal as we have read them for three centuries, for he wrote from the perspective of a perfectly ordered, completed, actual work, a work intended to serve faith, so much so that by writing them he made himself guilty of a double fault, that of giving too much to art by consecrating a great part of his existence to it, and that of giving too little to art by putting it in the service of a truth foreign to art and to language. Too much art, too little art, too much language, and yet a language that deceives and is deceived—this is the mixture of true and false that bothers Valéry. True. Yet there is nothing less true. In it, in fact, the role that existence plays in speech best shows itself. Yes, the aims of Pascal the writer, the designs of Pascal the apologist lead him toward a perfect masterpiece, worthy of his century, in which the zeal for language and the zeal for faith would triumph, in which everyone would win: Boileau, Arnauld, Louis XIV, and God himself. But against these aims dark existence works, in accordance with its truth that is the tomb, and it compensates for the emptiness that it sees in all this fullness of language by its own emptiness, which is the approach and presence of death. Little by little it ruins the work that is made, engulfing it with its own future, which is existence always more suffering and more threatened; from this book that is too sure of surviving it takes away its own future, to make of it a mass of little pieces of paper, more destroyed than written. But it is also then that language finds its truth again, which is the impenetrable spirit of death—and it listens to it, follows it, until eloquence is no longer eloquence but absolute distress, and terror deprived of speech continues to be terror until the surest and most admirable speech.

No one can say that the death that transforms the *Apology* into the *Pensées* is an accident that has nothing to do with the text as it was brought to light. The opposite sparkles with evidence. It is a living Pascal who projects and arranges the work, but it is a Pascal already dead who writes it. This hand of Pascal that Valéry thinks he sees at work is so little visible, so distanced from the work, that it is dead; and what it traces is the sign of its own disappearance, the proof of its incognito, this absence by presence in which "the strange secret" of God would also be revealed. And undoubtedly even this trace is too much. Detestable residue, forever irreducible with regard to a truth that is without sign and without trace (just as those who come to convince and who need wisdom and signs are nothing in comparison with those who, coming to convert, have neither sign nor wisdom, only madness and the cross). But this fault is inscribed in language, and to seek to surmount it, even in vain, that alone justifies language. Pascal is more guilty of that, and more justified, than anyone else. To him also we could, changing them a little, apply the words of Isaiah in which he tried to decipher the curse and the greatness of the Jewish people: "A book is given to someone who knows how to read, and he will say, I cannot read." In every book, written and read by someone worthy of writing it and worthy of reading it, there is this "I cannot write, I cannot read" that is at the heart of language. But the more the book that results from this *Non possum legere* is worthy of being read and written, the more this glory turns to its confusion and becomes its lie, which nullifies this glory and this book.

§ Valéry and Faust

Valéry, so distanced from the novelistic genre, although *Monsieur Teste* is nothing but a novel, was always tempted by theater sketches. They are not even absent from his poems. *The Young Fate* is a drama in which from one single character arise many who meet each other and speak secretly. His thinking aspires to dialogue—though scarcely dialogue, more a conversation in which the diversity of speeches is born from the echo of one single voice. *The Fixed Idea* is a conversation of men of the world; *Eupalinos*, a shadow of dialogue pursued among the shades; *My Faust*, the closest to theater, makes real replicas of comedy from these intersections of words.

"What a playwright you would make!" someone says to Monsieur Teste. That is because the metaphors that he uses to represent his mind change it into a spectacle, as subtle as one could wish, but a spectacle with the resources, the peripeteias, and conflicts of the dramatic genre. The division of the theater into an audience and a stage is always more or less present in the embarrassments and privileges that he recognizes in consciousness. This consciousness, he says, "makes one think naively of an audience living in the darkness of a theater." *Naively*, undoubtedly. But this naiveté is accepted with all the images that follow from it. The mind in us is like a character who might be inside us, "the being of the mind: the little man who is in man." These exchanges are exchanges between actors, and matter less because of what they are than because of their movement. In the theater, neither ideas nor words count in themselves, but in the relationships that they maintain, the passages that they assure, the general action whose moment-by-moment supports they provide. There is no genre in which language is closer to being thought of in the way that terms of mathematical analysis are. That is why Mallarmé loved the theater, and Valéry constantly returns to a certain form of intellectual comedy whose heroes he dreams or imagines: by turn Leonardo, Teste, Faust.

Why Faust? What undoubtedly interests him is the character of the cliché that he finds in him. We cannot seriously try to make Faust's character even more profound; he is already the image of profundity and seriousness, so much so, which is rather funny, that he has become the superficial symbol of profundity. But we see how an author, singularly mistrustful with regard to all profound thought (yet who, because of his problems, is always preoccupied with whatever is most profound in the world), can be drawn by the subject of Faust, not that Faust embodies the serious but that he discredits it by the excess with which he represents it, being no longer able from then on to express anything essential except beneath the veil of a shallow irony, offering the perfect form of discretion in his symbolic banality so excessively indiscreet and talkative.

My Faust is rather a little Faust. But that does not mean that it is an entertainment without ambition. It means that all the values which in his youth Valéry came to invest in Teste or Leonardo, ambitious characters if there ever were any, could no longer impose themselves on him except indirectly, by the detour of an ambiguous composition that perhaps smiles at itself, smiles at those who read it, and smiles no less at those who think only of smiling at it. Never have the enthusiasm and the kind of haughtiness that guided the twenty-year-old Valéry in writing *Introduction to the Method* joined again in his work. The vigor that carries him toward Leonardo, the intimacy of sympathy that makes him infinitely close to the hero that he imagines or discovers, are impulses that he will reject. Even Monsieur Teste is pale, distant, and cold compared with da Vinci. This enthusiasm for an individual whose superiority is to take away all value from enthusiasm, this naive pride in favor of an artist whom he places above all the others because naiveté is foreign to him, mark a period of excess and vertigo, a weak and audacious hour that will be renewed no more.

Leonardo da Vinci, a great artist whose works we know, who lived and created, is completely different from Faust, an obscure character from a very obscure time, whose actual existence matters infinitely less than the imaginary existence that it has been given by fiction. Yet both are very similar. The real man in da Vinci applies his life to conquest and to the exercise of all his abilities: being demands that he possess all the means to create, the real is all that he can do. Leonardo is a symbol because he represents a man whose entire reality is dedicated to the possible, who transforms all that he is into realizable and verifiable operations, and thus has at his disposal, in the form of an infinite capacity for acts, his entire story and that of humanity. But Faust, Valéry's Faust, is scarcely more. The soul of this character is that it has its own myth as its existence, that it lives consciously, as a real individual, all the imaginary lives that he has been given, adding to his history not only the events that we have made him live but, above all, the fact that these events were lent to him. This Faust makes from the unreality of his numerous lives the test and truth of his actual life. This amounts to saying he is everything he could have been; in him possibility, fiction, reality, are all indiscernible.

Is that a very intellectual, refined arrangement, one bordering on a jest? Perhaps. But in this ironic game let us acknowledge the move by which Valéry discovers himself. One could say that after having been the Leonardo da Vinci of history, after having become the key figure in *Introduction to the Method,* this mythical da Vinci wants, in a last episode, to try to live our life with all his load of myth and symbol. But didn't this second Leonardo really exist? Didn't he actually exist knowing very well that he could only be Valéry himself? So that the Faust of *My Faust,* with the alibi of a smile, is also the portrait of that twenty-year-old Valéry choosing actually to live the myth of the possibility of Leonardo, a life that, of course, could only give rise to a "comedy."

It might be vain to seek in such a work the expression of its author's real feelings. But it is nevertheless true that all the glory he attributes to Faust is very close to his own, so close that when Faust answers a disciple who says callowly to him, "There is no doubt about it, you are the guiding light of our time," "Of our time? . . . Then, it is possible, for our time is worth nothing, and its guiding light is the one it deserves," or again, "My friend, I do not think I am being modest, and I hope I am not being simple. . . . But I am tired of everything that prevents me from being it. It is annoying and tiresome to be thought of as the great man," we must recognize in this annoyance with his celebrity and in this weariness at seeing himself admired the feelings of one who, writing close to death and at the edge of the ruin of the world, could only have his eyes wounded by the brilliance of his twilight.

All Valéry's heroes resemble each other in this sense that, masters of the possible, they no longer have anything to do. Their work is to remain without work, beyond their own story. That is one of the singularities of Monsieur Teste. We know that he represents the highest ability to act, linked to the most complete mastery of himself: he is capable of as much as he wants, and his power is not a vague capacity but a virtuality of defined, determinable, and measurable abilities, like those of a machine whose output is subject to exact calculations. We are told about such a man that if he had turned the regular power of his mind against the world, "nothing could have resisted him." But his superiority is not only in his mastery, it is in his indifference to his superiority, in the anonymity that he preserves. Monsieur Teste must remain unknown, or else he is lost, he would lower himself to become Caesar or God ("Divinity is easy," he says with a magnificent contempt). He also does nothing. He plays at the Stock Exchange, goes often to cafés, lives, null and superb, in a sad room. But, doing nothing, condemned to doing nothing, since the smallest action would disclose him, what does his power amount to, if, conforming to the severity that is its rule, it has reality and value only insofar as it is exercised and verified? He is Monsieur Teste only as the place of realizable actions, and he can remain Monsieur Teste only if he refuses to act. If he were to seek to complete himself in the perfection of the banality of his life, even in this absolutely ordinary life that would be his own, he could not prevent being revealed, that is, to have himself recognized as superior and thus be destroyed as such. Monsieur Teste is not impossible because he comprises more abilities than is possible for a man, but because these abilities suppose the reality of the world where they are realized with all their consequences, and the distancing of the world to which they want to remain foreign. Pure abilities, vain abilities; real abilities, but "eaten by the others," the whole contradiction that animates Valéry is there, and in sum expresses itself in this little fact: Edmond Teste does not succeed at preserving his incognito, and finally has a friend and even a wife who admire him; recognized by them, he falls low enough to become one of the most famous characters of this time.

Monsieur Teste does nothing; anything he might do would be too much. Faust can no longer do anything, for he has exhausted and lived all things. "It is my fate to tread the full round of possible opinions on all points, to know successively all tastes and all distastes, and to make and unmake and remake all the knots that are the events of a life. . . . I no longer have an age." It is the reversal of the titanism symbolized by the Goethean Faust, who strives toward the All, aspires to the infinite, and no bounded moment, beautiful as it may be, can offer him rest: if he stops, he feels he is unfaithful to his need to be everything, and if he distances himself from it, he suffers being unfaithful to whatever eternity there also is in what does not last, and whatever infinite richness there is in that which is done with. Everywhere the Universe calls him, and everywhere he betrays it; whether he renounces it or seeks it, he finds it only as the boundary of what he cannot find. But for Valéry's Faust it is almost the opposite. He has had the All, infinity has been given to him. Not only is all that is present, present to him, but all that could be absent. He lives, says his young secretary, "in the intimacy at once of the nothingness and the totality of things." Titanism is thus behind him, and the only problem that remains to him, if it is one, is not to come forth from the finite to go toward the infinite, but, having everything, also to have something, and while being a man of the Universe, still to remain someone. Valéry's Faust seeks to assure himself of his existence starting from the greatest richness of possibilities that can be conceived. Like Saint Anselm's God, he has, in the way of perfections, all that it is possible to have, but he is not sure of existing. "That question is his soul."

In truth, if this uncertainty about his life is what remains to him of life, if he can live without knowing if he is still living, this indecision only partly affects him, and worries him hardly at all; he even willingly accommodates himself to it, finally finding in his power to be everything some compensation for the existence about which he sometimes regrets being less than sure. There is regarding this a passage in "Comédie de Lust"* that pushes very far the optimism of the intellectual construction and in which we see the man of just what is possible become the man of just what is present, the one who, being everything but alive, is no longer, because of that, anything but life, breathing, immediate sensation: "Might I be at the height of my art? I live. And I do nothing but live. That is a work. . . . Finally what I was has ended up constructing what I am. . . . Here I am, the present itself. My person marries exactly my presence, in a perfect exchange with whatever comes. Nothing else. There is no more profundity. . . . I am who I am. I am at the height of my art, at the classic period of the art of living. That is my work: living. Is that not everything? But I must know. . . . It is not a question of finding oneself on this high plateau of existence without knowing it. How many adventures, reasons, dreams, and mistakes to win the freedom of being what one is, nothing but what one is! What is perfection, if not the suppression of all that we lack? What is lacking is always too much. . . . But, now, the least look, the least sensation, the least acts and functions of life become for me of the same dignity as the designs and inner voices of my thought. . . .

* The first part of *My Faust*, translated as "Luste, or the Crystal Girl." —TRANS.

It is a supreme state in which everything is summed up in living, and, with a smile that comes to me, refuses all questions and all answers . . . LIVING . . . I feel, I breathe my masterpiece."

Truly a strange text. Contradictions are at their ease in it. The words move around in it outside of their meaning. Is it possible that Valéry holds as legitimate the illusion into which he plunges Faust, whom he crowns at the decline of his life with a proud challenge, which his youth had regarded only as unrealizable audacity? How can Faust, a man of pure mind, believe that this purity of mind suffices to give him things, or even better, to make him coincide exactly with whatever there is that is immediate and present in them? A man of the mind, he is nothing else, since he is, as he announces, "in perfect exchange with whatever happens." That is precisely this *indefinite refusal to be anything at all*, in which the study on Leonardo saw the definition of consciousness, "inexhaustible act, independent of the quality as of the quantity of apparent things." For Faust, it is his privilege, being capable of pursuing indefinitely the substitution of all things, to hold them as equal and to attribute the same value to the least sensation as to the supreme designs of thought. This is identical in all respects to the remark in the 1919 study (*Note and Digressions: Introduction to the Method of Leonardo*): "You must understand that nothing escapes the severity of this exhaustion; but that it is enough for our attention to put our most intimate movements on the level of exterior events and objects: from the instant that they can be observed, they are joined with all observed things.—Color and sorrow; memories, expectation, and surprises; that tree. . . . *It is all the same.* . . . All things substitute for each other.—Wouldn't that be a definition of things?"

We see that it is the same remark, because it is also the opposite remark. The Valéry of 1919, from this equivalence of things to the mind's eye, draws not their consecration but their condemnation, and concludes that they do not count. ("All phenomena, stricken there with a kind of equal repulsion and as if rejected by an identical gesture, appear in a certain equivalence. Feelings and thoughts are enveloped in this uniform condemnation, stretching out to all that is perceptible.") It is the "Take away all things so that I can see" of Monsieur Teste. But Faust, on the other hand, in this refusal of the mind to stop at any thing, recognizes his ability to answer to all things, to achieve the totality of things, and also to live this totality in each one. "What I see blinds me," said Teste. What Faust sees makes him perceptive of everything. "TO SEE, is just as much to see something else; to see that which is possible is to see that which is." And this universal vision, this gaze of the infinite, which is at the same time a gaze at one's gaze, in no way distances it from the vision of the present thing that it sees, from the clarity of forms, from their admirable singularity. He dares to say, "The infinite is definite." Thus the artist and the man of the Universe are reconciled.

Faust's character sketches thus a certain answer of Valéry to Titanism. If Titanism is a suffering, a suffering before the contradiction that consciousness and existence bring to us—our consciousness, by its infinite need to detach itself without rest from *all that appears to it, no matter what appears,* and our existence, by the desire to find itself in a determined presence, to enjoy itself in a definite, beautiful form—this contradiction does not stop being present in Valéry's thinking and work, but if it often disguises itself, if it sometimes defers appearing until Faust, in the subtlety of a skepticism that conceals itself, it never lays claim to an actual reconciliation. Faust is that Goethean hour in which tragic tension becomes harmony, that Hegelian time in which from the excess of opposition an agreement is born, in which the individual triumphs along with the universality of the mind, and pure possibility is exchanged with unique reality. There are, in truth, many common points in Faust's situation with the moment that for Hegel marks the end of history. Faust is not only the man for whom the time of the finished world began; he is the one for whom this very time is finished. His entire existence is to have finished with existence. And that is how he comes to add to what he knows the ignorance of what he knows, without disturbing his knowing, or can give himself for one self-same single act the fact of being empty of everything and of experiencing the fullness of each thing. His success, to the extent that it takes place when everything is over, dons a crepuscular appearance, a compensatory meaning of the end of the world that is not at all foreign to the Hegelian impulse. Faust has this ironic meaning: everything has ended, there is nothing now, but that is when the man of spirit begins to breathe, to see, to touch.

Valéry's entire work is drawn toward a contradiction between whose words it is loath to choose, loath even to recognize precisely as a contradiction. Having accepted as a method an analysis conceived by analogy with mathematic analysis, it arrives at a definite idea of the perfection of mental activity that it isolates to make pure, regarding it as a principle of transformation and substitution, separate from the contingency of things or notions that substitute for them. From this point of view, the purity and excellence of the mind are proportional to its ability to put itself to one side. "Its chief and hidden work" is to define itself, against everything, by a pure, unbiased, and unchanging relationship among all things, and to locate itself thus quite close to nothing. But at the same time, we have seen, this pure ability has value only if it exercises itself and acts in the world. Valéry, after having borrowed the ideal of the mind as a principle of substitution from mathematics, borrows the notion of pragmatic truth from the natural sciences: that which is proved is true, "knowing everything is valuable only as the description or formula of a verifiable ability." The great mind is thus at once uniquely in itself and uniquely outside of itself, absolutely separated from the world and absolutely present to the world. "It is a manner of luminous torture to feel that one sees everything, without ceasing to feel that one is still visible and the conceivable object of an alien attention." And Valéry adds: *Durus est hic sermo.** But it is the contradiction that is hard.

It is marked again in another way. A system of substitution forever in movement, rigorous ability of things to exchange and cancel out, of thoughts to dissolve, exterior and interior events to be put back into play, the mind recognizes itself as master of forms

---

* "This is a hard saying."—TRANS.

to the extent that the form is a rule, law, unity of the plurality of symbols, order of the undefined. For Valéry, "the most beautiful thing would be to think in a form that one has invented," for this discovery, equivalent to the creation of the mind by itself, would also be the creation by the mind of everything, creation of a universal law suppressing all things by accounting for them. The care about form is rigorously associated, thus, with the idea of the mind disengaging itself from everything and always returning to itself, in an incessant, closed, and empty movement. Only the notion of form is ambiguous, and this ambiguity makes a double contradictory movement possible: what is formal is that which goes beyond the diversity of contents, that which is superior and foreign to the variety and singularity of all modes, pure relationship. But that which is form is also definite form, exact contours, a thing given in the richness of nuances, the certainty of perspectives, the inexchangeable value of material modes. Form gives us an interest in materials, a concern for objects, if only to reconstruct them; it throws us back into the world, it reestablishes, as a new ideal, the alliance of the mind and the body, and exalts one at the expense of the other. It comes to recognize the source of wisdom and the power to know and to do (sometimes superior to the former) in unthinking instinct and the confused sleep of the flesh. We know that no writer has spoken better of the body and of the privilege, reserved to the artist, of being a scientist by his body alone. Who does not remember Eupalinos's prayer? "O my body, which reminds me every instant of this temperament of my tendencies, this equilibrium of your organs, these just proportions of your parts, which make you exist and establish you in the heart of moving things: take care of my work; silently teach me the demands of nature, and communicate to me this great art with which you are gifted, since you are made of it, of surviving the seasons and of withdrawing yourself from chance," *unparalleled prayer*, addressed to what the soul cannot lose without losing itself, yet a prayer coming from the same pen that writes: "I confess that I have made an idol of my mind, but I have not found any other." To make the ambiguity more complete, it is a perfect praise of the value and truth of our body, but symbolically expressed, in a place full of smoke, by shadows.

The commentators have shown how poetic themes in Valéry oscillate between what Eupalinos calls creative absence and invincibly actual presence, between the desire of the mind to be separate and its need to ask the body for proof of its abilities, between the nothingness that is the life of consciousness and the nothingness of consciousness that is living. But is this only an oscillation, a coming and going between contrary tendencies? For the one who has accepted the ideal of analysis, isn't there a paradoxical contradiction that he cannot claim to surmount and that divides him? The pathos of Valéry's work is that its recourse to analysis, a method that imposes on him an extreme care of intellectual and rigorous honesty, leads him to contradictions, equivocations, to a constant indecision, to the point that he must always be on appeal against himself, and that all he does, all that he creates, all that he thinks, however great the work may be, however strong the reflection, only makes work, theory, thought untenable, abusive, and superficial. That is why it is finally so moving to see this mind, careful above all not to be duped, seek in a compromise (sometimes denounced in an undertone, often passed in silence and as if ignored) the possibility of enduring, and of going to the fulfillment of its gifts. It is in these nuances that his exquisite art triumphs, not skillful but unstable, and at each instant on the point of falling and holding itself back from the fall. A nothing separates him from silence, a nothing distinguishes the man laden with the glory of what he is becoming from the obscure secretary of André Lebey that he could have gone on being. It is likewise a nothing that gives movement to his dialogues, that makes the two opposing interlocutors rise up in him, irreconcilable, complementary, and confused: in *Eupalinos* Socrates and Phaedra, the man who has no passion except for the mind of man, and the one who does not deny appearances; in "The Dialogue of the Tree," Lucretius and Tityrus; in *My Faust*, Faust and Lust.

Lust is Faust's secretary. She is at the dawn of a feeling for him, she is at that moment in which what stirs in the heart does not alter its transparency, Crystal lady, unaware of what she is experiencing because she is still only the future and imminence of her feelings. The episode is full of charm. Lust belongs to those ravishing figures of Valéry whose secret the Young Fate [in *The Young Fate*] herself has carried. Lust is the Young Fate before the Serpent, "myself harmonious . . . forehead clear . . . the equal and wife of the day," Eve before the Tree, "superb simplicity, transparency of gazes, stupidity pride bliss" and also Émilie Teste before marriage, like her, destined to make shine, between two thoughts, the soft brilliance of a rather pure shoulder, to cause to appear, beneath the distracted hand, a trinket, a familiar ivory. The same thoughts and almost the same words serve to describe the two couples, but something soft and tender remains in the young Lust that is absent from the one whom Monsieur Teste has "classed" under the rather hard names of *Being* and *Thing*. Lust, in herself, keeps an infinitesimal enigma, at least in the eyes of the devil whom this heart embarrasses, as Faust's mind embarrasses him, and perhaps even in Valéry's eyes, to the extent that, representing the immediate side of the mind before the increase of knowledge, the youth of consciousness involved purely in the world before all dealings with the self, it represents the hope that the poet seeks despite the severities of his analysis that deprive him of it.

If *My Faust* had wanted to become an actual play, one of its great difficulties would have been to make the movement of many protagonists possible. Faust, we have seen, is already beyond everything; he has everything and, moreover, this nothing that is awareness of everything; he has been young, he has been old, and then he has been young again. In his mythic past, he has triumphed over the devil, surmounted Titanism: what is left for him to do? What is he still capable of? Existing? He tells us sometimes that he wants "to assure himself of his existence," and he is like some homunculus, like the little man of glass born from too-alone intelligence and aspiring to be more than a pure possibility. But if his truth is to reconcile this too-much that is existence and this not-enough that is the mind, if his universe is so full that lack itself is present in it as that which completes it, then this last task must also leave him, and the only thing left to him will be to survive—that is, in an ironic form, to write his memoirs indefinitely, that *book* which evokes Mallarmé's but which also evokes the twilight song of Minerva's bird, Hegel's owl, when, night having taken the place of day, this owl can do nothing but tell, in eternity, the events of time, can be nothing but this very tale, richer and more important than all that has been lived.

Undoubtedly, Lust is going to love him. But, as he says, what's the use! The devil cannot hope to start another "Marguerite affair." Temptation is no longer possible, effort is suspended, action stops. Since, however, the work goes on, the subterfuge will consist of pursuing Faust's story by beginning it again on a lower level, among beings, no matter who. It is the disciple who becomes, in long, too long peripeteias, the new hero, the one at the sight of whom Mephistopheles finds again, at the same time as existence, the fullness of his means as tempter; in his turn the disciple, at Lust's side, will try to be what Faust was formerly at Marguerite's side; but Lust aims higher, at a death, at a higher fault, and she can only abandon him, "quite gently" annul him.

In *Faery*, which follows this first outline of the play, we see Faust trying rather dramatically to go beyond himself. Rising to "essential solitude," to the edge of the void, he meets a Solitary there, "worse than the devil," who represents the temptation above all others of the man of mind. This shouting Solitary, the extreme of Monsieur Teste, keeps himself well away from the naiveté of adoring the idol Mind: he has thrown his mind to the pigs, having understood perfectly that the perfection of pure intelligence, according to the rules of analysis, must also end up by dismissing itself. There is nothing cruder than his speech, nothing more absolute than his negation: masterpieces, songs, truth, even mathematics, everything is mocked, erased, everything "goes back to the sewers." Thus the demand of purity demands both rigorous will and the effort to put an end to illusion. And these demands are vain, for this terrible individual, strong enough to denounce whatever is an error, gets himself involved in a supreme error when, after having discredited speech, he grovels finally to invoke "voiceless Speech, speechless Voice, formless Forces, faceless smiles." From this mythical point, the last lie of ice, Faust can only fall: he falls. . . . Will he be finished? Forgetting what he was, introducing into his myth the forgetting of his myth, will he find in this subterfuge the means to go on being, he whose entire existence is without end, only to end continually and know itself ended? Or again, free of angels, conqueror of demons, will he be tempted by the image of his abilities, by the desire to develop again outreach and surprise, will he give way to the illusion of becoming a child again to know again the miracle of being a man? But how will he undergo the temptation to remake for himself, across the forgetting and ignorance of youth, a life that he already has at his disposal, as he wishes, in the double fullness of that which is and of that which is not?

Such is the paradox of Faust. Devil, angel, fairy, he leaves no chance and no existence for any Mind, good and bad, other than his own. He is not only Faust, he is Faust plus Mephistopheles, which limits the role of the latter to a perpetual record of inadequacy, to a bitter and comic disillusion in which, feeling that he is no longer Evil but only his mind, he sees himself fallen a little too much below nothing. This situation gives rise to scenes of perfect comedy whose dialogue is among the liveliest and most pleasant of Valéry's writings. It is in these scenes that the devil, suddenly aware of his disgrace, comes to sign a pact with Faust to obtain from him what Faust earlier wanted to obtain from the devil, the hope of renouncing his routine and renewing his ancient rebellion. In these scenes appear again wonders of the squalid little devils who pursue, like a minor pleasantry, the criticism of their own condition, criticism of the pure mind, too pure in its complete impurity, too clear in its darkness, and having as a fault only an excess of the absolute. These devils do not have the profound irony of the reasoning Serpent of "Outline of the Serpent." That serpent had made God his servant, and despised in him the Being guilty of having become aware of itself by creating, guilty of adding to Nothingness the "exploding fault" of the sun. But God was only God. Before Faust, the non-being has no more profundity, nothingness no more seduction, and the devil, condemned to remain superficial, sees himself reduced to the danger-free buffoonery of a character in comic opera.

My Faust is called an "outline." But, as an outline, it is complete; unfinished, it is accomplished. Its unsettling nature is to find its perfection in a state that visibly lacks all that makes a work of art. It has no end, but that is because it could not have one. It says everything, in each scene, in each line, in such a way that it can stop at any line, any scene, having said everything definitively. We sometimes begin to doubt that such a work could have begun: it begins when everything is already finished, its beginning is the end of all the others, and, far from wanting to prolong them, it has as its subject only the impossibility of being more than they are. In that consists its richness, for all is found in it, even that which may come after all; but because of that it also leaves the impression of pushing its self-mockery far: destitute by dint of fullness, frivolous insofar as profundity seems inconsequential in it. And certainly this appearance of being almost nothing, which the intellectual pastimes of the Evil Spirit confirm, the confessed intention of presenting itself like a form of joke, are part of the meaning of the work that would be infinitely less without this mystifying fringe. But that a work carries in itself, as its main design, the seed of its nothingness, that it recognizes this demon that denies it in the person of the one who creates it, this very claim can finally appear excessive, overly ambitious, and of the same nature as the mad humilities of the Solitary repeating vainly: Nothing, nothing, nothing.

What is a man capable of? asks Monsieur Teste. What is a work of art capable of? Incorporating this last doubt, thrusting away by greater reserve even the comforts of modesty and the alibi of nullity? Going from the sublime to the mediocre, from poetry to the last resort that is prose, from the brilliant mind that shows itself to the true mind that hides itself, from studied negligence to the composition of incoherence, from the disorder of ideas to the order of one and the same idea indefinitely asserted? All these perfections, all these imperfections are in Faust, and these, no less than those, make the work perfect, make of it Valéry's most exemplary work, into which he put himself completely, into which he put everything, and everything of him, even though we admit with Faust, "there is enormously nothing in the All." And that is why this book that "illuminates all that we love with a strange, cold light" is one of the most moving that has been written. What is more full of pathos than those last words, "No, no," that Faust addresses to life, rejecting all that it could still offer that is admirable and glorious and happy?

Je ne hais pas en moi cette immense amertume
De n'avoir pu trouver le feu qui me consume,
Et de tous les espoirs je me sens délié
Comme de ce passé dont j'ai tout oublié,
Mes crimes, mes ferveurs, mes vertus étouffées,
Mes triomphes de chair et tant de vils trophées
Que le monde a livrés à mes démons divers . . .
Non, non . . . N'égarez point vos complaisances, Fées . . .
Si grands soient les pouvoirs que l'on m'a découverts,
Ils ne me rendront pas le goût de l'Univers.
Le souci ne m'est point de quelque autre aventure,
Moi qui sus l'ange vaincre et le démon trahir,
J'en sais trop pour aimer, j'en sais trop pour haïr,
Et je suis excédé d'être une créature.

I do not hate this immense bitterness in me
Of not having been able to find the fire that consumes me,
And from all hopes I feel I am unbound
As of this past of which I have forgotten everything,
My crimes, my passions, my stifled virtues,
My triumphs of flesh and so many vile trophies
That the world has yielded to my various demons . . .
No, no . . . Do not waste your kindnesses, Fairies . . .
As great as the powers are that have been found in me,
They will give me no taste for the Universe.
My care is not at all for any other adventure,
I who knew the conquering angel and the betraying demon,
I know too much to love, I know too much to hate,
And I have gone beyond being a creature.

Thus speaks the last Faust, who has no end and does not die. But Valéry will die, and this death of which he is aware, death that he anticipates by taking leave of a too-glorious life, too satisfying and yet as if null, brings the single true conclusion to his work.

§ On Nietzsche's Side

Henri de Lubac's book *The Drama of Atheistic Humanism* is addressed undoubtedly only to Christians, and it has meaning only for them. But it also offers a more general interest in showing how honest, penetrating thinking can come close to another's thought or, more exactly, to a world that is radically hostile to it. It is a problem with very diverse aspects. Is it possible for a religious existence to enter into a situation in which, to come to actual understanding, it must lose itself as religious existence? Is the problem identical when someone who is unaware of the religious wants to know and express the religious? These questions send us back to another, that of the disinterested spectator: I live in a room, I cannot go out of it, and yet I speak of what happens in it as if I were looking at it from without, through the keyhole. The gaze through the keyhole has the most varied names. The Eye of God, the gaze of nothingness, of death (death with eyes awake, says Nietzsche); non-meaning, non-knowledge, phenomenological reduction. The quibbling is endless.

Father de Lubac states that the Christian world is undergoing a crisis. Instead of representing, as it did in the early centuries, a hope of liberation, Christianity's ideal signifies for many men an alienation and a yoke. This is a new and dramatic situation. "Drama" is everywhere. It is in the Church threatened by this crisis. It is in the world that, by losing all relationship to something beyond the world, can only be lost itself. It is in atheism, which destroys itself in endless problems. We must find out why we are in such a position, and question those who have led us there: Feuerbach, Nietzsche, Auguste Comte, all three prophets, initiators, or organizers of a Godless world.

To confine ourselves to the pages on Nietzsche, we do not see that the author has acknowledged the difficulties that the problem reserves for a religious interpreter. Or, at least, he has decided not to take them into account. Perhaps it seemed to him that ordinary critical probity would suffice. Perhaps he thought that, while studying the influence exercised by Nietzsche, as destroyer of the Christian world, over Christian consciousness, a Christian writer did not have to go beyond himself to appreciate and understand this influence. But even from that point of view, it is not certain that the method works. Nietzsche's influence is not limited to the outer forms that it has assumed; it is probably, on the contrary, the part of Nietzsche that has wielded no obvious influence, that part of him foreign to direct transmission that has exercised the most profound effects. As a Christian, the commentator can see what Nietzsche is to a Christian, the danger that he represents. But this danger is not the actual danger, for Nietzsche's real threat can be measured only from the point of view of Nietzsche himself, outside of all direct reference to the world of faith that he is at once both radically excluded from and extremely close to. The Christian perceives the Nietzsche who has an effect on him, but Nietzsche has perhaps had most effect where his influence was not perceived.

Father de Lubac's analysis returns to this: Nietzsche's atheism is not an ordinary atheism; it is not to be confused with the atheism of those for whom the negation of God has never been a problem or is a resolved problem; he does not assert the absence of God but chooses this absence; he takes sides, he decides to make God die. God is dead because we have killed Him. This revolt is necessary for the affirmation of man. For as long as man regards the stars as placed above him, one can say that he lacks the gaze; and these stars are not only God, they are all that accompanies God: truth, morality, reason. The death of God allows man to know himself in his real limits, to leave his refuge and experience his unique possibilities, to become fully responsible for himself, that is, to become a creator. A short critical conclusion, somewhat superficial in the use it makes of texts by Heidegger and Sartre, recalls that atheist humanism can only end in failure, since, as Nicolas Berdyayev says, "Where there is no God, there is no man either."

After having read these pages, one will feel how difficult it is to approach Nietzsche. There is nothing to be said against the analysis; it goes straight to the essential assertion, which is that of the death of God, which it describes in dramatic form inseparable from the analysis. All that is Nietzsche is the replica of Nietzsche, yet it makes the breadth and profundity of his influence incomprehensible. It is not enough to add remarks on the lyricism of the writer or the nobility of his attitude. One could push such praises to exaltation without advancing the problem. Nietzsche's case gains nothing from the confusion of literary evocations. It demands, on the contrary, the seriousness and patience of an infinite reflection, one that never stops working while it recognizes the movement that escapes it. Father de Lubac has written an excellent study on Nietzsche's atheism with a view to clarifying the role that he played in the formation of a world from which God is absent, yet, despite his exactitude, this attempt lets Nietzsche's presence, and perhaps the meaning of his deed, escape, a deed exceptional from all points of view, since it was the deed of an exceptional being who nevertheless had an effect on many other beings who were not exceptional. Such is the problem; it calls into question not the individual merits of the commentator but the possibility of any commentary on a passionate thinker, written from outside.

Perhaps Nietzsche's atheism is particularly difficult to circumscribe because in appearance it isolates itself rather easily. The death of God seems to dominate Nietzsche's existence and work, and if there are fundamental thoughts in this philosophy, this death seems to envelop them all. Moreover, such an assertion, in a work in which everything is moving, has a relative fixity; it clarifies itself sometimes in a different way, but it never turns against itself, and keeps to the end this sense that God, legislator and foundation of the world, is dead. This advantage, though, is not an advantage. The theme of the death of God can be considered apart, insofar as the whole movement of Nietzsche's thinking and existence is to be found in it: it is enough because it absorbs the whole. Hence the gravity of such a theme, its force that never stops provoking uneasiness. It owes its power to the catastrophe that it announces and that tears history apart, but even more to the fact that, expressing the impossibility of any repose, it becomes the place of such a violent, stormy movement that the very contradiction that could ease it is excluded.

Jaspers has shown, as no commentator has before him, that all interpretation of Nietzsche is faulty if it does not seek out the contradictions. The essential impulse of such a way of thinking is to contradict itself. It is a movement that is all the more important since, unusually methodical, it is not the play of a capricious or confused mind, and is linked to the passion for truth. This impulse is an impulse of existence as well as of thought. Life and knowledge are one. Knowledge, says Jaspers, wants to commit itself to all its possibilities, to go beyond each one of them, and cannot linger over them. First it seems to touch, seize something, as if it were absolute; it seems to find this the unique truth; its affirmations raise it to the highest level, going beyond the relative and embracing the whole. Then, by a reversal to the opposite, it rejects what it has just affirmed, does so with the same passion and the same force. This calling into question in its turn goes beyond that which it denies, destroys yet maintains what it destroys, ruins the movement yet in the end leaves it possible. There is no reconciliation of opposites: oppositions, contradictions do not get to rest in some higher synthesis, but hold themselves together by an increasing tension, by a choice that is at once an exclusive choice and a choice of contradiction. This questioning is not only an intellectual act. Even in Nietzsche's life, attempted negation is constantly fulfilled, and that which is denied, instead of being rejected as an empty, dead possibility that would be of no concern to him, is on the contrary experienced and lived as real. Thus he was all that he fought against: "Although I can create and love, I must soon become its adversary, rebel against my love. . . . To travel the entire circle of the modern soul, to have sat in all its innermost recesses—that is my ambition, my torture and my happiness." And thus he comes to recommend patience against oneself as a technique, the will to "take sides against one's inclinations," the search in oneself for what is dangerously opposed to oneself. "There is in Nietzsche," writes Charles du Bos, "a courage of logic as fertile as such courage is elsewhere sterile most of the time. This movement is properly called 'thinking against oneself,' and nothing indicates more the strength and validity of the Nietzschean organism than the fact that it could become itself starting from such an act."

In no way can the idea of the Death of God be the expression of a definitive knowledge, or the outline of a stable proposition. Anyone who wants to draw certainty from it, some "There is no God" in the dogmatic sense of banal atheism, it cunningly deflects away from complacency and calm. "God is dead" is an enigma, an assertion ambiguous because of its religious origin, its dramatic form, the literary myths it follows upon (Jean-Paul's, for example, or Hölderlin's). The parodic parable that Nietzsche once used proclaims this ambiguous quality. In the parable, men are prisoners. Jesus is the son of their warden. Yet this warden dies just at the instant when his son announces to the men: "I will make all those who believe in me free, as surely as my father lives." We see the entangled nature of the situation: to be free, one must have faith in the warden's son and that this warden is alive; but if he is dead, the men are not freed, Christ's promise is no longer worth anything; without a warden, the prison becomes eternal. Naturally, the parable also has this other meaning: that men cannot win their freedom from a strange phrase, but from the awareness that the warden is dead. It is again through symbols that Nietzsche answers the question, Why is God dead? "God died from his pity for men. . . . When the Gods die, they always die of all kinds of deaths. . . . God saw man's depths, all his hidden shame and ugliness. Man does not permit such a witness to live." We also know that this "God is dead," while it marks a historic break, the arrival of a phase of the world in which solitude and wilderness will be for everyone tasks to survive and surmount, does not signify that humanity has once and for all gone beyond its fundamental moment. First, there is the eternal Return. Then, "humanity in its entirety has no destination," which means that, not being able to fly above the total course of human affairs, we can only figuratively suppose there to be a Great Noon or a Great Midnight to man's day. But above all, this Death of God is infinite: the madman who cries, "We have killed him," must in the end necessarily throw his lamp on the ground to break it and extinguish it, he must necessarily say, "I come too soon . . . I did not come when I should have. This monstrous event is always on the way . . . it goes forward, and it has not yet reached anyone's ears." In a way, the madman will never come at the right time, he will always be ahead of the event; questioned and driven out, he can be only the mad witness of an action that will always seem more distant than the farthest stars and that nevertheless is present, complete. That is why "God is dead" cannot live in Nietzsche as knowledge bringing an answer, but as the refusal of an answer, the negation of a salvation, the "no" he utters to this grandiose permission to rest, to unload oneself onto an eternal truth, which is God for him. "God is dead" is a task, and a task that has no end. History carries with it the moment that it goes beyond. "God is dead, but men are such that there will still, perhaps for millennia, be caves in which one will show his shadow. . . . And we . . . we still must conquer his shadow." The Death of God keeps the sacred, enigmatic quality of the sacrifice that its name evokes: after the time when man offered himself as a sacrifice to God, after that other time when we sacrificed our strongest instincts to God, now God himself is the victim of the sacrifice, he is sacrificed, and to whom? "To nothing"—"That is the paradoxical mystery of supreme cruelty, reserved for the generation that is coming now." A very equivocal expression, for if it means that the sacrifice of God is necessary so that man can become aware of this nothing that invests him and is the foundation of his freedom, if it means again that instead of God comes the reign of Nothing (which is the temptation of nihilism in its dogmatic form), it also suggests that God is complicit with the sacrificial act, that it is accomplished in agreement with him, and that, included in the nothingness in view of which it is realized, it is in some way intercepted by this nothingness and itself reduced to nothing. God is not only sacrificed to nothing, but the sacrifice is involved in this nothing and, consequently, is nothing, is not, does not take place (similarly, the pope says to Zarathustra, "It must be some god that converted you to your atheism").

Father de Lubac notes that atheism has a positive sense. Nietzsche wants to leave the field clear to affirm man and, even more, to affirm in man this more-than-man that until now was alienated by God. That is what the expression of current Nietzscheanism translates: God is dead, long live the Superman. The positive quality of the Death of God is hardly arguable: one can even believe that negation, to be possible, must be not only the negation of god but also the affirmation of something. Still, the meaning of this affirmation remains to be sorted out. It is not actually certain, as Jaspers believes, that the negation of transcendence must be enclosed in a dogmatic affirmation of immanence. He himself shows that all of Nietzsche's positive philosophy, that of the Will to power as well as that of the Superman, without speaking of the eternal Return, remains constantly suspended, and serves to maintain moment by moment, with historic examples and realities, a position that, once sure of a point of stability, reverses itself and succumbs to its own equilibrium. In principle, the Superman replaces God. But, finally, what does Nietzsche say about the Superman? Exactly what he says about the gods: "Always, we are lured higher, up to the realm of the clouds: there we put our motley empty theories, and now they take on the name of Gods and Supermen—are they not pleasurably light, just what is right for such thrones, all these gods and supermen? Ah, how tired I am of all that is insufficient!" And of the eternal Return? "Perhaps there is nothing true in that—let others fight about it." And of the Will to power? "Power makes one stupid. . . . Power is tiresome. . . . Would we want a world in which the action of the weak, their freedom, their reserve, their spirituality, their adaptability would be lacking?" And of the possibility of renouncing God? "You would never pray again. . . . Never again would you rest in an infinite confidence, you renounce abiding with a last wisdom, a last goodness, a last power, and unharnessing your thoughts. Man of renouncing, are you ready to renounce everything? Who will give you the strength? No one has yet had this strength." And finally of the collection of his "truths"? "My life is now all in this wish that things be very much other than the way I conceive them, and that someone would make me disbelieve my truths."

There is nevertheless in this negation of God an affirmation, and precisely the affirmation that runs through all Nietzsche's existence and thought, that which God makes impossible and questions infinitely, and that for this reason is never completely finished with God. This affirmation is that of man as infinite power of negation, ability to be always equal to what surpasses him, other than he is, different from himself; it is the measureless, limitless dissatisfaction, questioning become passion and will to sacrifice; it is, against all the forms of being, revolt, united to the search for a form to be capable of putting this revolt in danger and starting it again. Thus the negation of God is indeed linked to something positive, but this positive is man as negativity without rest, power to deny God without end: freedom. And we see why the negation of God never arrives at its end. It is because all that is question in God, exhausting enigma, interrogation, remains valid for Nietzsche, who adopts it as his own, under other names and often under the name of God. (Thus he writes, "The refutation of God: in sum, it is only the moral God that is refuted.") On the contrary, all that is answer in God, solution to his enigma, cure for his wound, is pushed away as a cowardly, deceiving subterfuge, an illusory base thrown into the abyss. On the other hand, as God is never an answer separated from the question, affirmation without negation, the movement of surpassing endlessly finds obliquely what it rejects, by its ambiguous tendency to give itself and experience itself as absolute. Jaspers wonders if the negation of God, in Nietzsche, is not the restlessness, always in movement, of a search for God that no longer understands itself. And it is the same movement that Georges Bataille translates in terms where the determined plays with the indeterminate, in which the universal takes the form of the particular, in which a perpetual equivocation, an oscillation between immanence and transcendence endlessly open and close words to the absolute: "If the whole of mankind, that is, their integral existence, incarnated in one single being, obviously as solitary and abandoned as the ensemble, the head of the incarnated being would be the scene of an irreconcilable battle, so violent that sooner or later it would fly into fragments. For it is difficult to conceive to what tempestuous extremes the visions of this incarnate being would reach, a being who would see God but at the same instant kill him, then become God himself, only to hurl himself immediately into nothingness: then he would find that he was a man stripped of meaning as the first passerby who happens along, but deprived of all possibility of rest" ("Nietzsche's Madness," in *Acephalous*).

Nietzsche, hardly sensitive to the plastic arts, always expressed his predilection for the Dürer engraving *The Knight, Death, and the Devil*: "This image is close to me, I cannot say how close." In such a liking, we recognize his original choice, the one by which he links himself to the courageous, inflexible "Even so . . . ," to the bravery that pushes away all guarantees, and of which the Death of God is the touchstone. It is the "Do you have courage?—Not courage before witnesses but the courage of the solitary, of the eagle upon whom no god looks any more." Such courage cannot be an inverted faith or a simple will to deny, in risk, the affirmations of belief. It must be real faith, having a dogmatic, rational content (the eternal Return, Dionysios, etc.); this courage would be cowardliness at bottom, a dramatic leap—as is all faith—toward a refuge and toward rest. And empty faith, pure and simple choice of risk in the face of God representing the certainty of being, courage would still be only the affirmation of courage as a value, heroic daring, "the good will to lose oneself"; and undoubtedly Nietzsche placed heroic greatness very high, but questioned it like the rest. "As for the hero," he writes to Heinrich von Stein, "I do not think as well of him as you. I'll go this far: it is the most acceptable form of human existence, especially when one has no other choice." Yet we are thrown back to such interpretations when we content ourselves with recognizing in the Nietzschean negation of God either a pure heroic negation (the opposite of Pascal's wager) or "the field left clear" for subsequent affirmations of a dogmatic or mystical nature. In the first case, we see in the revolt against God only the negation of God (without a compensatory positive view). In the second case, we base the negation on affirmations of immanence that are necessarily debatable.

The Death of God is less a negation aiming at the infinite than an affirmation of the infinite power to deny and to live to the end of this power. In the Death of God, it is not atheism that counts (whether positive or not) but the experience of man as freedom or, more exactly, the fact that in one and the same experience is disclosed the absence of all recourse to an unconditioned being, along with the structure of human freedom as unconditioned ability to separate oneself from oneself, to escape oneself, to free oneself by means of an infinite questioning. The mutual confrontation of God who disappears and of man who is responsible for this disappearance is necessary for Nietzsche to live this ability in a pure way, in anguish and in risk, and also in the full, actual situation of the historical world to which he is confined. The infinite collapse of God allows freedom to become aware of the nothing that is its foundation, without making an absolute of this nothing (for nothingness is only the nothingness of God, rejection of the absolute). And the infinite ability to deny remains an ability to deny the infinite, and escapes the temptation to place oneself outside of questioning, to turn petrified by choosing oneself as the inarguable value. Such is certainly one of Nietzsche's dramas: he feels he is God's accomplice, not because he seeks God without knowing it, as Jaspers tends to say, or because he cannot do without the affirmation of God, but because he cannot do without the negation of God. Transcendence obsesses him, as that which he must endlessly surmount to be free. Freedom is to God what Ariadne is to Theseus and Dionysios: first, it annihilates him, as Ariadne annihilates Theseus: "That is the sign of my supreme love, to reduce him to nothing." But then, Ariadne needs Dionysios, the god torn apart, who tells her, "I am your labyrinth." She needs to tear God apart; for against God who is the end, the outcome above all others, she asserts herself as refusal, refusal ever to accept an alien end. And she needs the torn-apart God who is the labyrinth, and against the labyrinth she affirms her free movement, her ability to separate herself. Under the veil of enigmas, we are led to think that, in Nietzsche, freedom and the final truth are linked to death. Thus he becomes, in the end, Dionysios and the Crucified One, not God but his double, Death of God.

Every assertion of Nietzsche or about Nietzsche must be balanced with its opposite assertion. It is quite true that, in another movement of his thought, Nietzsche definitively dismisses God or takes the Death of God as a historic event that will one day be gone beyond, but starting from which we must take responsibility for this world. (For Nietzsche, the beyond cancels responsibility.) His interpretation of the world, his preference for becoming, his concern with a full life, removed from the vicious glance of morality, are linked to this inflexible conviction. On this level of his thinking, all that we have said is overturned: here, he discredits anguish as only the sign of a tired existence; he takes away from death its privilege: "There is no greater banality in mankind than death." And he asserts the radical immanence of man (notably by an immoderate use of scientific explanations). This entire perspective everywhere causes certainties to arise such that Nietzsche seems really to believe that he touches the heart of things, and that there is nothing more to be said. Then this perspective disappears in its turn. The notions that he uses are undermined by the worst equivocations. What is life? What is power? A more than life? A Will to become more, that is, to have, as we choose, a purer value or a greater strength? Even at the instant that he condemns anguish before death, he rehabilitates it in an even more ambiguous form, that of joy and drunkenness: "We must make a celebration of our death." And we know his "Die at the right time,"* which is on one side a simple Stoic apology for voluntary death, but which also

---

* "*Au moment voulu*," literally "at the willed moment."—TRANS.

conceals an agonizing temptation, since it recommends the impossible to me, by linking my decision to a moment that no one can recognize, the best moment, the deliberate moment, one that I could perceive only after I am dead, by going back over the whole of my complete existence, so that finally the choice of the moment of death implies that I leap above death and from there look at my whole life, implies that I am already dead.

Father de Lubac, in the most remarkable study in his book, the one devoted to Dostoyevsky, notes that the entire work of the novelist is filled with doublings and enigmas: the characters are always different from what they are, and when they are relatively simple, they share with each other and receive from other characters reflections that make them invisible. Thus Smerdyakov is the vile double of Ivan Karamazov; thus Verkhovensky is "the ape" of Stavrogin; and Shatov and Kirilov live, in our mind, separate and confused, as they lived themselves, side by side, dying of hunger, in a hate born from their closeness. And this is why so many of these characters seem to us an expression of anguish—their ambiguity, an ambiguity that is not only for us but also for themselves: Raskolnikov, Kirilov, Stavrogin, Prince Myshkin answer, in the dramatic richness of their story, to an emptiness without history, to something frozen that the burning of their passions makes unbearable. "Dostoyevsky did not hand over his thinking all at once," Father de Lubac says. (He believes perhaps too willingly that what Dostoyevsky thought—for instance, his faith in the resurrection of Christ—gives us the meaning of his work. But the meaning the work has for us is not linked to what Dostoyevsky thought.) For the strongest reason, that must be said of Nietzsche, who also, moreover, used not only masks to express himself but also characters, figures, either historical or fictional—Heraclitus, Socrates, Napoleon, Wagner, the Superman, Zarathustra—whom he always ends up rejecting. ("Above all do not believe," he writes to his sister, "that my son Zarathustra expresses what I think. He is one of my prologues and one of my interludes.") There again, we must listen to Jaspers: when we think we see Nietzsche, he says, he is not this but something else. And, at the same time, this Other seems each time to escape us. The fundamental characteristic of Nietzsche's truth is that it can only be misunderstood, can only be the object of an endless misunderstanding. "Above all," says Nietzsche, "do not take me for another. . . . People have the habit, I confess, of taking me for someone else. It would render me a great service to defend me against such misunderstandings." But it is not enough to see this confusion to clarify it: infinite confusion is part of his existence. Without it, without the ambiguity that constantly makes unknown to us what we think we know, there would remain of this *grosse Zweideutige*, this great figure with a double meaning, only what he wanted to avoid being.

§ Literature and the Right to Death

One can certainly write without asking why one writes. As a writer watches his pen form the letters, does he even have a right to lift it and say to it: "Stop! What do you know about yourself? Why are you moving forward? Why can't you see that your ink isn't making any marks, that although you may be moving ahead freely, you're moving through a void, that the reason you never encounter any obstacles is that you never left your starting place? And yet you write—you write on and on, disclosing to me what I dictate to you, revealing to me what I know; as others read, they enrich you with what they take from you and give you what you teach them. Now you have done what you did not do; what you did not write has been written: you are condemned to be indelible."

Let us suppose that literature begins at the moment when literature becomes a question. This question is not the same as a writer's doubts or scruples. If he happens to ask himself questions as he writes, that is his concern; if he is absorbed by what he is writing and indifferent to the possibility of writing it, if he is not even thinking about anything, that is his right and his good luck. But one thing is still true: as soon as the page has been written, the question which kept interrogating the writer while he was writing—though he may not have been aware of it—is now present on the page; and now the same question lies silent within the work, waiting for a reader to approach—any kind of reader, shallow or profound; this question is addressed to language, behind the person who is writing and the person who is reading, by language which has become literature.

This concern that literature has with itself may be condemned as an infatuation. It is useless for this concern to speak to literature about its nothingness, its lack of seriousness, its bad faith; this is the very abuse of which it is accused. Literature professes to be important while at the same time considering itself an object of doubt. It confirms itself as it disparages itself. It seeks itself: this is more than it has a right to do, because literature may be one of those things which deserve to be found but not to be sought.

Perhaps literature has no right to consider itself illegitimate. But the question it contains has, properly speaking, nothing to do with its value or its rights. The reason the meaning of this question is so difficult to discover is that the question tends to turn into a prosecution of art and art's capacities and goals. Literature is built on top of its own ruins: this paradox has become a cliché to us. But we must still ask whether the challenge brought against art by the most illustrious works of art in the last thirty years is not based on the redirection, the displacement, of a force laboring in the secrecy of works and loath to emerge into broad daylight, a force the thrust of which was originally quite distinct from any deprecation of literary activity or the literary Thing.

We should point out that as its own negation, literature has never signified the simple denunciation of art or the artist as mystification or deception. Yes, literature is unquestionably illegitimate, there is an underlying deceitfulness in it. But certain people have discovered something beyond this: literature is not only illegitimate, it is also null, and as long as this nullity is isolated in a state of purity, it may constitute an extraordinary force, a marvelous force. To make literature become the exposure of this emptiness inside, to make it open up completely to its nothingness, realize its own unreality—this is one of the tasks undertaken by surrealism. Thus we are correct when we recognize surrealism as a powerful negative movement, but no less correct when we attribute to it the greatest creative ambition, because if literature coincides with nothing for just an instant, it is immediately everything, and this everything begins to exist: what a miracle!

It is not a question of abusing literature, but rather of trying to understand it and to see why we can only understand it by disparaging it. It has been noted with amazement that the question "What is literature?" has received only meaningless answers. But what is even stranger is that something about the very form of such a question takes away all its seriousness. People can and do ask, "What is poetry?" "What is art?" and even "What is the novel?" But the literature which is both poem and novel seems to be the element of emptiness present in all these serious things, and to which reflection, with its own gravity, cannot direct itself without losing its seriousness. If reflection, imposing as it is, approaches literature, literature becomes a caustic force, capable of destroying the very capacity in itself and in reflection to be imposing. If reflection withdraws, then literature once again becomes something important, essential, more important than the philosophy, the religion, or the life of the world which it embraces. But if reflection, shocked by this vast power, returns to this force and asks it what it is, it is immediately penetrated by a corrosive, volatile element and can only scorn a Thing so vain, so vague, and so impure, and in this scorn and this vanity be consumed in turn, as the story of Monsieur Teste has so clearly shown us.

It would be a mistake to say that the powerful negative contemporary movements are responsible for this volatizing and volatile force which literature seems to have become. About one hundred fifty years ago, a man who had the highest idea of art that anyone can have—because he saw how art can become religion and religion, art—this man (called Hegel) described all the ways in which someone who has chosen to be a man of letters condemns himself to belong to the "animal kingdom of the mind."* From his very

* In this argument, Hegel is considering human work in general. It should be understood that the remarks which follow are quite remote from the text of the *Phenomenology* and make no attempt to illuminate it. The text can be read in Jean Hippolyte's translation and pursued further through his important book, *Origin and Structure of Hegel's 'Phenomenology of the Spirit.'*

first step, Hegel virtually says, a person who wishes to write is stopped by a contradiction: in order to write, he must have the talent to write. But gifts, in themselves, are nothing. As long as he has not yet sat down at his table and written a work, the writer is not a writer and does not know if he has the capacity to become one. He has no talent until he has written, but he needs talent in order to write.

This difficulty illuminates, from the outset, the anomaly which is the essence of literary activity and which the writer both must and must not overcome. A writer is not an idealistic dreamer, he does not contemplate himself in the intimacy of his beautiful soul, he does not submerse himself in the inner certainty of his talents. He puts his talents to work; that is, he needs the work he produces in order to be conscious of his talents and of himself. The writer only finds himself, only realizes himself, through his work; before his work exists, not only does he not know who he is, but he is nothing. He exists only as a function of the work; but then how can the work exist? "An individual," says Hegel, "cannot know what he [really] is until he has made himself a reality through action. However, this seems to imply that he cannot determine the *End* of his action until he has carried it out; but at the same time, since he is a *conscious* individual, he must have the action in front of him beforehand as *entirely his* own, i.e., as an *End*."* Now, the same is true for each new work, because everything begins again from nothing. And the same is also true when he creates a work part by part: if he does not see his work before him as a project already completely formed, how can he make it the conscious end of his conscious acts? But if the work is already present in its entirety in his mind and if this presence is the essence of the work (taking the words, for the time being, to be inessential), why would he realize it any further? Either as an interior project it is everything it ever will be, and from that moment the writer knows everything about it that he can learn, and so will leave it to lie there in its twilight,

* Hegel, *Phenomenology of Spirit*, trans. A. V. Miller (Oxford University Press, 1977, p. 240); chap. V, sec. 1a, "The spiritual animal kingdom and deceit or the 'matter in hand' itself."—TRANS.

without translating it into words, without writing it—but then he won't ever write; and he won't be a writer. Or, realizing that the work cannot be planned, but only carried out, that it has value, truth, and reality only through the words which unfold it in time and inscribe it in space, he will begin to write, but starting from nothing and with nothing in mind—like a nothingness working in nothingness, to borrow an expression of Hegel's.

In fact, this problem could never be overcome if the person writing expected its solution to give him the right to begin writing. "For that very reason," Hegel remarks, "he has to start immediately, and, whatever the circumstances, without further scruples about beginning, means, or End, proceed to action."* This way, he can break the circle, because in his eyes the circumstances under which he begins to write become the same thing as his talent, and the interest he takes in writing, and the movement which carries him forward, induce him to recognize these circumstances as his own, to see his own goal in them. Valéry often reminded us that his best works were created for a chance commission and were not born of personal necessity. But what did he find so remarkable about that? If he had set to work on *Eupalinos* of his own accord, what reasons would he have had for doing it? That he had held a piece of shell in his hand? Or that opening a dictionary one morning, he happened to read the name Eupalinos in *La Grande Encyclopédie*? Or that he wanted to try dialogue as a form and happened to have on hand a piece of paper that lent itself to that form? One can imagine the most trivial circumstance as the starting point of a great work; nothing is compromised by that triviality: the act by which the author makes it into a crucial circumstance is enough to incorporate it into his genius and his work. In this sense, the publication *Architectures*, which commissioned *Eupalinos* from Valéry, was really the form in which he originally had the talent to write it: that commission was the beginning of that talent, was that talent itself, but we must also add that that commission only became real, only became a true project through Valéry's

* Ibid.—TRANS.

existence, his talent, his conversations in the world, and the interest he had already shown in this sort of subject. Every work is an occasional work: this simply means that each work has a beginning, that it begins at a certain moment in time and that that moment in time is part of the work, since without it the work would have been only an insurmountable problem, nothing more than the impossibility of writing it.

Let us suppose that the work has been written: with it the writer is born. Before, there was no one to write it; starting from the book, an author exists and merges with his book. When Kafka chances to write the sentence "He was looking out the window," he is—as he says—in a state of inspiration such that the sentence is already perfect. The point is that he is the author of it—or rather that, because of it, he is an author: it is the source of his existence, he has made it and it makes him, it is himself and he is completely what it is. This is the reason for his joy, his pure and perfect joy. Whatever he might write, "the sentence is already perfect." This is the reason for his joy, his pure and perfect joy. This is the strange and profound certainty which art makes into a goal for itself. What is written is neither well nor badly written, neither important nor frivolous, memorable nor forgettable: it is the perfect act through which what was nothing when it was inside emerges into the monumental reality of the outside as something which is necessarily true, as a translation which is necessarily faithful, since the person it translates exists only through it and in it. One could say that this certainty is in some sense the writer's inner paradise and that *automatic writing* has been only one way of making this golden age real—what Hegel calls the pure joy of passing from the night of possibility into the daytime of presence—or again, the certainty that what bursts into the light is none other than what was sleeping in the night. But what is the result of this? The writer who is completely gathered up and enclosed in the sentence "He was looking out the window" apparently cannot be asked to justify this sentence, since for him nothing else exists. But at least the sentence exists, and if it really exists to the point of making the person who wrote it a writer, this is because it is not just his sentence, but a sentence that belongs to other people, people who can read it—it is a universal sentence.

At this point, a disconcerting ordeal begins. The author sees other people taking an interest in his work, but the interest they take in it is different from the interest that made it a pure expression of himself, and that different interest changes the work, transforms it into something different, something in which he does not recognize the original perfection. For him the work has disappeared, it has become a work belonging to other people, a work which includes them and does not include him, a book which derives its value from other books, which is original if it does not resemble them, which is understood because it is a reflection of them. Now the writer cannot disregard this new stage. As we have seen, he exists only in his work, but the work exists only when it has become this public, alien reality, made and unmade by colliding with other realities. So he really is inside the work, but the work itself is disappearing. This is a particularly critical moment in the experiment. All sorts of interpretations come into play in getting beyond it. The writer, for example, would like to protect the perfection of the written Thing by keeping it as far away from life outside as possible. The work is what he created, not the book that is being bought, read, ground up, and praised or demolished in the marketplace of the world. But then where does the work begin, where does it end? At what moment does it come into existence? Why make it public if the splendor of the pure self must be preserved in the work, why take it outside, why realize it in words which belong to everyone? Why not withdraw into an enclosed and secret intimacy without producing anything but an empty object and a dying echo? Another solution—the writer himself agrees to do away with himself: the only one who matters in the work is the person who reads it. The reader makes the work; as he reads it, he creates it; he is its real author, he is the consciousness and the living substance of the written thing; and so the author now has only one goal, to write for that reader and to merge with him. A hopeless endeavor. Because the reader has no use for a work written for him, what he wants is precisely an alien work in which he can discover something unknown, a different reality, a separate mind capable of transforming him and which he can transform into himself. An author who is writing specifically for a public is not really writing: it is the public that is writing, and for this reason the public can no longer be a reader; reading only appears to exist, actually it is nothing. This is why works created to be read are meaningless: no one reads them. This is why it is dangerous to write for other people, in order to evoke the speech of others and reveal them to themselves: the fact is that other people do not want to hear their own voices; they want to hear someone else's voice, a voice that is real, profound, troubling like the truth.

A writer cannot withdraw into himself, for he would then have to give up writing. As he writes, he cannot sacrifice the pure night of his own possibilities, because his work is alive only if that night—and no other—becomes day, if what is most singular about him and farthest removed from existence as already revealed now reveals itself within shared existence. It is true that the writer can try to justify himself by setting himself the task of writing—the simple operation of writing, made conscious of itself quite independently of its results. As we know, this was Valéry's way of saving himself. Let us accept this. Let us accept that a writer may concern himself with art as pure technique, with technique as nothing more than the search for the means by which what was previously not written comes to be written. But if the experiment is to be a valid one, it cannot separate the operation from its results, and the results are never stable or definitive, but infinitely varied and meshed with a future which cannot be grasped. A writer who claims he is concerned only with how the work comes into being sees his concern get sucked into the world, lose itself in the whole of history; because the work is also made outside of him, and all the rigor he put into the consciousness of his deliberate actions, his careful rhetoric, is soon absorbed into the workings of a vital contingency which he cannot control or even observe. Yet his experiment is not worthless: in writing, he has put himself to the test as a nothingness at work, and after having written, he puts his work to the test as something in the act of disappearing. The work disappears, but the fact of disappearing remains and appears as the essential thing, the movement which allows the work to be realized as it enters the stream of history, to be realized as it disappears. In this experiment, the writer's real goal is no longer the ephemeral work but something beyond that work: the truth of the work, where the individual who writes—a force of creative negation—seems to join with the work in motion through which this force of negation and surpassing asserts itself.

This new notion, which Hegel calls the Thing Itself, plays a vital role in the literary undertaking. No matter that it has so many different meanings: it is the art which is above the work, the ideal that the work seeks to represent, the World as it is sketched out in the work, the values at stake in the creative effort, the authenticity of this effort; it is everything which, above the work that is constantly being dissolved in things, maintains the model, the essence, and the spiritual truth of that work just as the writer's freedom wanted to manifest it and can recognize it as its own. The goal is not what the writer makes but the truth of what he makes. As far as this goes, he deserves to be called an honest, disinterested conscience—*the honest man.* But here we run into trouble: as soon as honesty comes into play in literature, imposture is already present. Here bad faith is truth, and the greater the pretension to morality and seriousness, the more surely will mystification and deceit triumph. Yes, literature is undoubtedly the world of values, since above the mediocrity of the finished works everything they lack keeps appearing as their own truth. But what is the result of this? A perpetual enticement, an extraordinary game of hide-and-seek in which the writer claims as an excuse that what he has in mind is not the ephemeral work but the spirit of that work and of every work— no matter what he does, no matter what he has not been able to do, he adapts himself to it, and his honest conscience derives knowledge and glory from it. Let us listen to that honest conscience; we are familiar with it because it is working in all of us. When the work has failed, this conscience is not troubled: it says to itself, "Now it has been fully completed, for failure is its essence; its disappearance constitutes its realization," and the conscience is happy with this;

lack of success delights it. But what if the book does not even manage to be born, what if it remains a pure nothing? Well, this is still better: silence and nothingness are the essence of literature, "the Thing Itself." It is true: the writer is willing to put the highest value on the meaning his work has for him alone. Then it does not matter whether the work is good or bad, famous or forgotten. If circumstances neglect it, he congratulates himself, since he wrote it only to negate circumstances. But when a book that comes into being by chance, produced in a moment of idleness and lassitude, without value or significance, is suddenly made into a masterpiece by circumstantial events, what author is not going to take credit for the glory himself, in his heart of hearts, what author is not going to see his own worth in that glory, and his own work in that gift of fortune, the working of his mind in providential harmony with his time?

A writer in his own first dupe, and at the very moment he fools other people he is also fooling himself. Listen to him again: now he states that his function is to write for others, that as he writes he has nothing in mind but the reader's interest. He says this and he believes it. But it is not true at all. Because if he were not attentive first and foremost to what *he* is doing, if he were not concerned with literature as his own action, he could not even write: he would not be the one who was writing—the one writing would be no one. This is why it is futile for him to take the seriousness of an ideal as his guarantee, futile for him to claim to have stable values: this seriousness is not his own seriousness and can never settle definitively where he thinks he is. For example: he writes novels, and these novels imply certain political statements, so that he seems to side with a certain Cause. Other people, people who directly support the Cause, are then inclined to recognize him as one of themselves, to see his work as proof that the Cause is really his cause, but as soon as they make this claim, as soon as they try to become involved in this activity and take it over, they realize that the writer is not on their side, that he is only on his own side, that what interests him about the Cause is the operation he himself has carried out—and they are puzzled. It is easy to understand why men who have committed themselves to a party, who have made a decision, distrust writers who share their views; because these writers have also committed themselves to literature, and in the final analysis literature, by its very activity, denies the substance of what it represents. This is its law and its truth. If it renounces this in order to attach itself permanently to a truth outside itself, it ceases to be a literature and the writer who still claims he is a writer enters into another aspect of bad faith. Then must a writer refuse to take an interest in anything, must he turn his face to the wall? The problem is that if he does this, his equivocation is just as great. First of all, looking at the wall is also turning toward the world; one is making the wall into the world. When a writer sinks into the pure intimacy of a work which is no one's business but his own, it may seem to other people—other writers and people involved in other activities—that at least they have been left at peace in their Thing and their own work. But not at all. The work created by this solitary person and enclosed in solitude contains within itself a point of view which concerns everyone, implicitly passing judgment on other works, on the problems of the times, becoming the accomplice of whatever it neglects, the enemy of whatever it abandons, and its indifference mingles hypocritically with everyone's passion.

What is striking is that in literature, deceit and mystification not only are inevitable but constitute the writer's honesty, whatever hope and truth are in him. Nowadays people often talk about the sickness of words, and we even become irritated with those who talk about it, and suspect them of making words sick so they can talk about it. This could be the case. The trouble is that this sickness is also the words' health. They may be torn apart by equivocation, but this equivocation is a good thing—without it there would be no dialogue. They may be falsified by misunderstanding—but this misunderstanding is the possibility of our understanding. They may be imbued with emptiness—but this emptiness is their very meaning. Naturally, a writer can always make it his ideal to call a cat a cat. But what he cannot manage to do is then believe that he is on the way to health and sincerity. On the contrary, he is causing more mystification than ever, because the cat is not a cat, and anyone who claims that it is has nothing in mind but this hypocritical violence: Rolet is a rascal.*

There are many reasons for this imposture. We have just been discussing the first reason: literature is made up of different stages which are distinct from one another and in opposition to one another. Honesty, which is analytical because it tries to see clearly, separates these stages. Under the eyes of honesty pass in succession the author, the work, and the reader; in succession the art of writing, the thing written, and the truth of that thing or the Thing Itself; still in succession, the writer without a name, pure absence of himself, pure idleness, then the writer who is work, who is the action of a creation indifferent to what it is creating, then the writer who is the result of this work and is worth something because of this result and not because of the work, as real as the created thing is real, then the writer who is no longer affirmed by this result but denied by it, who saves the ephemeral work by saving its ideal, the truth of the work, etc. The writer is not simply one of these stages to the exclusion of the others, nor is he even all of them put together in their unimportant succession, but the action which brings them together and unifies them. As a result, when the honest conscience judges the writer by immobilizing him in one of these forms, when, for instance, it attempts to condemn the work because it is a failure, the writer's other honesty protests in the name of the other stages, in the name of the purity of art, which sees its own triumph in the failure—and likewise, every time a writer is challenged under one of his aspects, he has no choice but to present himself as someone else, and when addressed as the author of a beautiful work, disown that work, and when admired as an inspiration and a genius, see in himself only application and hard work, and when read by everyone, say: "Who can read me? I haven't written anything." This shifting on the part of the writer makes him into someone who is perpetually absent, an irresponsi-

---

* Blanchot is referring to a remark made by Nicolas Boileau (1637–1711) in his first *Satire*: "J'appelle un chat un chat et Rolet un fripon" ("I call a cat a cat and Rolet a rascal"). Rolet was a notorious figure of the time.—TRANS.

ble character without a conscience, but this shifting also forms the extent of his presence, of his risks and responsibility.

The trouble is that the writer is not only several people in one, but each stage of himself denies all the others, demands everything for itself alone, and does not tolerate any conciliation or compromise. The writer must respond to several absolute and absolutely different commands at once, and his morality is made up of the confrontation and opposition of implacably hostile rules.

One rule says to him: "You will not write, you will remain nothingness, you will keep silent, you will not know words."

The other rule says: "Know nothing but words."

"Write to say nothing."

"Write to say something."

"No works; rather, the experience of yourself, the knowledge of what is unknown to you."

"A work! A real work, recognized by other people and important to other people."

"Obliterate the reader."

"Obliterate yourself before the reader."

"Write in order to be true."

"Write for the sake of truth."

"Then be a lie, because to write with truth in mind is to write what is not yet true and perhaps never will be true."

"It doesn't matter, write in order to act."

"Write—you who are afraid to act."

"Let freedom speak in you."

"Oh! do not let freedom become a word in you."

Which law should be obeyed? Which voice should be listened to? But the writer must listen to them all! What confusion! Isn't clarity his law? Yes, clarity, too. He must therefore oppose himself, deny himself even as he affirms himself, look for the deepness of the night in the facility of the day, look in the shadows which never begin, to find the sure light which cannot end. He must save the world and be the abyss, justify existence and allow what does not exist to speak; he must be at the end of all eras in the universal plenitude, and he is the origin, the birth of what does nothing but come into being. Is he all that? Literature is all that, in him. But isn't all that what literature would *like* to be, what in reality it is not? In that case, literature is nothing. But is it nothing?

Literature is not nothing. People who are contemptuous of literature are mistaken in thinking they are condemning it by saying it is nothing. "All that is only literature." This is how people create an opposition between action, which is a concrete initiative in the world, and the written word, which is supposed to be a passive expression on the surface of the world; people who are in favor of action reject literature, which does not act, and those in search of passion become writers so as not to act. But this is to condemn and to love in an abusive way. If we see work as the force of history, the force that transforms man while it transforms the world, then a writer's activity must be recognized as the highest form of work. When a man works, what does he do? He produces an object. That object is the realization of a plan which was unreal before then: it is the affirmation of a reality different from the elements which constitute it and it is the future of new objects, to the extent that it becomes a tool capable of creating other objects. For example, my project might be to get warm. As long as this project is only a desire, I can turn it over every possible way and still it will not make me warm. But now I build a stove: the stove transforms the empty ideal which was my desire into something real; it affirms the presence in the world of something which was not there before, and in so doing, denies something which was there before; before, I had in front of me stones and cast iron; now I no longer have either stones or cast iron, but instead the product of the transformation of these elements—that is, their denial and destruction—by work. Because of this object, the world is now different. All the more different because this stove will allow me to make other objects, which will in turn deny the former condition of the world and prepare its future. These objects, which I have produced by changing the states of things, will in turn change me. The idea of heat is nothing, but actual heat will make my life a different kind of life, and every new thing I am able to do from now on because of this heat will also make me someone different. Thus is history formed, say Hegel and Marx—by work which realizes being in denying it, and reveals it at the end of the negation.*

But what is a writer doing when he writes? Everything a man does when he works, but to an outstanding degree. The writer, too, produces something—a work in the highest sense of the word. He produces this work by transforming natural and human realities. When he writes, his starting point is a certain state of language, a certain form of culture, certain books, and also certain objective elements—ink, paper, printing presses. In order to write, he must destroy language in its present form and create it in another form, denying books as he forms a book out of what other books are not. This new book is certainly a reality: it can be seen, touched, even read. In any case, it is not nothing. Before I wrote it, I had an idea of it, at least I had the project of writing it, but I believe there is the same difference between that idea and the volume in which it is realized as between the desire for heat and the stove which makes me warm. For me, the written volume is an extraordinary, unforeseeable innovation—such that it is impossible for me to conceive what it is capable of being without writing it. This is why it seems to me to be an experiment whose effects I cannot grasp, no matter how consciously they were produced, and in the face of which I shall be unable to remain the same, for this reason: in the presence of something other, I become other: But there is an even more decisive reason: this other thing—the book—of which I had only an idea and which I could not possibly have known in advance, is precisely myself become other.

The book, the written thing, enters the world and carries out its work of transformation and negation. It, too, is the future of many other things, and not only books: by the projects which it can give rise to, by the undertakings it encourages, by the totality of the world of which it is a modified reflection, it is an infinite source of new realities, and because of these new realities existence will be something it was not before.

* Alexandre Kojève offers this interpretation of Hegel in his *Introduction to the Reading of Hegel* (Readings on *The Phenomenology of the Spirit*, selected and published by Raymond Queneau).

So is the book nothing? Then why should the act of building a stove pass for the sort of work which forms and produces history, and why should the act of writing seem like pure passivity which remains in the margins of history and which history produces in spite of itself? The question seems unreasonable, and yet it weighs on the writer and its weight is crushing. At first sight one has the impression that the formative power of written works is incomparably great; one has the impression that the writer is endowed with more power to act than anyone else since his actions are immeasurable, limitless: we know (or we like to believe) that one single work can change the course of the world. But this is precisely what makes us think twice. The influence authors exert is very great, it goes infinitely far beyond their actions, to such an extent that what is real in their actions does not carry over into their influence and that tiny bit of reality does not contain the real substance that the extent of their influence would require. What is an author capable of? Everything—first of all, everything: he is fettered, he is enslaved, but as long as he can find a few moments of freedom in which to write, he is *free* to create a world without slaves, a world in which the slaves become the masters and formulate a new law; thus, by writing, the chained man immediately obtains freedom for himself and for the world; he denies everything he is, in order to become everything he is not. In this sense, his work is a prodigious act, the greatest and most important there is. But let us examine this more closely. Insofar as he *immediately* gives himself the freedom he does not have, he is neglecting the actual conditions for his emancipation, he is neglecting to do the real thing that must be done so that the abstract idea of freedom can be realized. His negation is *global.* It not only negates his situation as a man who has been walled into prison but bypasses time that will open holes in these walls; it negates the negation of time, it negates the negation of limits. This is why this negation negates nothing, in the end, why the work in which it is realized is not a truly negative, destructive act of transformation, but rather the realization of the inability to negate anything, the refusal to take part in the world; it transformed the freedom which would have to be embodied in things in the process of time into an ideal above time, empty and inaccessible.

A writer's influence is linked to this privilege of being master of everything. But he is only master of everything, he possesses only the infinite; he lacks the finite, limit escapes him. Now, one cannot act in the infinite, one cannot accomplish anything in the unlimited, so that if a writer acts in quite a real way as he produces this real thing which is called a book, he is also discrediting all action by this action, because he is substituting for the world of determined things and defined work a world in which *everything* is *instantly* given and there is nothing left to do but read it and enjoy it.

In general, the writer seems to be subjected to a state of inactivity because he is the master of the imaginary, and those who follow him into the realm of the imaginary lose sight of the problems of their true lives. But the danger he represents is much more serious. The truth is that he ruins action, not because he deals with what is unreal but because he makes *all* of reality available to us. Unreality begins with the whole. The realm of the imaginary is not a strange region situated beyond the world, it is the world itself, but the world as entire, manifold, the world as a whole. That is why it is not in the world, because it is the world, grasped and realized in its entirety by the global negation of all the individual realities contained in it, by their disqualification, their absence, by the realization of that absence itself, which is how literary creation begins, for when literary creation goes back over each thing and each being, it cherishes the illusion that it is creating them, because now it is seeing and naming them from the starting point of *everything*, from the starting point of the *absence* of everything, that is, from nothing.

Certainly that literature which is said to be "purely imaginative" has its dangers. First of all, it is not pure imagination. It believes that it stands apart from everyday realities and actual events, but the truth is that it has stepped aside from them; it is that distance, that remove from the everyday which necessarily takes the everyday into consideration and describes it as separateness, as pure strangeness. What is more, it makes this distance into an absolute value, and then this separateness seems to be a source of general understanding, the capacity to grasp everything and attain everything immediately, for those who submit to its enchantment enough to emerge from both their life, which is nothing but limited understanding, and time, which is nothing but a narrow perspective. All this is the lie of a fiction. But this kind of literature has on its side the fact that it is not trying to deceive us: it presents itself as imaginary; it puts to sleep only those who want to go to sleep.

What is far more deceitful is the literature of action. It calls on people to do something. But if it wants to remain authentic literature, it must base its representation of this "something to do," this predetermined and specific goal, on a world where such an action turns back into the unreality of an abstract and absolute value. "Something to do," as it may be expressed in a work of literature, is never more than "everything remains to be done," whether it presents itself as this "everything," that is, as an absolute value, or whether it needs this "everything," into which it vanishes, to justify itself and prove that it has merit. The language of a writer, even if he is a revolutionary, is not the language of command. It does not command, it presents; and it does not present by causing whatever it portrays to be present, but by portraying it behind everything, as the meaning and the absence of this everything. The result is either that the appeal of the author to the reader is only an empty appeal, and expresses only the effort which a man cut off from the world makes to reenter the world, as he stands discreetly at its periphery—or that the "something to do," which can be recovered only by starting from absolute values, appears to the reader precisely as that which cannot be done or as that which requires neither work nor action in order to be done.

As we know, a writer's main temptations are called stoicism, skepticism, and the unhappy consciousness. These are all ways of thinking that a writer adopts for reasons he believes he has thought out carefully, but which only literature has thought out in him. A stoic: he is the man of the universe, which itself exists only on paper, and, a prisoner or a poor man, he endures his condition stoically because he can write and because the one minute of freedom in which he writes is enough to make him powerful and free, is enough to give him not his own freedom, which he derides, but universal freedom. A nihilist, because he does not simply negate this and that by methodical work which slowly transforms each thing: he negates everything at once, and he is obliged to negate everything, since he deals only with everything. The unhappy consciousness! It is only too evident that this unhappiness is his most profound talent, since he is a writer only by virtue of his fragmented consciousness divided into irreconcilable moments called inspiration—which negates all work; work—which negates the nothingness of genius; the ephemeral work—in which he creates himself by negating himself; the work as everything—in which he takes back from himself and from other people everything which he seems to give to himself and to them. But there is one other temptation.

Let us acknowledge that in a writer there is a movement which proceeds without pause, and almost without transition, from nothing to everything. Let us see in him that negation that is not satisfied with the unreality in which it exists, because it wishes to realize itself and can do so only by negating something real, more real than words, more true than the isolated individual in control: it therefore keeps urging him toward a worldly life and a public existence in order to induce him to conceive how, even as he writes, he can become that very existence. It is at this point that he encounters those decisive moments in history when everything seems put in question, when law, faith, the State, the world above, the world of the past—everything sinks effortlessly, without work, into nothingness. The man knows he has not stepped out of history, but history is now the void, the void in the process of realization; it is *absolute* freedom which has become an event. Such periods are given the name Revolution. At this moment, freedom aspires to be realized in the *immediate* form of *everything* is possible, everything can be done. A fabulous moment—and no one who has experienced it can completely recover from it, since he has experienced history as his own history and his own freedom as universal freedom. These moments are, in fact, fabulous moments: in them, fable speaks; in them, the speech of fable becomes action. That the writer should be tempted by them is completely appropriate. Revolutionary action is in every respect analogous to action as embodied in literature: the passage from nothing to everything, the affirmation of the absolute as event and of every event as absolute. Revolutionary action explodes with the same force and the same facility as the writer who has only to set down a few words side by side in order to change the world. Revolutionary action also has the same demand for purity, and the certainty that everything it does has absolute value, that it is not just any action performed to bring about some desirable and respectable goal, but that it is itself the ultimate goal, the Last Act. This last act is freedom, and the only choice left is between freedom and nothing. This is why, at that point, the only tolerable slogan is Freedom or Death. Thus the Reign of Terror comes into being. People cease to be individuals working at specific tasks, acting here and only now: each person is universal freedom, and universal freedom knows nothing about elsewhere or tomorrow, or work or a work accomplished. At such times there is nothing left for anyone to do, because everything has been done. No one has a right to a private life any longer, everything is public, and the most guilty person is the suspect—the person who has a secret, who keeps a thought, an intimacy to himself. And in the end no one has a right to his life any longer, to his actually separate and physically distinct existence. This is the meaning of the Reign of Terror. Every citizen has a right to death, so to speak: death is not a sentence passed on him, it is his most essential right; he is not suppressed as a guilty person—he needs death so that he can proclaim himself a citizen, and it is in the disappearance of death that freedom causes him to be born. Where this is concerned, the French Revolution has a clearer meaning than any other revolution. Death in the Reign of Terror is not simply a way of punishing seditionaries; rather, since it becomes the unavoidable, in some sense the desired lot of everyone, it appears as the very operation of freedom in free men. When the blade falls on Saint-Just and Robespierre, in a sense it executes no one. Robespierre's virtue, Saint-Just's relentlessness, are simply their existences already suppressed, the anticipated presence of their deaths, the decision to allow freedom to assert itself completely in them and through its universality to negate the particular reality of their lives. Granted, perhaps they caused the Reign of Terror to take place. But the Terror they personify does not come from the death they inflict on others but from the death they inflict on themselves. They bear its features, they do their thinking and make their decisions with death sitting on their shoulders, and this is why their thinking is cold, implacable; it has the freedom of a decapitated head. The Terrorists are those who desire absolute freedom and are fully conscious that this constitutes a desire for their own death, they are conscious of the freedom they affirm, as they are conscious of their death, which they realize, and consequently they behave during their lifetimes not like people living among other living people but like beings deprived of being, like universal thoughts, pure abstractions beyond history, judging and deciding in the name of all of history.

Death as an event no longer has any importance. During the Reign of Terror individuals die and it means nothing. In the famous words of Hegel, "It is thus the coldest and meanest of all deaths, with no more significance than cutting off a head of cabbage or swallowing a mouthful of water."* Why? Isn't death the achievement of freedom—that is, the richest moment of meaning? But it is also only the empty point in that freedom, a manifestation of the fact that such a freedom is still abstract, ideal (literary), that it is only poverty and platitude. Each person dies, but everyone is alive, and that really also means everyone is dead. But "is dead" is the positive side of freedom which has become the world: here, being is revealed as absolute. "Dying," on the other hand, is pure insignificance, an event without concrete reality, one which has lost all value as a personal and interior drama because there is no longer any interior. It is the moment when *I die* signifies to me as I die a banality which there is no way to take into consideration: in the liberated world and in these moments when freedom is an absolute apparition, dying is unimportant and death has no depth. The Reign of Terror and revolution—not war—have taught us this.

* Hegel, *Phenomenology of the Spirit*, p. 360.—TRANS.

The writer sees himself in the Revolution. It attracts him because it is the time during which literature becomes history. It is his truth. Any writer who is not induced by the very fact of writing to think, "I am the revolution, only freedom allows me to write," is not really writing. In 1793 there is a man who identifies himself completely with revolution and the Reign of Terror. He is an aristocrat clinging to the battlements of his medieval castle, a tolerant man, rather shy and obsequiously polite: but he writes, all he does is write, and it does not matter that freedom puts him back into the Bastille after having brought him out, he is the one who understands freedom the best, because he understands that it is a time when the most insane passions can turn into political realities, a time when they have a right to be seen, and are the law. He is also the man for whom death is the greatest passion and the ultimate platitude, who cuts off people's heads the way you cut a head of cabbage, with such great indifference that nothing is more unreal than the death he inflicts, and yet no one has been more acutely aware that death is sovereign, that freedom is death. Sade is the writer par excellence, he combines all the writer's contradictions. Alone: of all men he is the most alone, and yet at the same time a public figure and an important political personage; forever locked up and yet absolutely free, theoretician and symbol of absolute freedom. He writes a vast body of work, and that work exists for no one. Unknown: but what he portrays has an immediate significance for everyone. He is nothing more than a writer, and he depicts life raised to the level of a passion, a passion which has become cruelty and madness. He turns the most bizarre, the most hidden, the most unreasonable kind of feeling into a universal affirmation, the reality of a public statement which is consigned to history to become a legitimate explanation of man's general condition. He is, finally, negation itself: his oeuvre is nothing but the work of negation, his experience the action of a furious negation, driven to blood, denying other people, denying God, denying nature, and, within this circle in which it runs endlessly, reveling in itself as absolute sovereignty.

Literature contemplates itself in revolution, it finds its justification in revolution, and if it has been called the Reign of Terror, this is because its ideal is indeed that moment in history, that moment when "life endures death and maintains itself in it" in order to gain from death the possibility of speaking and the truth of speech. This is the "question" that seeks to pose itself in literature, the "question" that is its essence. Literature is bound to language. Language is reassuring and disquieting at the same time. When we speak, we gain control over things with satisfying ease. I say, "This woman," and she is immediately available to me, I push her away, I bring her close, she is everything I want her to be, she becomes the place in which the most surprising sorts of transformations occur and actions unfold: speech is life's ease and security. We cannot do anything with an object that has no name. Primitive man knows that the possession of words gives him mastery over things, but for him the relationship between words and the world is so close that the manipulation of language is as difficult and as fraught with peril as contact with living beings: the name has not emerged from the thing, it is the inside of the thing which has been dangerously brought out into the open and yet it is still the hidden depths of the thing; the thing has therefore not yet been named. The more closely man becomes attached to a civilization, the more he can manipulate words with innocence and composure. Is it that words have lost all relation to what they designate? But this absence of relation is not a defect, and if it is a defect, this defect is the only thing that gives language its full value, so that of all languages the most perfect is the language of mathematics, which is spoken in a rigorous way and to which no entity corresponds.

I say, "This woman." Hölderlin, Mallarmé, and all poets whose theme is the essence of poetry have felt that the act of naming is disquieting and marvelous. A word may give me its meaning, but first it suppresses it. For me to be able to say, "This woman," I must somehow take her flesh-and-blood reality away from her, cause her to be absent, annihilate her. The word gives me the being, but it gives it to me deprived of being. The word is the absence of that being, its nothingness, what is left of it when it has lost being—the very fact that it does not exist. Considered in this light, speaking is a curious right. In a text dating from before *The Phenomenology*, Hegel, here the friend and kindred spirit of Hölderlin, writes:

"Adam's first act, which made him master of the animals, was to give them names, that is, he annihilated them in their existence (as existing creatures)."* Hegel means that from that moment on, the cat ceased to be a uniquely real cat and became an idea as well. The meaning of speech, then, requires that before any word is spoken, there must be a sort of immense hecatomb, a preliminary flood plunging all of creation into a total sea. God had created living things, but man had to annihilate them. Not until then did they take on meaning for him, and he in turn created them out of the death into which they had disappeared; only instead of beings (*êtres*) and, as we say, existants (*existants*), there remained only being (*l'être*), and man was condemned not to be able to approach anything or experience anything except through the meaning he had to create. He saw that he was enclosed in daylight, and he knew this day could not end, because the end itself was light, since it was from the end of beings that their meaning—which is being—had come.

Of course my language does not kill anyone. And yet, when I say, "This woman," real death has been announced and is already present in my language; my language means that this person, who is here right now, can be detached from herself, removed from her existence and her presence, and suddenly plunged into a nothingness in which there is no existence or presence; my language essentially signifies the possibility of this destruction; it is a constant, bold allusion to such an event. My language does not kill anyone. But if this woman were not really capable of dying, if she were not threatened by death at every moment of her life, bound and joined to death by an essential bond, I would not be able to carry out that ideal negation, that deferred assassination which is what my language is.

Therefore it is accurate to say that when I speak, death speaks in me. My speech is a warning that at this very moment death is loose

* From a collection of essays titled *System of 1803–1804*. A. Kojève, in his *Introduction to the Reading of Hegel*, interpreting a passage from the *Phenomenology*, demonstrates in a remarkable way how for Hegel comprehension was equivalent to murder.

in the world, that it has suddenly appeared between me, as I speak, and the being I address: it is there between us as the distance that separates us, but this distance is also what prevents us from being separated, because its contains the condition for all understanding. Death alone allows me to grasp what I want to attain; it exists in words as the only way they can have meaning. Without death, everything would sink into absurdity and nothingness.

This situation has various consequences. Clearly, in me, the power to speak is also linked to my absence from being. I say my name, and it is as though I were chanting my own dirge: I separate myself from myself, I am no longer either my presence or my reality, but an objective, impersonal presence, the presence of my name, which goes beyond me and whose stonelike immobility performs exactly the same function for me as a tombstone weighing on the void. When I speak, I deny the existence of what I am saying, but I also deny the existence of the person who is saying it: if my speech reveals being in its nonexistence, it also affirms that this revelation is made on the basis of the nonexistence of the person making it, out of his power to remove himself from himself, to be other than his being. This is why, if true language is to begin, the life that will carry this language must have experienced its nothingness, must have "trembled in the depths; and everything in it that was fixed and stable must have been shaken." Language can begin only with the void; no fullness, no certainty can ever speak; something essential is lacking in anyone who expresses himself. Negation is tied to language. When I first begin, I do not speak in order to say something; rather, a nothing demands to speak, nothing speaks, nothing finds its being in speech, and the being of speech is nothing. This formulation explains why literature's ideal has been the following: to say nothing, to speak in order to say nothing. That is not the musing of a high-class kind of nihilism. Language perceives that its meaning derives not from what exists but from its own retreat before existence, and it is tempted to proceed no further than this retreat, to try to attain negation in itself and to make everything of nothing. If one is not to talk about things except to say what makes them nothing, then to say nothing is really the only hope of saying everything about them.

A hope which is naturally problematic. Everyday language calls a cat a cat, as if the living cat and its name were identical, as if it were not true that when we name the cat, we retain nothing of it but its absence, what it is not. Yet for a moment everyday language is right, in that even if the word excludes the existence of what it designates, it still refers to it through the thing's nonexistence, which has become its essence. To name the cat is, if you like, to make it into a non-cat, a cat that has ceased to exist, has ceased to be a living cat, but this does not mean one is making it into a dog, or even a non-dog. That is the primary difference between common language and literary language. The first accepts that once the nonexistence of the cat has passed into the word, the cat itself comes to life again fully and certainly in the form of its idea (its being) and its meaning: on the level of being (idea), the word restores to the cat all the certainty it had on the level of existence. And in fact that certainty is even much greater: things can change if they have to, sometimes they stop being what they are—they remain hostile, unavailable, inaccessible; but the being of these things, their idea, does not change: the idea is definitive, it is sure, we even call it eternal. Let us hold on to words, then, and not revert back to things, let us not let go of words, not believe they are sick. Then we shall be at peace.

Common language is probably right, this is the price we pay for our peace. But literary language is made of uneasiness; it is also made of contradictions. Its position is not very stable or secure. On the one hand, its only interest in a thing is in the meaning of the thing, its absence, and it would like to attain this absence absolutely in itself and for itself, to grasp in its entirety the infinite movement of comprehension. What is more, it observes that the word "cat" is not only the nonexistence of the cat but a nonexistence made *word*, that is, a completely determined and objective reality. It sees that there is a difficulty and even a lie in this. How can it hope to have achieved what it set out to do, since it has transposed the unreality of the thing into the reality of language? How could the infinite absence of comprehension consent to be confused with the limited, restricted presence of a single word? And isn't everyday language mistaken when it tries to persuade us of this? In fact, it is deceiving itself and it is deceiving us, too. Speech is not sufficient for the truth it contains. Take the trouble to listen to a single word: in that word, nothingness is struggling and toiling away, it digs tirelessly, doing its utmost to find a way out, nullifying what encloses it—it is infinite disquiet, formless and nameless vigilance. Already the seal which held this nothingness within the limits of the word and within the guise of its meaning has been broken; now there is access to other names, names which are less fixed, still vague, more capable of adapting to the savage freedom of the negative essence—they are unstable groups, no longer terms but the movement of terms, an endless sliding of "turns of phrase" which do not lead anywhere. Thus is born the image that does not directly designate the thing but, rather, what the thing is not; it speaks of a dog instead of a cat. This is how the pursuit begins in which all of language, in motion, is asked to give in to the uneasy demands of one single thing that has been deprived of being and that, after having wavered between each word, tries to lay hold of them all again in order to negate them all at once, so that they will designate the void as they sink down into it—this void which they can neither fill nor represent.

Even if literature stopped here, it would have a strange and embarrassing job to do. But it does not stop here. It recalls the first name which would be the murder Hegel speaks of. The "existant" was called out of its existence by the word, and it became being. This *Lazare, veni foras* summoned the dark, cadaverous reality from its primordial depths and in exchange gave it only the life of the mind. Language knows that its kingdom is day and not the intimacy of the unrevealed; it knows that in order for the day to begin, for the day to be that Orient which Hölderlin glimpsed—not light that has become the repose of noon but the terrible force that draws beings into the world and illuminates them—something must be left out. Negation cannot be created out of anything but the reality of what it is negating; language derives its value and its pride from the fact that it is the achievement of this negation; but in the beginning, what was lost? The torment of language is what it lacks because of the necessity that it be the lack of precisely this. It cannot even name it.

Whoever sees God dies. In speech what dies is what gives life to speech; speech is the life of that death, it is "the life that endures death and maintains itself in it." What wonderful power. But something was there and is no longer there. Something has disappeared. How can I recover it, how can I turn around and look at what exists *before*, if all my power consists of making it into what exists *after*? The language of literature is a search for this moment which precedes literature. Literature usually calls it existence; it wants the cat as it exists, the pebble *taking the side of things*, not man but the pebble, and in this pebble what man rejects by saying it, what is the foundation of speech and what speech excludes in speaking, the abyss, Lazarus in the tomb and not Lazarus brought back into the daylight, the one who already smells bad, who is Evil, Lazarus lost and not Lazarus saved and brought back to life. *I say a flower*! But in the absence where I mention it, through the oblivion to which I relegate the image it gives me, in the depths of this heavy word, itself looming up like an unknown thing, I passionately summon the darkness of this flower, I summon this perfume that passes through me though I do not breathe it, this dust that impregnates me though I do not see it, this color which is a trace and not light. Then what hope do I have of attaining the thing I push away? My hope lies in the materiality of language, in the fact that words are things, too, are a kind of nature—this is given to me and gives me more than I can understand. Just now the reality of words was an obstacle. Now, it is my only chance. A name ceases to be the ephemeral passing of nonexistence and becomes a concrete ball, a solid mass of existence; language, abandoning the sense, the meaning which was all it wanted to be, tries to become senseless. Everything physical takes precedence: rhythm, weight, mass, shape, and then the paper on which one writes, the trail of the ink, the book. Yes, happily language is a thing: it is a written thing, a bit of bark, a sliver of rock, a fragment of clay in which the reality of the earth continues to exist. The word acts not as an ideal force but as an obscure power, as an incantation that coerces things, makes them *really* present outside of themselves. It is an element, a piece barely detached from its subterranean surroundings: it is no longer a name, but rather one moment in the universal anonymity, a bald statement, the stupor of a confrontation in the depths of obscurity. And in this way language insists on playing its own game without man, who created it. Literature now dispenses with the writer: it is no longer this inspiration at work, this negation asserting itself, this idea inscribed in the world as though it were the absolute perspective of the world in its totality. It is not beyond the world, but neither is it the world itself: it is the presence of things before the *world* exists, their perseverance after the world has disappeared, the stubbornness of what remains when everything vanishes and the dumbfoundedness of what appears when nothing exists. That is why it cannot be confused with consciousness, which illuminates things and makes decisions; it is *my* consciousness *without me*, the radiant passivity of mineral substances, the lucidity of the depths of torpor. It is not the night, it is the obsession of the night; it is not the night but the consciousness of the night, which lies awake watching for a chance to surprise itself and because of that is constantly being dissipated. It is not the day, it is the side of the day that day has rejected in order to become light. And it is not death either, because it manifests existence without being, existence which remains below existence, like an inexorable affirmation, without beginning or end—death as the impossibility of dying.

By turning itself into an inability to reveal anything, literature is attempting to become the revelation of what revelation destroys. This is a tragic endeavor. Literature says, "I no longer represent, I am; I do not signify, I present." But this wish to be a thing, this refusal to mean anything, a refusal immersed in words turned to salt; in short, this destiny which literature becomes as it becomes the language of no one, the writing of no writer, the light of a consciousness deprived of self, this insane effort to bury itself in itself, to hide itself behind the fact that it is visible—all this is what literature now manifests, what literature now shows. If it were to become as mute as a stone, as passive as the corpse enclosed behind that stone, its decision to lose the capacity for speech would still be legible on the stone and would be enough to wake that bogus corpse.

Literature learns that it cannot go beyond itself toward its own end: it hides, it does not give itself away. It knows it is the movement through which whatever disappears keeps appearing. When it names something, whatever it designates is abolished; but whatever is abolished is also sustained, and the thing has found a refuge (in the being which is the word) rather than a threat. When literature refuses to name anything, when it turns a name into something obscure and meaningless, witness to the primordial obscurity, what has disappeared in this case—the meaning of the name—is really destroyed, but signification in general has appeared in its place, the meaning of the meaninglessness embedded in the word as expression of the obscurity of existence, so that although the precise meaning of the terms has faded, what asserts itself now is the very possibility of signifying, the empty power of bestowing meaning—a strange impersonal light.

By negating the day, literature re-creates day in the form of fatality; by affirming the night, it finds the night as the impossibility of the night. This is its discovery. When day is the light of the world, it illuminates what it lets us see: it is the capacity to grasp, to live, it is the answer "understood" in every question. But if we call the day to account, if we reach a point where we push it away in order to find out what is prior to the day, under it we discover that the day is already present, and that what is prior to the day is still the day, but in the form of an inability to disappear, not a capacity to make something appear: the darkness of necessity, not the light of freedom. The nature, then, of what is prior to the day, of prediurnal existence, is the dark side of the day, and that dark side is not the undisclosed mystery of its beginning but its inevitable presence—the statement "There is no day," which merges with "There is already day," its appearance coinciding with the moment when it has not yet appeared. In the course of the day, the day allows us to escape from things, it lets us comprehend them, and as it lets us comprehend them, it makes them transparent and as if null—but what we cannot escape from is the day: within it we are free, but it, itself, is fatality, and day in the form of fatality is the being of what is prior to the day, the existence we must turn away from in order to speak and comprehend.

If one looks at it in a certain way, literature has two slopes. One side of literature is turned toward the movement of negation by which things are separated from themselves and destroyed in order to be known, subjugated, communicated. Literature is not content to accept only the fragmentary, successive results of this movement of negation: it wants to grasp the movement itself and it wants to comprehend the results in their totality. If negation is assumed to have gotten control of everything, then real things, taken one by one, all refer back to that unreal whole which they form together, to the world which is their meaning as a group, and this is the point of view that literature has adopted—it looks at things from the point of view of this still *imaginary* whole which they would *really* constitute if negation could be achieved. Hence its non-realism— the shadow which is its prey. Hence its distrust of words, its need to apply the movement of negation to language itself and to exhaust it by realizing it as that totality on the basis of which each term would be nothing.

But there is another side to literature. Literature is a concern for the reality of things, for their unknown, free, and silence existence; literature is their innocence and their forbidden presence, it is the being which protests against revelation, it is the defiance of what does not want to take place outside. In this way, it sympathizes with darkness, with aimless passion, with lawless violence, with everything in the world that seems to perpetuate the refusal to come into the world. In this way, too, it allies itself with the reality of language, it makes language into matter without contour, content without form, a force that is capricious and impersonal and says nothing, reveals nothing, simply announces—through its refusal to say anything—that it comes from night and will return to night. In itself, this metamorphosis is not unsuccessful. It is certainly true that words are transformed. They no longer *signify* shadow, earth, they no longer represent the absence of shadow and earth which is meaning, which is the shadow's light, which is the transparency of the earth: opacity is their answer; the flutter of closing wings is their speech; in them, physical weight is present as the stifling density of an accumulation of syllables that has lost all meaning. The metamorphosis has taken place. But beyond the change that has solidified, petrified, and stupefied words two things reappear in this metamorphosis: the meaning of this metamorphosis, which illuminates the words, and the meaning the words contain by virtue of their apparition as things or, if it should happen this way, as vague, indeterminate, elusive existences in which nothing appears, the heart of depth without appearance. Literature has certainly triumphed over the meaning of words, but what it has found in words considered apart from their meaning is meaning that has become thing: and thus it is meaning detached from its conditions, separated from its moments, wandering like an empty power, a power no one can do anything with, a power without power, the simple inability to cease to be, but which, because of that, appears to be the proper determination of indeterminate and meaningless existence. In this endeavor, literature does not confine itself to rediscovering in the interior what it tried to leave behind on the threshold. Because what it finds, as the interior, is the outside which has been changed from the outlet it once was into the impossibility of going out—and what it finds as the darkness of existence is the being of day which has been changed from explicatory light, creative of meaning, into the aggravation of what one cannot prevent oneself from understanding and the stifling obsession of a reason without any principle, without any beginning, which one cannot account for. Literature is that experience through which the consciousness discovers its being in its inability to lose consciousness, in the movement whereby, as it disappears, as it tears itself away from the meticulousness of an I, it is re-created beyond unconsciousness as an impersonal spontaneity, the desperate eagerness of a haggard knowledge which knows nothing, which no one knows, and which ignorance always discovers behind itself as its own shadow changed into a gaze.

One can, then, accuse language of having become an interminable resifting of words instead of the silence it wanted to achieve. Or one can complain that it has immersed itself in the conventions of literature when what it wanted was to be absorbed into existence. That is true. But this endless resifting of words without content, this continuousness of speech through an immense pillage of words, is precisely the profound nature of a silence that talks even in its dumbness, a silence that is speech empty of words, an echo speaking on and on in the midst of silence. And in the same way literature, a blind vigilance which in its attempt to escape from itself plunges deeper and deeper into its own obsession, is the only rendering of the obsession of existence, if this itself is the very impossibility of emerging from existence, if it is being which is always flung back into being, that which in the bottomless depth is already at the bottom of the abyss, a recourse against which there is no recourse.*

Literature is divided between these two slopes. The problem is that even though they are apparently incompatible, they do not lead toward distinctly different works or goals, and that an art which purports to follow one slope is already on the other. The first slope is meaningful prose. Its goal is to express things in a language that designates things according to what they mean. This is the way everyone speaks; and many people write the way we speak. But still on this side of language, there comes a moment when art realizes that everyday speech is dishonest and abandons it. What is art's complaint about everyday speech? It says it lacks meaning: art feels it is madness to think that in each word some thing is completely

---

* In his book *Existence and Existents*, Emmanuel Lévinas uses the term *il y a* ("there is") to throw some "light" on this anonymous and impersonal flow of being that precedes all being, being that is already present in the heart of disappearance, that in the depths of annihilation still returns to being, being as the fatality of being, nothingness as existence: when there is nothing, *il y a being*. See also *Deucalion I*. (*Existence and Existents*, trans. A. Lingis, Boston: Kluwer, 1978).—TRANS.

present through the absence that determines it, and so art sets off in quest of a language that can recapture this absence itself and represent the endless movement of comprehension. We do not need to discuss this position again, we have described it at length already. But what can be said about this kind of art? That it is a search for a pure form, that it is a vain preoccupation with empty words? Quite the contrary: its only concern is true meaning; its only preoccupation is to safeguard the movement by which this meaning becomes truth. To be fair, we must consider it more significant than any ordinary prose, which only subsists on false meanings: it represents the world for us, it teaches us to discover the total being of the world, it is the work of the negative in the world and for the world. How can we help admiring it as preeminently active, lively, and lucid art? Of course we must. But then we must appreciate the same qualities in Mallarmé, who is the master of this art.

Mallarmé is on the other slope of literature, too. In some sense all the people we call poets come together on that slope. Why? Because they are interested in the reality of language, because they are not interested in the world, but in what things and beings would be if there were no world; because they devote themselves to literature as to an impersonal power that only wants to be engulfed and submerged. If this is what poetry is like, at least we will know why it must be withdrawn from history, where it produces a strange insectlike buzzing in the margins, and we will also know that no work which allows itself to slip down this slope toward the chasm can be called a work of prose. Well, what is it, then? Everyone understands that literature cannot be divided up, and that if you choose exactly where your place in it is, if you convince yourself that you really are where you wanted to be, you risk becoming very confused, because literature has already insidiously caused you to pass from one slope to the other and changed you into something you were not before. This is its treachery; this is also its cunning version of the truth. A novelist writes in the most transparent kind of prose, he describes men we could have met ourselves and actions we could have performed; he says his aim is to express the reality of a human world the way Flaubert did. In the end, though, his work really has only one subject. What is it? The horror of existence deprived of the world, the process through which whatever ceases to be continues to be, whatever is forgotten is always answerable to memory, whatever dies encounters only the impossibility of dying, whatever seeks to attain the beyond is always still here. This *process* is day which has become fatality, consciousness whose light is no longer the lucidity of the vigil but the stupor of lack of sleep, it is existence without being, as poetry tries to recapture it behind the meaning of words, which reject it.

Now here is a man who does more observing than writing: he walks in a pine forest, looks at a wasp, picks up a stone. He is a sort of scholar, but this scholar fades away in the face of what he knows, sometimes in the face of what he wants to know; he is a man who learns for the sake of other men: he has gone over to the side of objects, sometimes he is water, sometimes a pebble, sometimes a tree, and when he observes things, he does it for the sake of things, and when he describes something, it is the thing itself that describes itself. Now, this is the surprising aspect of the transformation, because no doubt it is possible to become a tree, and is there any writer who could not succeed in making a tree talk? But Francis Ponge's tree is a tree that has observed Francis Ponge and that describes itself as it imagines Ponge might describe it. These are strange descriptions. Certain traits make them seem completely human: the fact is that the tree knows the weakness of men who only speak about what they know; but all these metaphors borrowed from the picturesque human world, these images which form an image, really represent the way things regard man, they really represent the singularity of human speech animated by the life of the cosmos and the power of seeds; this is why other things slip in among these images, among certain objective notions— because the tree knows that science is a common ground of understanding between the two worlds: what slip in are vague recollections rising from deep down in the earth, expressions that are in the process of metamorphosing, words in which a thick fluidity of vegetable growth insinuates itself under the clear meaning. Doesn't everyone think he understands these descriptions, written in perfectly meaningful prose? Doesn't everyone think they belong to the clear and human side of literature? And yet they do not belong to the world but to the underside of the world; they do not attest to form but to lack of form, and they are clear only to a person who does not penetrate them, the opposite of the oracular words of the tree of Dodona—another tree—which were obscure but concealed a meaning: these are clear only because they hide their lack of meaning. Indeed, Ponge's descriptions begin at that hypothetical moment after the world has been achieved, history completed, nature almost made human, when speech advances to meet the thing and the thing learns to speak. Ponge captures this touching moment when existence, which is still mute, encounters speech at the edge of the world, speech which as we know, is the murderer of existence. From the depths of dumbness, he hears the striving of an antediluvian language and he recognizes the profound work of the elements in the clear speech of the concept. In this way he becomes the will that mediates between that which is rising slowly to speech and speech which is descending slowly to the earth, expressing not existence as it was before the day but existence as it is after the day: the world of the end of the world.

Where in a work lies the beginning of the moment when the words become stronger than their meaning and the meaning more physical than the word? When does Lautréamont's prose lose the name of prose? Isn't each sentence understandable? Isn't each group of sentences logical? And don't the words say what they mean? At what moment, in this labyrinth of order, in this maze of clarity, did meaning stray from the path? At what turning did reason become aware that it had stopped "following," that something else was continuing, progressing, concluding in its place, something like it in every way, something reason thought it recognized as itself, until the moment it woke up and discovered this other that had taken its place? But if reason now retraces its steps in order to denounce the intruder, the illusion immediately vanishes into thin air, reason finds only itself there, the prose is prose again, so that reason starts off again and loses its way again, allowing a sickening physical substance to replace it, something like a walking staircase, a corridor that unfolds ahead—a kind of reason whose infallibility excludes all reasoners, a logic that has become the "logic of things." Then where is the work? Each moment has the clarity of a beautiful language being spoken, but the work as a whole has the opaque meaning of a thing that is being eaten and that is also eating, that is devouring, being swallowed up, and re-creating itself in a vain effort to change itself into nothing.

Lautréamont is not a true writer of prose? But what is Sade's style, if it isn't prose? And does anyone write more clearly than he does? Is there anyone less familiar than he—who grew up in the least poetic century—with the preoccupations of a literature in search of obscurity? And yet in what other work do we hear such an impersonal, inhuman sound, such a "gigantic and haunting murmur" (as Jean Paulhan says)? But this is simply a defect! The weakness of a writer who cannot be brief! It is certainly a serious defect—literature is the first to accuse him of it. But what it condemns on one side becomes a merit on the other; what it denounces in the name of the work it admires as an experience, what seems unreadable, is really the only thing worth being written. And at the end of everything is fame; beyond, there is oblivion; farther beyond, anonymous survival as part of a dead culture; even farther beyond, perseverance in the eternity of the elements. Where is the end? Where is that death which is the hope of language? But language is *the life that endures death and maintains itself in it.*

If we want to restore literature to the movement which allows all its ambiguities to be grasped, that movement is here: literature, like ordinary speech, *begins* with the *end*, which is the only thing that allows us to understand. If we are to speak, we must see death, we must see it behind us. When we speak, we are leaning on a tomb, and the void of that tomb is what makes language true, but at the same time void is reality and death becomes being. There is being— that is to say, a logical and expressible truth—and there is a world, because we can destroy things and suspend existence. This is why we can say that there is being because there is nothingness: death is man's possibility, his chance, it is through death that the future of a finished world is still there for us; death is man's greatest hope, his only hope of being man. This is why existence is his only real dread, as Emmanuel Lévinas has clearly shown;* existence frightens him, not because of death, which could put an end to it, but because it excludes death, because it is still there underneath death, a presence in the depths of absence, an inexorable day in which all days rise and set. And there is no question that we are preoccupied by dying. But why? It is because when we die, we leave behind not only the world but also death. That is the paradox of the last hour. Death works with us in the world; it is a power that humanizes nature, that raises existence to being, and it is within each one of us as our most human quality; it is death only in the world—man knows death only because he is man, and he is man only because he is death in the process of becoming. But to die is to shatter the world; it is the loss of the person, the annihilation of the being; and so it is also the loss of death, the loss of what in it and for me made it death. As long as I live, I am a mortal man, but when I die, by ceasing to be a man I also cease to be mortal, I am no longer capable of dying, and my impending death horrifies me because I see it as it is: no longer death but the impossibility of dying.

Certain religions have taken the impossibility of death and called it immortality. That is, they have tried to "humanize" the very event which signifies "I cease to be a man." But it is only the opposite thrust that makes death impossible: through death I lose the advantage of being mortal, because I lose the possibility of being man; to be man beyond death could only have this strange meaning—to be, in spite of death, still capable of dying, to go on as though nothing had happened, with death as a horizon and the same hope—death which would have no outcome beyond a "go on as though nothing had happened," etc. This is what other religions have called the curse of being reborn: you die, but you die badly

* He writes, "Isn't dread in the face of being—horror of being—just as primordial as dread in the face of death? Isn't fear of being just as primordial as fear for one's being? Even more primordial, because one could account for the latter by means of the former" (*Existence and Existents*).

because you have lived badly, you are condemned to live again, and you live again until, having become a man completely, in dying you become a truly blessed man—a man who is really dead. Kafka inherited this idea from the Cabala and Eastern traditions. A man enters the night, but the night ends in awakening, and there he is, an insect. Or else the man dies, but he is actually alive; he goes from city to city, carried along by rivers, recognized by some people, helped by no one, the mistake made by old death snickering at his bedside; his is a strange condition, he has forgotten to die. But another man thinks he is alive, when the fact is, he has forgotten his death, and yet another, knowing he is dead, struggles in vain to die; death is over there, the great unattainable castle, and life was over there, the native land he left in answer to a false summons; now there is nothing to do but to struggle, to work at dying completely, but if you struggle, you are still alive; and everything that brings the goal closer also makes the goal inaccessible.

Kafka did not make this theme the expression of a drama about the next world, but he did try to use it to capture the present fact of our condition. He saw in literature the best way of trying to find a way out for this condition, not only of describing it. This is high praise, but does literature deserve it? It is true that there is powerful trickery in literature, a mysterious bad faith that allows it to play everything both ways and gives the most honest people an unreasonable hope of losing and yet winning at the same time. First of all, literature, too, is working toward the advent of the world; literature is civilization and culture. In this way, it is already uniting two contradictory movements. It is negation, because it drives the inhuman, indeterminate side of things back into nothingness; it defines them, makes them finite, and this is the sense in which literature is really the work of death in the world. But at the same time, after having denied things in their existence, it preserves them in their being; it causes things to have a meaning, and the negation which is death at work is also the advent of meaning, the activity of comprehension. Besides this, literature has a certain privilege: it goes beyond the immediate place and moment, and situates itself at the edge of the world and as if at the end of time, and it is from this position that it speaks about things and concerns itself with men. From this new power, literature apparently gains a superior authority. By revealing to each moment the whole of which it is a part, literature helps it to be aware of the whole that it is not and to become another moment that will be a moment within another whole, and so forth; because of this, literature can be called the greatest ferment in history. But there is one inconvenient consequence: this whole which literature represents is not simply an idea, since it is *realized* and not formulated abstractly— but it is not realized in an objective way, because what is real in it is not the whole but the particular language of a particular work, which is itself immersed in history; what is more, the whole does not present itself as real but as fictional, that is, precisely as whole, as everything: perspective of the world, grasp of that *imaginary* point where the world can be seen in its entirety. What we are talking about, then, is a view of the world which realizes itself as unreal using language's peculiar reality. Now, what is the consequence of this? As for the task which is the world, literature is now regarded more as a bother than as a serious help; it is not the result of any true work, since it is not reality but the realization of a point of view which remains unreal; it is foreign to any true culture, because culture is the work of a person changing himself little by little over a period of time, and not the immediate enjoyment of a fictional transformation which dispenses with both time and work.

Spurned by history, literature plays a different game. If it is not really in the world, working to make the world, this is because its lack of being (of intelligible reality) causes it to refer to an existence that is still inhuman. Yes, it recognizes that this is so, that in its nature there is a strange slipping back and forth between being and not being, presence and absence, reality and nonreality. What is a work? Real words and an imaginary story, a world in which everything that happens is borrowed from reality, and this world is inaccessible; characters who are portrayed as living—but we know that their life consists of not living (of remaining a fiction); pure nothingness, then? But the book is there, and we can touch it, we read the words and we cannot change them; is it the nothingness of an idea, then, of something which exists only when understood? But the fiction is not understood, it is experienced through the words with which it is realized, and for me, as I read it or write it, it is more real than many real events, because it is impregnated with all the reality of language and it substitutes itself for my life simply by existing. Literature does not act: but what it does is plunge into this depth of existence which is neither being nor nothingness and where the hope of doing anything is completely eliminated. It is not explanation, and it is not pure comprehension, because the inexplicable emerges in it. And it expresses without expressing, it offers its language to what is murmured in the absence of speech. So literature seems to be allied with the strangeness of that existence which being has rejected and which does not fit into any category. The writer senses that he is in the grasp of an impersonal power that does not let him either live or die: the irresponsibility he cannot surmount becomes the expression of that death without death which awaits him at the edge of nothingness; literary immortality is the very movement by which the nausea of a survival which is not a survival, a death which does not end anything, insinuates itself into the world, a world sapped by crude existence. The writer who writes a work eliminates himself as he writes that work and at the same time affirms himself in it. If he has written it to get rid of himself, it turns out that the work engages him and recalls him to himself, and if he writes it to reveal himself and live in it, he sees that what he has done is nothing, that the greatest work is not as valuable as the most insignificant act, and that his work condemns him to an existence that is not his own existence and to a life that has nothing to do with life. Or again he has written because in the depths of language he heard the work of death as it prepared living beings for the truth of their name: he worked for this nothingness and he himself was a nothingness at work. But as one realizes the void, one creates a work, and the work, born of fidelity to death, is in the end no longer capable of dying; and all it brings to the person who was trying to prepare an unstoried death for himself is the mockery of immortality.

Then where is literature's power? It plays at working in the world, and the world regards its work as a worthless or dangerous game. It opens a path for itself toward the obscurity of existence and does not succeed in pronouncing the "Never more" which would suspend its curse. Then where is its force? Why would a man like Kafka decide that if he had to fall short of his destiny, being a writer was the only way to fall short of it truthfully? Perhaps this is an unintelligible enigma, but if it is, the source of the mystery is literature's right to affix a negative or positive sign indiscriminately to each of its moments and each of its results. A strange right—one linked to the question of ambiguity in general. Why is there ambiguity in the world? Ambiguity is its own answer. We cannot answer it except by rediscovering it in the ambiguity of our answer, and an ambiguous answer is a question about ambiguity. One of the ways it reduces us is by making us want to clear it up, a struggle that is like the struggle against evil Kafka talks about, which ends in evil, "like the struggle with women, which ends in bed."

Literature is language turning into ambiguity. Ordinary language is not necessarily clear, it does not always say what it says; misunderstanding is also one of its paths. This is inevitable. Every time we speak, we make words into monsters with two faces, one being reality, physical presence, and the other meaning, ideal absence. But ordinary language limits equivocation. It solidly encloses the absence in a presence, it puts *a term* to understanding, to the indefinite movement of comprehension; understanding is limited, but misunderstanding is limited, too. In literature, ambiguity is in some sense abandoned to its excesses by the opportunities it finds and exhausted by the extent of the abuses it can commit. It is as though there were a hidden trap here to force ambiguity to reveal its own traps, and as though in surrendering unreservedly to ambiguity, literature were attempting to keep it—out of sight of the world and out of the thought of the world—in a place where it fulfills itself without endangering anything. Here ambiguity struggles with itself. It is not just that each moment of language can become ambiguous and say something different from what it is saying, but that the general meaning of language is unclear: we do not know if it is expressing or representing, if it is a thing or means that thing; if it is there to be forgotten or if it only makes us forget it so that we will see it; if it is transparent because what it says has so little meaning or clear because of the exactness with which it says it, obscure because it says too much, opaque because it says nothing. There is ambiguity everywhere: in its trivial exterior—but what is most frivolous may be the mask of the serious; in its disinterestedness—but behind this disinterestedness lie the forces of the world, and it connives with them without knowing them, or again, ambiguity uses this disinterestedness to safeguard the absolute nature of the values without which action would stop or become mortal; its unreality is therefore both a principle of action and the incapacity to act, in the same way that the fiction in itself is truth and also indifference to truth; in the same way that if it allies itself with morality, it corrupts itself, and if it rejects morality, it still perverts itself; in the same way that it is nothing if it is not its own end, but it cannot have its end in itself, because it is without end, it ends outside itself, in history, etc.

All these reversals from *pro* to *contra*—and those described here—undoubtedly have very different causes. We have seen that literature assigns itself irreconcilable tasks. We have seen that in moving from the writer to the reader, from the labor to the finished work, it passes through contradictory moments and can only place itself in the affirmation of all the opposing moments. But all these contradictions, these hostile demands, these divisions and oppositions, so different in origin, kind, and meaning, refer back to an ultimate ambiguity whose strange effect is to attract literature to an unstable point where it can indiscriminately change both its meaning and its sign.

This ultimate vicissitude keeps the work in suspense in such a way that it can choose whether to take on a positive or a negative value and, as though it were pivoting invisibly around an invisible axis, enter the daylight of affirmations or the backlight of negations, without its style, genre, or subject being accountable for the radical transformation. Neither the content of the words nor their form is involved here. Whether the work is obscure or clear, poetry or prose, insignificant or important, whether it speaks of a pebble or of God, there is something in it that does not depend on its qualities and that deep within itself is always in the process of changing the work from the ground up. It is as though in the very heart of literature and language, beyond the visible movements that transform them, a point of instability were reserved, a power to work substantial metamorphoses, a power capable of changing everything about it without changing anything. This instability can appear to be the effect of a disintegrating force, since it can cause the strongest, most forceful work to become a work of unhappiness and ruin, but this disintegration is also a form of construction, if it suddenly causes distress to turn into hope and destruction into an element of the indestructible. How can such imminence of change, present in the depths of language quite apart from the meaning that affects it and the reality of that language, nevertheless be present in that meaning and in that reality? Could it be that the meaning of a word introduces something else into the word along with it, something which, although it protects the precise signification of the word and does not threaten that signification, is capable of completely modifying the meaning and modifying the material value of the word? Could there be a force at once friendly and hostile hidden in the intimacy of speech, a weapon intended to build and to destroy, which would act behind signification rather than upon signification? Do we have to suppose a meaning for the meaning of words that, while determining that meaning, also surrounds this determination with an ambiguous indeterminacy that wavers between yes and no?

But we cannot suppose anything: we have questioned this meaning of the meaning of words at length, this meaning which is as much the movement of a word toward its truth as it is its return through the reality of language to the obscure depths of existence; we have questioned this absence by which the thing is annihilated, destroyed in order to become being and idea. It is *that life which supports death and maintains itself in it*—death, the amazing power of the negative, or freedom, through whose work existence is detached from itself and made significant. Now, nothing can prevent this power—at the very moment it is trying to understand things and, in language, to specify words—nothing can prevent it from continuing to assert itself as continually differing possibility, and nothing can stop it from perpetuating an irreducible *double meaning*, a choice whose terms are covered over with an ambiguity that makes them identical to one another even as it makes them opposite.

If we call this power negation or unreality or death, then presently death, negation, and unreality, at work in the depths of language, will signify the advent of truth in the world, the construction of intelligible being, the formation of meaning. But just as suddenly, the sign changes: meaning no longer represents the marvel of comprehension, but instead refers us to the nothingness of death, and intelligible being signifies only the rejection of existence, and the absolute concern for truth is expressed by an incapacity to act in a real way. Or else death is perceived as a civilizing power which results in a comprehension of being. But at the same time, a death that results in being represents an absurd insanity, the curse of existence—which contains within itself both death and being and is neither being nor death. Death ends in being: this is man's hope and his task, because nothingness itself helps to make the world, nothingness is the creator of the world in man as he works and understands. Death ends in being: this is man's laceration, the source of his unhappy fate, since by man death comes to being and by man meaning rests on nothingness; the only way we can comprehend is by denying ourselves existence, by making death *possible*, by contaminating what we comprehend with the nothingness of death, so that if we emerge from being, we fall outside the possibility of death, and the way out becomes the disappearance of every way out.

This original double meaning, which lies deep inside every word like a condemnation that is still unknown and a happiness that is still invisible, is the source of literature, because literature is the form in which this double meaning has chosen to show itself behind the meaning and value of words, and the question it asks is the question asked by literature.

TRANSLATED BY LYDIA DAVIS

M E R I D I A N

Crossing Aesthetics

Library of Congress
Cataloging-in-Publication Data

Blanchot, Maurice.
[Part du feu. English]
The work of fire / Maurice Blanchot ;
translated by Charlotte Mandell.
p.   cm. — (Meridian)
ISBN 0-8047-2432-6 (alk. paper) : —
ISBN 0-8047-2493-8 (pbk. : alk. paper) :
1. Literature—History and criticism—Theory, etc.   I. Title.
II. Series: Meridian (Stanford, Calif.)
PN81.B544713   1995
809—dc20 —dc 20
[809'.91]   94-32418   CIP

♾ This book is printed on acid-free paper.
It was typeset in Adobe Garamond and
Lithos by Keystone Typesetting, Inc.